The Trusts of Land
and Appointment of
Trustees Act 1996

AUSTRALIA
LBC Information Services
Brisbane • Sydney • Melbourne • Perth

CANADA
Carswell
Ottawa • Toronto • Calgary • Montreal • Vancouver

AGENTS:
Steimatzky's Agency Ltd, Tel Aviv;
N. M. Tripathi (Private) Ltd, Bombay;
Eastern Law House (Private) Ltd, Calcutta;
M.P.P. House, Bangalore;
Universal Book Traders, Delhi;
Aditya Books, Delhi;
MacMillan Shuppan KK, Tokyo;
Pakistan Law House, Karachi

The Trusts of Land and Appointment of Trustees Act 1996

with annotations by

Professor Phillip H. Kenny

and

Ann Kenny

LONDON
SWEET & MAXWELL
1997

Published in 1997 by
Sweet & Maxwell Limited of
100 Avenue Road
London NW3 3PF
Typeset by MFK Information Services Ltd
Hitchin, Herts.
Printed and bound in Great Britain by
Butler & Tanner Ltd, Frome and London

**A CIP catalogue record for this book is available
from the British Library**

ISBN 0-421 584602

CONTENTS

Contents

PREFACE

The Trusts of Land and Appointment of Trustees Act 1996 is the product of the Law Commission. It is the first piece of fundamental reform there has been of the 1925 property legislation. The first part of the Act replaces the dual system of trusts for sale and strict settlements with Trusts of Land. It contains a plethora of amendments to the 1925 legislation.

The second part of the Act contains some important new measures dealing with the appointment of trustees.

Overall the Act contains many unnecessary and some quite surprising alterations to legislation which is well known to property lawyers and which works very efficiently in practice. Unwanted as these continued attempts at law reform are by the profession they contain provisions which practising lawyers need to know. This Act is a good example of unwelcome legislation for the property lawyer. Its basic premise is an unsettling change to well understood concepts. It is carried through by a series of odd changes in abolishing entails, abolishing in part the doctrine of conversion and so on. The Act will find a necessary place on the lawyer's book shelf but it will never find a place in the conveyancer's heart.

Phillip H. Kenny
Ann Kenny

October 16, 1996

TABLE OF CASES

References are either to the Introduction or the General Note to the specified section of the Act (found in Part I of the book) or to a paragraph in Part II of the book.

Table of Cases

TABLE OF STATUTES

References are either to the Introduction or the General Note to the specified section of the Act (found in Part I of the book) or to a paragraph in Part II of the book.

Table of Statutes

PART I: THE TRUSTS OF LAND AND APPOINTMENT OF TRUSTEES ACT 1996

(1996 c. 47)

ARRANGEMENT OF SECTIONS

PART I

TRUSTS OF LAND

Introductory

26. Power to make consequential provision.
27. Short title, commencement and extent.

SCHEDULES:
Schedule 1—Provisions consequential on section 2.
Schedule 2—Amendments of statutory provisions imposing trust for sale.
Schedule 3—Minor and consequential amendments.
Schedule 4—Repeals.

An Act to make new provision about trusts of land including provision phasing out the Settled Land Act 1925, abolishing the doctrine of conversion and otherwise amending the law about trusts for sale of land; to amend the law about the appointment and retirement of trustees of any trust; and for connected purposes.   [24th July 1996]

PARLIAMENTARY DEBATES
Hansard, H.L. Vol. 567, col. 417; Vol. 569, col. 1717; Vol. 570, col. 1532; Vol. 571, col. 954; Vol. 572, col. 94; Vol. 574, col. 1174. H.C. Vol. 279, col. 787; Vol. 281, col. 1052.

INTRODUCTION AND GENERAL NOTE
The Trusts of Land and Appointment of Trustees Act 1996 is in two distinct parts.

Part I—Trusts of land
Part I derives largely from the Law Commission Report entitled *Transfer of Land: Trusts of Land* (Law Comm. No. 181) although there are some amendments. As with so much Law Commission legislation, hurried changes were made during the passage of the Bill and, as a result, the effect of some parts was not clarified.
The purpose of Pt. I is to replace the existing dual system of trusts for sale and strict settlements by a single system. The Explanatory Memorandum to the Bill claims that this is "an entirely new single system". This claim is quite untrue. The Bill proceeds in reality by a clever, but piecemeal, series of amendments of the 1925 legislation. Most of the problems "resolved" by this legislation have existed in land law text books since 1925 without impeding the efficient practice of law. An overall conclusion on this Part must be that it provides cerebral activity for lawyers without ameliorating the position of consumers of their services in any way sufficient to be worth the trouble of Parliament in enacting the legislation.
The immediate effect of the Act coming into force will be that nearly all new trusts which include land will fall under the new nomenclature—as a "trust of land". Nearly all existing trusts which include land will also fall under this new statutory regime. To this clear picture there are two exceptions. Existing strict settlements under the Settled Land Act 1925 (c. 18) will continue to be governed by that Act. Additionally Pt. I does not apply to land to which the Universities and College Estates Act 1925 (c. 24) applies.
The Act seeks to make some small and surprisingly unnecessary alterations to existing law. The doctrine of conversion is abolished in respect of trusts for sale. An attempt is made to abolish the creation of new entailed interests. A wide power to postpone the exercise of trusts for sale is imposed. The power of trustees to partition land is rewritten.
Less trivially, extensive powers of management are conferred on trustees of land replacing the position under the Law of Property Act 1925 (c. 20) whereby trustees for sale had only the same powers as a tenant for life under Pt. II of the Settled Land Act 1925. These new powers can be limited by the trust instrument. Trustees are given the duty in exercising their powers to consult beneficiaries who are *sui juris* and entitled in possession.
Of limited practical significance is a new power of delegation given to the trustees by s.9. This allows delegation to a beneficiary of full age and capacity with an interest in possession. It will allow such a beneficiary to be in much the same position as a tenant for life under a strict settlement. Trustees are (as a result largely due to the influence of the Law Society on the final wording of this section) more or less exempted from the consequences of such delegation. The anomalous position of professional trustees as providers of services to consumers for the poor performance of which they are largely unaccountable is, thus, not affected by this Act. Such steps as the Law Commission took in the direction of consumer protection were by amendment to this section and others undone by Parliament. This can be put down to the fact that the Law Society's advisers understood the effect of the changes made to the Bill and Parliament did not.
Of interest to litigators is the demise of s.30 of the Law of Property Act 1925. This is replaced by ss.14 and 15 of the Act which provide a similar mechanism for applications to the court where there are disputes about the interests under a trust of land or the exercise of the trustee's powers. It may be noted that s.17 of the Married Women's Property Act 1882 (c. 75) (which provides a

similar jurisdiction to s.30 of the Law of Property Act 1925) is unaffected by this Act.

An entirely new provision in this part of the Act is found in ss.12 and 13. Section 12 gives a right of occupation to certain beneficiaries. Section 13 provides rules for dealing with situations where more than one beneficiary claims this statutory right of occupation. This provision is intended to assist in co-ownership trusts of dwelling houses where there are frequent arguments over occupation. It is a nuisance for family investment trusts and will provide some difficulties of application in this contex.

Part II—Appointment of new trustees

The purpose of this part of the Act, which applies to all trusts whenever created, was to give beneficiaries greater powers over the appointment of trustees. As the law previously stood, the trustees did not have to consult the beneficiaries' wishes in making an appointment (*Re Brockbank* [1948] Ch. 206). Nor, in the absence of an action for maladministration of the trust, could the beneficiaries force the trustees to retire. These new provisions are meant to provide an alternative to the otherwise drastic course of action open to the beneficiaries who want to control the appointment of the trustees, namely to end the trust under the rule in *Saunders v. Vautier* (1841) 3 Bear 115.

Now beneficiaries are able to give trustees a written direction to retire from the trust, or to appoint a particular person as a trustee. Such are the limitations upon the operation of this right that it must be doubted whether it will make a vast change in practice. First, the provisions relating to appointment and retirement do not apply if there is a person nominated by the trustees to appoint new trustees. Secondly, the beneficiaries can only give a direction if they are of full age and capacity and absolutely entitled to the property subject to the trust. This makes Pt. II inapplicable to the many discretionary trusts or where there are infant beneficiaries. Thirdly, the direction to retire is only effective where all the co-trustees are ready to consent to the discharge. Finally, but most importantly, these powers can be excluded in relation to trusts created both before and after the Act came into force.

As many settlors or testators will wish to exclude the operation of Pt. II, its main applicability will be in relation to the family home or other constructive or resulting trusts where there is a sole legal owner holding on trust for another who has contributed to the purchase price.

Part III

Part III (ss.22–27) is a collection of supplementary provisions including those commonly found at the end of an Act. These sections are largely self-explanatory.

Sections 22 and 23 provide for definitions (in addition to those in s.17) and are discussed below. Section 24 generally excludes the application of the Act to the Crown (except so far as it related to undivided shares and joint tenancies). Amendments and repeals are provided for by s.25, and referred to as appropriate earlier in these annotations with a short additional note below. Section 26 contains the power in favour of the Lord Chancellor to make consequential provision and s.27 gives details of the short title, commencement and extent.

ABBREVIATIONS

1996 Act: Trusts of Land and Appointment of Trustees Act 1996.
AEA: Administration of Estates Act 1925.
LPA 1925 : Law of Property Act 1925.
SLA 1925 : Settled Land Act 1925.
TA: Trustee Act 1925.

PART I

TRUSTS OF LAND

Introductory

Meaning of "trust of land"

1.—(1) In this Act—
(a) "trust of land" means (subject to subsection (3)) any trust of property which consists of or includes land, and
(b) "trustees of land" means trustees of a trust of land.
(2) The reference in subsection (1)(a) to a trust—
(a) is to any description of trust (whether express, implied, resulting or constructive), including a trust for sale and a bare trust, and
(b) includes a trust created, or arising, before the commencement of this Act.

(3) The reference to land in subsection (1)(a) does not include land which (despite section 2) is settled land or which is land to which the Universities and College Estates Act 1925 applies.

GENERAL NOTE

This section introduces the new system for trusts of land. Any trust of property which has land in it will (subject to subs. (3)) be known as a trust of land. The importance of the change is that there will be now (subject to subs. (3)) a unified conveyancing system for trusts of land. The same conveyancing procedures will be used for all trusts of land. The change made is retrospective and applies to trusts whenever created. It also applies to implied, resulting and constructive trusts.

Subs. (2)

The purpose of this subsection is to make clear that the new rules should, so far as possible, apply to all trusts.

Subs. (3)

Land which is settled land, despite s.2, is land which is in a settlement to which the SLA 1925 applies. The statutory route to discovering the definition of settled land is as follows. Subsection (3) applies to *settled land*. Section 23(2) of this Act incorporates the definitions from s.205 of the LPA 1925. Section 205(1)(xxvi) provides that "settled land" has the same meaning as in the SLA 1925. Section 2 of the SLA 1925 provides that: "Land which is or is deemed to be the subject of a settlement is, for the purposes of this Act, settled land". Section 1 of that Act then contains the well known provision intended to ensure that settlements of land which are not trusts for sale fall within the SLA 1925.

It should be noted that the Universities and College Estates Act 1925 applies only to certain Universities. It has no application to Universities or Colleges which are designated as Higher Education Corporations or Further Education Corporations under the Education Reform Act 1988 (c. 40), or as the case may be. The land owned by these statutory corporations is not usually held on trust. However, such a University or College may enjoy the benefit of established trusts and, if these include land, then this Act applies.

Settlements and trusts for sale as trusts of land

Trusts in place of settlements

2.—(1) No settlement created after the commencement of this Act is a settlement for the purposes of the Settled Land Act 1925; and no settlement shall be deemed to be made under that Act after that commencement.

(2) Subsection (1) does not apply to a settlement created on the occasion of an alteration in any interest in, or of a person becoming entitled under, a settlement which—

(a) is in existence at the commencement of this Act, or

(b) derives from a settlement within paragraph (a) or this paragraph.

(3) But a settlement created as mentioned in subsection (2) is not a settlement for the purposes of the Settled Land Act 1925 if provision to the effect that it is not is made in the instrument, or any of the instruments, by which it is created.

(4) Where at any time after the commencement of this Act there is in the case of any settlement which is a settlement for the purposes of the Settled Land Act 1925 no relevant property which is, or is deemed to be, subject to the settlement, the settlement permanently ceases at that time to be a settlement for the purposes of that Act.

In this subsection "relevant property" means land and personal chattels to which section 67(1) of the Settled Land Act 1925 (heirlooms) applies.

(5) No land held on charitable, ecclesiastical or public trusts shall be or be deemed to be settled land after the commencement of this Act, even if it was or was deemed to be settled land before that commencement.

(6) Schedule 1 has effect to make provision consequential on this section (including provision to impose a trust in circumstances in which, apart from this section, there would be a settlement for the purposes of the Settled Land Act 1925 (and there would not otherwise be a trust)).

GENERAL NOTE

This section has as its principal objective the prevention of the creation of any new settlements under the SLA 1925. Any attempt (should there ever be one) to create a strict settlement with structures that mimic the provisions of a SLA 1925 settlement will simply produce a settlement which is a trust of land and governed by the new Act. It will, nevertheless, be a very long time before there is no land subject to SLA 1925 and, indeed, it is not necessarily the case that this sad day will ever arrive.

Subs. (1)

This is a clear provision preventing the creation of new strict settlements. The circumstances where settlements were deemed to be made require particular provisions to bring them into line with this Act and these provisions are found in Sched. 1 and explained in the notes on that Schedule.

Subs. (2)

This is a very important provision for those solicitors who manage the legal affairs of the remaining settled estates. Existing settlements can continue in the following ways:

- succession of a new tenant for life, or to other trusts, on the termination of an interest in possession.
- exercise of a power of appointment under an existing settlement. This will frequently be exercised so as to create an alternative settlement and such a settlement will be settled land (unless the land is appointed on a trust for sale which takes it outside s.1 of the SLA 1925 in which case the derivative settlement will be a trust of land).
- once a derivative settlement has been created which is a SLA 1925 settlement then it can be varied or settlements derived from it without the land ceasing to be settled land.

Subs. (3)

This allows a new settlement created out of an existing SLA 1925 settlement to be a trust of land. This provision will doubtless be used extremely rarely, and its operation is not so straightforward as appears at first sight.

This provision confers no new powers upon trustees and they will still only be able to vary or appoint under a settlement in the manner permitted by the settlement, otherwise there will be a breach of trust. Providing these powers are sufficient to allow creation of a derivative settlement which is not a settled land settlement, this subsection can be relied upon.

The conveyancing machinery to give effect to this subsection is not obvious. The instrument exercising the power should state, if that is the desired result, "that the trusts hereby created are not a settlement under the Settled Land Act 1925". However, it is important that a purchaser of land from the new derivative trust should know that he is dealing with a trust of land and not a strict settlement—because in the former, the trustees exercise the conveyancing powers and in the latter, the tenant for life.

Subs. (4)

Once there is no land in an existing strict settlement, then it becomes a trust of land. For this purpose personal property settled as land (heirlooms) counts as land. The world which gave rise to s.67 of the SLA 1925 (sale and purchase of heirlooms) is nearly gone. In the uncommon cases where such pleasant relics exist, trustees should be careful to ensure the new rule is correctly applied: if there are such heirlooms remaining, then if capital money in trustees' hands is used to acquire land, that land is settled land. It should be vested in the tenant for life or statutory owner under s.10 of the SLA 1925.

Subs. (5)

This provision is consequential on the repeal of s.29 of the SLA 1925. Section 29 provided that land held on charitable, ecclesiastical or public trusts was deemed to be settled land. The purpose of this was to confer upon such trustees the powers conferred on SLA 1925 tenants for life and trustees. In respect of these trusts, created before or after the present Act, they will in future be trusts of land and the trustees will have the extensive powers of managing land conferred by ss.6 and 7 of this Act.

There is no particular problem with the definition of charitable trusts. The concepts of ecclesiastical or public trusts may cause more difficulty. All three are discussed further in the General Note on s.8(3) in which the same expression is used.

Abolition of doctrine of conversion

3.—(1) Where land is held by trustees subject to a trust for sale, the land is not to be regarded as personal property; and where personal property is subject to a trust for sale in order that the trustees may acquire land, the personal property is not to be regarded as land.

(2) Subsection (1) does not apply to a trust created by a will if the testator died before the commencement of this Act.

(3) Subject to that, subsection (1) applies to a trust whether it is created, or arises, before or after that commencement.

GENERAL NOTE

The first thing to note is that the marginal note for this section is misleading. It refers to the "Abolition of doctrine of conversion". The wording of s.3 has no such effect. It is intended to prevent the doctrine of conversion operating in the case of a trust for sale. The mischief at which this damage is aimed is that persons who have interests under trusts for sale could inadvertently leave the property to the wrong person by describing the gift in their will as one of personalty or realty when, because of the operation of the doctrine of conversion, it has a different legal description. This is a very small and virtually non-existent problem. It is not possible to compliment the proposers of this change for its sense or the draftsperson for the wording. For the section to apply there must be a trust for sale. It has no application, therefore, to any implied, resulting or constructive trust because there is no trust for sale in respect of these whether they came into being before or after this Act. In other cases where there was, before the Act, an implied trust for sale on the statutory trusts, these cases are now all trusts of land and the statutory trusts abolished by the repeal of s.35 of the LPA 1925.

The section, therefore, applies to cases, whether before or after the coming into force of the Act, where there is an express trust for sale. In such cases, land under trust is to be regarded as land, and money (or other personal property) which is held to be laid out on land is not to be regarded as land. This does not, however, although it may have been intended by the draftsperson so to do, have the effect that the interest of the beneficiary is necessarily an interest in land where land is held by the trustees. This will depend on the nature of the beneficiary's interest.

First, it may help to look at the doctrine of conversion itself. The doctrine is an equitable doctrine and part of the fundamental principle that equity looks upon that as done which ought to be done. One conclusion to which this doctrine was pressed was that if land was held on trust for sale then it was to be regarded as personalty. Conversely, if money was expressed as having to be laid out on land then it was to be regarded as having been so spent. A good example was the case of *Lechmere v. Earl of Carlisle* 3.P.Wms 211. Lord Lechmere promised in his marriage settlement to lay out £30,000 on land. When he died he had not done so and that sum passed as realty to his heir. The doctrine was of great importance in circumstances such as *Lechmere v. Carlisle* where the fortunes of great estates turned on whether property passed to the heir at law (realty) or to the next of kin (personalty) or whether it passed under specific gifts of realty or personalty. A failure to take account of this notorious role could have surprising consequences—see for example *Re Kempthorne* [1930] 1 Ch. 268 where an interest under a trust for sale passed with a specific gift of personalty.

The partial abolition of the doctrine of conversion by this section means it will be necessary to examine the terms of an express trust to see if a particular interest is land or not. This may be very important for applying other provisions of this Act—particularly s.12 where this issue is returned to and discussed at length.

Express trusts for sale as trusts of land

4.—(1) In the case of every trust for sale of land created by a disposition there is to be implied, despite any provision to the contrary made by the disposition, a power for the trustees to postpone sale of the land; and the trustees are not liable in any way for postponing sale of the land, in the exercise of their discretion, for an indefinite period.

(2) Subsection (1) applies to a trust whether it is created, or arises, before or after the commencement of this Act.

(3) Subsection (1) does not affect any liability incurred by trustees before that commencement.

GENERAL NOTE

This is a surprising but largely insignificant change. Under the present law (s.25 of the LPA 1925) trustees for sale have a power to postpone the sale but this can be disapplied by the trust instrument. The power to postpone cannot now ever be excluded. Thus, even if the trust says: "Upon trust to sell and an auction sale of the land must be held at by the latest January 1 2000" the trustees can with impunity ignore this direction and postpone the sale indefinitely.

Implied trusts for sale as trusts of land

5.—(1) Schedule 2 has effect in relation to statutory provisions which impose a trust for sale of land in certain circumstances so that in those circumstances there is instead a trust of the land (without a duty to sell).

(2) Section 1 of the Settled Land Act 1925 does not apply to land held on any trust arising by virtue of that Schedule (so that any such land is subject to a trust of land).

GENERAL NOTE
    This introduces Sched. 2 which deals in detail with the statutory provisions under which formerly a trust for sale was implied.

Functions of trustees of land

General powers of trustees

6.—(1) For the purpose of exercising their functions as trustees, the trustees of land have in relation to the land subject to the trust all the powers of an absolute owner.

(2) Where in the case of any land subject to a trust of land each of the beneficiaries interested in the land is a person of full age and capacity who is absolutely entitled to the land, the powers conferred on the trustees by subsection (1) include the power to convey the land to the beneficiaries even though they have not required the trustees to do so; and where land is conveyed by virtue of this subsection—
    (a) the beneficiaries shall do whatever is necessary to secure that it vests in them, and
    (b) if they fail to do so, the court may make an order requiring them to do so.

(3) The trustees of land have power to purchase a legal estate in any land in England or Wales.

(4) The power conferred by subsection (3) may be exercised by trustees to purchase land—
    (a) by way of investment,
    (b) for occupation by any beneficiary, or
    (c) for any other reason.

(5) In exercising the powers conferred by this section trustees shall have regard to the rights of the beneficiaries.

(6) The powers conferred by this section shall not be exercised in contravention of, or of any order made in pursuance of, any other enactment or any rule of law or equity.

(7) The reference in subsection (6) to an order includes an order of any court or of the Charity Commissioners.

(8) Where any enactment other than this section confers on trustees authority to act subject to any restriction, limitation or condition, trustees of land may not exercise the powers conferred by this section to do any act which they are prevented from doing under the other enactment by reason of the restriction, limitation or condition.

DEFINITIONS
    "beneficiary": s.22.

GENERAL NOTE
    The powers conferred on trustees for sale were found in s.28 of the LPA 1925 which is repealed by this Act. They are "all the powers of a tenant for life and the trustees of a settlement under the Settled Land Act 1925". The problems caused by the somewhat limited nature of

these powers was in truth largely theoretical and had little significance in practical conveyancing. Trustees of land now have (subject to s.8) considerably enlarged powers. A significant change is that the trustees will have power to raise the purchase price of land by mortgage.

Subs. (1)

The main point to note is that the powers granted are powers "in relation to the land". There is no enlargement of the trustees' powers concerned with, for example, investment. For a section which is clearly intended to be an unproblematical extension of trustees' powers the opening words are unhelpfully ambiguous. The new powers are given "for the purpose of exercising their functions as trustees". Anything they do for any other purpose is not an exercise of their powers. Presumably this means the actual purpose for which the trustees exercise their powers. Where there are several trustees, who would ever be sure of the actual purpose of any one of them? The subsection would operate perfectly well without these words and any exercise by the trustees of their powers for a wrongful purpose would in any event be a breach of trust (see subs. (6)). If the words add anything to the sense (which may be doubted) they must add this—the trustees (**who must still act as trustees**) have, in relation to the land, the powers conferred by s.6. Thus, in exercising them they are still circumscribed by the rules of equity which apply to trustees. This, in any event, is made explicit by subs. (6).

Subs. (2)

This applies as follows. It may happen under a trust that all the beneficiaries are *sui juris* (of full age and capacity) and absolutely entitled to the land. The trustees may, in such a case, force them to take a conveyance of the land. Paragraph (a) requires the beneficiaries to co-operate with such a transfer and para. (b) gives the court power to make them co-operate. There will be many trusts of land where thought will have to be given as to whether this curious power is appropriate. Much land is held by partnerships on trust for sale or by nominees in a commercial context. There may be occasions when it is desirable to exclude s.6(2) in such cases.

Where there is more than one beneficiary, the land will be conveyed to them on a trust of land and they will become the beneficiaries of the trust on which they hold the land.

Subss. (3) and (4)

The power to purchase land given by these subsections is very wide. However, unless wider powers are given in the trust instrument these subsections contain the only powers to purchase land; s.6(1) applies only to land already in the trust. This means that there is no power to purchase an equitable interest in land. The examples of purposes for which the power to purchase land is given are listed because of the previous doubts surrounding the purchase of land by trustees for investment or for occupation. In fact subs. (4)(a) and (b) seem unnecessary in the face of subs. 4(c).

Subs. (5)

This is an odd, even gnomic, utterance from the legislature. If the beneficiaries have **rights** then clearly the trustees must anyway have regard to them. Subsections (1) to (4) confer **powers** upon the trustees. No-one could interpret that as allowing the trustees to divest a beneficiary of an established right. If a trust instrument gives, say, the settlor's wife a right to live in the trust property for her life, then it is perfectly clear that the trustees cannot exercise their powers to defeat this right. To that extent this subsection is otiose.

Subs. (6)

This subsection is caused by the same failure of nerve by the draftsperson as the previous one. The powers which trustees have do in any event have to be exercised properly and no more is added by this provision. It is in fact a misconceived provision. The court has power to intervene in the case of misconduct by a trustee. This does not mean that any breach of a rule of law or equity is misconduct. However, the literal effect of s.6(6) is that any exercise of a power in breach of any rule of law or equity is void. Doubts will arise in practice as to the relationship between the wide powers given by subs. (1) and the need to conform with existing rules of law and equity. The resolution is as follows. In form the trustees have unrestricted powers of management. These must be exercised in conformity with principles of equity such as sound business management, holding the balance between capital and income and between the interests of different beneficiaries. Any breach of such a principle will not affect an innocent purchaser relying upon the width of the statutory powers, but a purchase with an improper purpose may, as it always has been, be challenged by the beneficiaries.

Subs. (7)
It is hard to see that this subsection adds anything to subs. (6), and the same comments apply.

Partition by trustees

7.—(1) The trustees of land may, where beneficiaries of full age are absolutely entitled in undivided shares to land subject to the trust, partition the land, or any part of it, and provide (by way of mortgage or otherwise) for the payment of any equality money.

(2) The trustees shall give effect to any such partition by conveying the partitioned land in severalty (whether or not subject to any legal mortgage created for raising equality money), either absolutely or in trust, in accordance with the rights of those beneficiaries.

(3) Before exercising their powers under subsection (2) the trustees shall obtain the consent of each of those beneficiaries.

(4) Where a share in the land is affected by an incumbrance, the trustees may either give effect to it or provide for its discharge from the property allotted to that share as they think fit.

(5) If a share in the land is absolutely vested in a minor, subsections (1) to (4) apply as if he were of full age, except that the trustees may act on his behalf and retain land or other property representing his share in trust for him.

DEFINITION
"beneficiary": s.22.

GENERAL NOTE
This section replaces s.28(3) of the LPA 1925 which is repealed. Neither this new provision nor s.28(3) was or is actually necessary. The adult beneficiaries of full age who are absolutely entitled may direct the determination of the trust and the destination of the trust properly in any event under the well known rule in *Saunders v. Vautier* (1841) Cr. & Ph. 240. Section 28(3) was to all intents and purposes a dead letter and rewording the provision in modern legislative form, as is done here, is essentially an academic curiosity.

Subs. (3)
This is a rephrasing of proviso (ii) to the former s.28(3). Notably it replaces "as they may consider expedient" with "as they think fit". Comment on such "law reform" is as superfluous as the exercise itself.

Subs. (5)
This replaces s.28(4) of the LPA 1925 which is repealed.

Exclusion and restriction of powers

8.—(1) Sections 6 and 7 do not apply in the case of a trust of land created by a disposition in so far as provision to the effect that they do not apply is made by the disposition.

(2) If the disposition creating such a trust makes provision requiring any consent to be obtained to the exercise of any power conferred by section 6 or 7, the power may not be exercised without that consent.

(3) Subsection (1) does not apply in the case of charitable, ecclesiastical or public trusts.

(4) Subsections (1) and (2) have effect subject to any enactment which prohibits or restricts the effect of provision of the description mentioned in them.

GENERAL NOTE
This allows the powers conferred by s.6 and s.7 to be excluded from any particular trust.

Subs. (1)
This provision applies only to a trust of land created by a **disposition**. The term **disposition** has been much discussed by courts and academics in trust cases—notably *Vandervell v. I.R.C.* [1967]

2 A.C. 291; *Vandervell's Trusts, Re (No. 2)*; *White v. Vandervell Trustees* [1974] Ch. 269. It is unclear from this very murky case law whether a simple declaration of trust is a disposition. It would appear that it probably is not. This would have the odd effect that s.8 would apply where a settlor conveys land to trustees but not where the settlor executes a declaration that he holds the land on trust—for there the land is not disposed of. That is clearly an unfortunate ambiguity in the drafting of this subsection. The definition of conveyance in s.205 of the LPA 1925, however, does include a disposition. It is a wide definition and could easily be read as including a declaration of trust. That definition is included in this Act by virtue of s.23 and could lead to the more sensible view that a declaration of trust is a disposition.

Equally puzzling is the statement that ss.6 and 7 do not apply "so far as **provision** to the effect that they do not apply is made ... ". This tends a little to suggest that s.6 and/or s.7 need to be **expressly** disapplied in whole or in part. But, the sensible assumption is that that is not so. Sections 6 or 7 are simply disapplied to the extent that there are directions to the contrary in the disposition, however expressed.

The third puzzle in s.8 is that the limitation of ss.6 or 7 must be made "by the disposition". A typical example of a trust of land for commercial purposes is a partnership. Here there will be a partnership deed, or very often, several. Land acquired by the partnership will be conveyed by the seller to the partners upon these trusts. Amongst the partners any limitation or direction as to the powers of the trustees will be contained in the trust instrument. However, to comply with s.8 the limitation must be contained in the disposition which created the trust land, *i.e.* it must be contained in the conveyance to the nominee partners.

Subs. (2)
This has to be read together with s.10. If the disposition requires the consent of more than two people, then a failure to obtain all the required consents will be a breach of trust. However, s.10 deals with the position so far as a purchaser is concerned. The oddity is that it is sensible for the position so far as a purchaser is concerned to be related to the **disposition**, that is, a document that is part of the title. However, there is no reason why a limitation on the powers of the trustees as between them and the beneficiaries should be actually contained in "the disposition creating such a trust". Nevertheless, failure to comply with it will still be a breach of trust, s.8(2) is simply declaratory of an obvious proposition but it only states part of the obvious principle applicable.

Subs. (3)
The definition of "charitable, ecclesiastical or public trust" is also relevant to s.2(5) of this Act.
Charitable Trusts. These are presently dealt with by the Charities Act 1992 (c. 41). Despite the extension of the powers of all trustees of land contained in s.6 of the new Act the requirements of the Charities Act 1992 must still be complied with see s.6(6) to (8) of this Act. The most accessible account of the rules for dealing with charity land is found in Sweet and Maxwell's *Conveyancing Practice.*
Ecclesiastical Trusts. So far as ecclesiastical or public trusts are concerned this expression derives from s.29 of the SLA 1925. The meaning of ecclesiastical trusts was discussed inconclusively in *St Swithin's Norwich, Re* [1960] P.78. It does not include land vested in an incumbent but beyond that the case gives little assistance. It suggests "Parliament intended no more than to include ... those ecclesiastical and public trusts which are not charitable in the legal sense". Examples given are *Re Stratton* [1931] Ch. 197, a gift to a vicar to divide among parochial institutions or purposes; *Re Cleveland Literary and Philosophical Society's Land* [1931] Ch. 247; *Oxford Group v. I.R.C.* [1949] W.N. 343, a trust for religious purposes which was not charitable. *Re Cleveland* involved an unincorporated society for encouraging literature, science and art. The court (Farwell J.) said "this property is held primarily on trust for the encouragement of literature, science and art, and not for the benefit of the members; and since the encouragement of literature, science and art is a public purpose, the primary purpose for which the land is held is public. Under these circumstances I think that this is a case of a public and not a private trust, and that it comes within s.29".

Delegation by trustees

9.—(1) The trustees of land may, by power of attorney, delegate to any beneficiary or beneficiaries of full age and beneficially entitled to an interest in possession in land subject to the trust any of their functions as trustees which relate to the land.

(2) Where trustees purport to delegate to a person by a power of attorney under subsection (1) functions relating to any land and another person in good faith deals with him in relation to the land, he shall be presumed in favour of that other person to have been a person to whom the functions could be delegated unless that other person has knowledge at the time of the transaction that he was not such a person.

And it shall be conclusively presumed in favour of any purchaser whose interest depends on the validity of that transaction that that other person dealt in good faith and did not have such knowledge if that other person makes a statutory declaration to that effect before or within three months after the completion of the purchase.

(3) A power of attorney under subsection (1) shall be given by all the trustees jointly and (unless expressed to be irrevocable and to be given by way of security) may be revoked by any one or more of them; and such a power is revoked by the appointment as a trustee of a person other than those by whom it is given (though not by any of those persons dying or otherwise ceasing to be a trustee).

(4) Where a beneficiary to whom functions are delegated by a power of attorney under subsection (1) ceases to be a person beneficially entitled to an interest in possession in land subject to the trust—

(a) if the functions are delegated to him alone, the power is revoked,

(b) if the functions are delegated to him and to other beneficiaries to be exercised by them jointly (but not separately), the power is revoked if each of the other beneficiaries ceases to be so entitled (but otherwise functions exercisable in accordance with the power are so exercisable by the remaining beneficiary or beneficiaries), and

(c) if the functions are delegated to him and to other beneficiaries to be exercised by them separately (or either separately or jointly), the power is revoked in so far as it relates to him.

(5) A delegation under subsection (1) may be for any period or indefinite.

(6) A power of attorney under subsection (1) cannot be an enduring power within the meaning of the Enduring Powers of Attorney Act 1985.

(7) Beneficiaries to whom functions have been delegated under subsection (1) are, in relation to the exercise of the functions, in the same position as trustees (with the same duties and liabilities); but such beneficiaries shall not be regarded as trustees for any other purposes (including, in particular, the purposes of any enactment permitting the delegation of functions by trustees or imposing requirements relating to the payment of capital money).

(8) Where any function has been delegated to a beneficiary or beneficiaries under subsection (1), the trustees are jointly and severally liable for any act or default of the beneficiary, or any of the beneficiaries, in the exercise of the function if, and only if, the trustees did not exercise reasonable care in deciding to delegate the function to the beneficiary or beneficiaries.

(9) Neither this section nor the repeal by this Act of section 29 of the Law of Property Act 1925 (which is superseded by this section) affects the operation after the commencement of this Act of any delegation effected before that commencement.

DEFINITION
"beneficiary": s.22.

GENERAL NOTE
This section contains a new power of delegation by the trustees to a beneficiary. It enables all trustees of land to delegate any of their functions in relation to the land as trustee to a beneficiary in possession. It replaces the powers of a tenant for life under the SLA 1925 and the powers of delegation under s.29 of the LPA 1925. Section 9 contains a much wider power of delegation than either of these provisions as the trustees can choose to delegate all their powers which, under s.6, are those of an absolute owner. Unlike the position of the tenant for life under the SLA 1925, delegation is at the trustees' discretion (subject to the possibility of an application by the beneficiary to the court to enforce delegation under s.14). The section gives trustees generous protection from the improvident acts of the beneficiary attorney (subs. (8)), being liable if and only if they failed to exercise reasonable care in making the appointment. A further safeguard arises under subs. (3) allowing the trustees to revoke the appointment at any time.

Section 9 permits the trustees to delegate their functions as a body. If individual trustees want to delegate their trusteeship, they will still have to make use of s.25 of the Trustee Act 1925 (c. 19) or the Enduring Power of Attorney Act 1985 (c. 29).

It should be noted that s.9 cannot be excluded. There is no reference to a contrary intention, either in relation to existing trusts or those arising after the commencement of the Act.

Subs. (1)

The Power of Delegation. The trustees can delegate all or any of their functions to one or more beneficiaries of full age who are beneficially entitled to an interest in land. This would include a beneficiary with an immediate life interest, but not a beneficiary, even of full age, with a contingent interest. Nor would it allow delegation to a beneficiary whose interest is in the income of land held on trust for sale. It must be a joint delegation by all the trustees (subs. (3)). Delegation can be of all or any of the trustees' functions, jointly or separately, to one or more beneficiaries, with the possibility of splitting the functions between the beneficiaries. As only functions which relate to the land can be delegated, powers of investment, even of the proceeds of sale, cannot be delegated under this provision.

Subs. (2)

Protection of Purchasers and others. The person dealing in good faith with an attorney is protected from a delegation to a person who does not fulfil the requirements of being of full age or beneficially entitled in possession. It is presumed that delegation could be made to the purported attorney unless the person dealing with the attorney knew that he was not a person to whom the trustees could delegate their powers. This means that a transaction will be valid in favour of a person dealing with the attorney providing they take the normal steps, *i.e.* purchasers can rely on normal proof of the power of attorney. As it is only *presumed* that such a person did not know of a failure to comply with the requirements of subs. (1), the transaction will be invalidated by proof of actual knowledge of such irregularity. Where the person who originally dealt with the attorney (who did not fit the description in subs. (1)) enters into a transaction with a purchaser, there is further protection available for that purchaser. It is conclusively presumed in favour of the purchaser that the person dealing with the attorney did not have knowledge of such invalidity if the person dealing with the attorney makes a statutory declaration to that effect before or within three months of the purchase. The presumption here is conclusive and cannot be rebutted. A purchaser is protected, even if it can be established that the person dealing with the attorney knew of the irregularity.

The protection given by this subsection to purchasers and those dealing with the attorney is very similar to that given to those people under the Powers of Attorney Act 1971 (c. 27). Section 5 of the 1971 Act will govern the position of, and protection available to such people, where there has been a revocation of the power.

Subss. (3) and (4)

Revocation. Although the power must be given jointly, any one trustee can revoke it at any time (except for a security power expressed to be irrevocable). This allows a new trustee to decide whether to adopt the attorney, as his appointment revokes the power automatically. He, and the continuing trustees, can then grant a renewed power, if so desired. Where a person simply ceases to be a trustee (by dying or retiring) but without a substitutional appointment being made, there is no automatic revocation.

Where a power is given by way of security and is expressed to be irrevocable, it cannot be revoked by a trustee. Nor would the appointment of a new trustee have that effect.

The effect of subs. (4) is that where a beneficiary loses his beneficial entitlement to an interest in possession in land, any delegation in his favour, whether alone or jointly, will be revoked. Other beneficiaries still within that beneficial entitlement will be able to continue to exercise a joint power of delegation, or a power which has been delegated for separate exercise to them and the disentitled beneficiary.

Subss. (5) and (6)

Delegation Period. Delegation can be for whatever fixed period the trustees deem appropriate, or indefinite (subs. (5)). As it cannot be an enduring power (subs. (6)), it will be revoked by a trustee's mental incapacity. This is because there is nothing in the Act to displace the normal rule that a power of attorney is revoked by the mental incapacity of the donor.

Subs. (7)

Liability of the Attorney. This places the beneficiary-attorney, in the exercise of the delegated functions, in the same position as the trustees, with the same duties and liabilities. They have the same standard of care as the trustees and are directly liable for actions which, if carried out by the trustees, would be a breach of trust. For example, the beneficiary would not (without further authority) be able to sell to him/herself and, in effecting a sale, would have a duty to obtain the best price.

Where issues of duty and liability do not relate to the exercise of the delegated functions, attornies under this section do not have the responsibilities of a trustee. They would not, for example, be liable for the wrongful investment by the trustees of the proceeds of sale, even if the power of sale had been delegated to them. The subsection expressly preserves the present position regarding over-reaching, *i.e.* payment must be made to two trustees or a trust corporation. The beneficiary-attorney cannot give a good receipt alone for capital money or be one of the two trustees necessary for a good receipt.

Subs. (8)

Trustees' Liability. This restricts the trustees' liability for delegation, which is joint and several, to the situation where they did not exercise reasonable care in deciding to delegate their function(s). For example, delegation to an 18-year-old with no experience of property management, or to someone with a track record of mismanaging their own affairs, might be considered unreasonable. The intention was to force trustees to adopt the standard of the ordinary prudent person in deciding whether to delegate the functions to the particular beneficiary (*Hansard*, H.L., April 22, 1996 p.960).

If the reference to failure to take reasonable care refers solely to trustees' liability for the appointment, their supervisory duties would continue (in the absence of an appropriate indemnity clause). Against this interpretation is the reference in subs. (8) to the trustees being liable "only if" they did not exercise reasonable care in delegating. It seems to have the effect of removing all other responsibility, and liability, for the actions of the attorney-beneficiary. This does not accord with the proposals made by the Law Commission in its Report—*Transfer of Land: Trusts of Land* (Law Comm. No. 181) that "trustees of land will be liable to the other beneficiaries for the acts or defaults of the donee(s). Therefore, the trustees will have a clear incentive to adopt a supervisory role" (para. 11.3).

Whatever their liability, trustees will be able to continue to exercise a measure of control over the attorney through the requirements that they receive capital money (subs. (7)). In this respect the provisions reflect the position of the tenant for life. The ambiguity, however, about the extent of their duties may cause difficulties in the future of the sort reflected in the discussions on *Re Vickery* [1931] 1 Ch. 572.

Consents and consultation

Consents

10.—(1) If a disposition creating a trust of land requires the consent of more than two persons to the exercise by the trustees of any function relating to the land, the consent of any two of them to the exercise of the function is sufficient in favour of a purchaser.

(2) Subsection (1) does not apply to the exercise of a function by trustees of land held on charitable, ecclesiastical or public trusts.

(3) Where at any time a person whose consent is expressed by a disposition creating a trust of land to be required to the exercise by the trustees of any function relating to the land is not of full age—

 (a) his consent is not, in favour of a purchaser, required to the exercise of the function, but

 (b) the trustees shall obtain the consent of a parent who has parental responsibility for him (within the meaning of the Children Act 1989) or of a guardian of his.

DEFINITIONS

 "disposition": s.17(6).
 "purchase": s.23(1).

GENERAL NOTE

This section protects a purchaser from any requirement in the trust instrument to obtain more than two consents to a disposition, or from the need to obtain the consent of an infant. Section 26 of the LPA 1925 is repealed (Sched. 4) and these new provisions apply to any "disposition creating a trust of land" (subs. (1)) which makes the exercise of the trustees' powers subject to the consent of others. It is therefore now possible for the trust instrument to state that the trustees must obtain such consent whether the interests under the trust are concurrent or successive. This represents a radical change from the position under the SLA 1925 where, in the case of successive interests and in the absence of a trust for sale, it was impossible to fetter the exercise in any way of the powers of a tenant for life.

The LPA 1925, s.26(1) and (2) provided a model for s.10.

There are two significant differences:

(i) s.10 does not apply to charitable, ecclesiastical or public trusts, where the purchasers will be bound to ensure that all consents are obtained (see the note on s.8(3) for discussion of these phrases).
(ii) s.10 does not state what is to happen where the person whose consent is required becomes mentally incapable.

In that case the trustees would have to obtain the consent of any attorney acting under an enduring power created by the mentally disordered person, his receiver, or make an application under s.14 to dispense with the consent.

The rules in s.10 apply to dispositions after the commencement date, whatever the date of the trust. Dispositions before the commencement date are governed by s.26 LPA 1925. There is no provision for excluding the operation of s.10.

Subs. (1)
The Purchaser. The trust instrument may stipulate that any number of consents shall be obtained to the exercise by the trustees of any function. If the consent of more than two is required the consent of any two is sufficient in favour of the purchaser. By s.23(1) "purchaser" has the same meaning as in Pt. I of the LPA 1925. Section 205(1)(xx) states that in Pt. I "purchaser" only means a person who acquires an interest in or charge on property for money or money's worth. It makes no difference whether the purchaser acquires a legal or an equitable interest. Whilst the purchaser is relieved of the need to obtain more than two consents, if so required, the trustees have a duty to obtain all the specified consents. Failure to do so will constitute a breach of trust unless an order has been made under s.14 relieving them of this duty.

Subs. (3)
Infancy. The purchaser is relieved of the need to see the consent of an infant. However, the trustees cannot ignore that child's consent if it is required by the trust instrument. They must obtain instead the consent of a parent or guardian (or make the appropriate application under s.14).

Consultation with beneficiaries

11.—(1) The trustees of land shall in the exercise of any function relating to land subject to the trust—
  (a) so far as practicable, consult the beneficiaries of full age and beneficially entitled to an interest in possession in the land, and
  (b) so far as consistent with the general interest of the trust, give effect to the wishes of those beneficiaries, or (in case of dispute) of the majority (according to the value of their combined interests).
  (2) Subsection (1) does not apply—
  (a) in relation to a trust created by a disposition in so far as provision that it does not apply is made by the disposition,
  (b) in relation to a trust created or arising under a will made before the commencement of this Act, or
  (c) in relation to the exercise of the power mentioned in section 6(2).
  (3) Subsection (1) does not apply to a trust created before the commencement of this Act by a disposition, or a trust created after that commencement by reference to such a trust, unless provision to the effect that it is to apply is made by a deed executed—
  (a) in a case in which the trust was created by one person and he is of full capacity, by that person, or
  (b) in a case in which the trust was created by more than one person, by such of the persons who created the trust as are alive and of full capacity.
  (4) A deed executed for the purposes of subsection (3) is irrevocable.

DEFINITIONS
"beneficiary": s.22.
"disposition": s.17(6).

GENERAL NOTE
This section imposes on trustees of land a duty to consult the beneficiaries before exercising their powers. It applies to all three types of trusts of land: express, implied and constructive, and

also applies whether the interests are concurrent or successive. It extends to express trusts a rule that formerly applied to implied trusts for sale under the now repealed s.26(3) of the LPA 1925.

Subs. (1)

The duty to consult. This is limited in para. (a) to beneficiaries of full age and beneficially entitled to an interest *in possession in the land*. This is a change from the wording of s.26(3) of the LPA 1925, which referred to trustees consulting all beneficiaries with interests in "possession in the rents and profits of the land". Section 11 excludes a requirement to consult beneficiaries under a trust of land whose interests are expressly stated to be only in the rents and profits. The duty is *as far as practicable* to consult the beneficiaries (para. (a)). There is, for example, no need to make disproportionately expensive or vigorous efforts to consult absent beneficiaries.

The trustees do not necessarily have to accede to the beneficiaries' views. By para. (b) the duty to give effect to the wishes of the beneficiaries is limited to where this will be consistent with the general interest of the trust. There will be no need to apply to court under s.14 to ignore the beneficiaries' wishes if they do not accord with such interest. If there is a dispute between the beneficiaries as to the course of action, the trustees must follow the wishes of the majority in value.

Subss. (2) to (4)

Application of s.11. The duty to consult will never apply in relation to the exercise of the trustees' powers under s.6(2) (subs. (2)(c)). Otherwise, it applies to all trusts created after the commencement of the Act unless there is express provision for its exclusion in the trust instrument. This possibility of exclusion applies to "dispositions" (subs. (2)(a)), and will not apply to implied, resulting or constructive trusts. It is likely that this is the main type of trust to which s.11 will apply.

For trusts created before the commencement date, the position depends upon whether the trust was created in a will or by deed. Section 11 never applies to trusts created or arising under a will made before the Act (subs. 2(b)). Where a trust created before the Act, or after the Act by reference to a trust created before, was made by deed, the provisions of s.11 can be expressly incorporated into the trust. The settlor or surviving settlors (subs. (3)(a)(b)) must expressly execute a deed to that effect. The deed is irrevocable (subs. (4)). If this deed is not executed, and as s.26 of the LPA 1925 has been repealed, there will be no duty to consult the beneficiaries in respect of such a trust.

Right of beneficiaries to occupy trust land

The right to occupy

12.—(1) A beneficiary who is beneficially entitled to an interest in possession in land subject to a trust of land is entitled by reason of his interest to occupy the land at any time if at that time—

(a) the purposes of the trust include making the land available for his occupation (or for the occupation of beneficiaries of a class of which he is a member or of beneficiaries in general), or

(b) the land is held by the trustees so as to be so available.

(2) Subsection (1) does not confer on a beneficiary a right to occupy land if it is either unavailable or unsuitable for occupation by him.

(3) This section is subject to section 13.

DEFINITION

"beneficiary": s.22.

GENERAL NOTE

There has been much uncertainty over whether a person with a beneficial interest in land held on trust for sale has a right to occupy the land. This entirely new provision clarifies the position.

It applies where a beneficiary is entitled to an interest *in possession in land*. For a beneficiary under a trust this becomes the crucial question. The difference is between a situation where the beneficiary has an interest in the land and where the beneficiary has only an interest in the income and proceeds of sale. Note that s.22(3) provides that an annuitant is not a person with an interest in possession in land subject to the trust.

Where there is an express trust for sale, the interest of the beneficiary will usually be an interest in the proceeds and not in the land. This precise distinction was clearly intended by the Law Commission in its Report—*Transfer of Land: Trusts of Land* (Law Comm. No. 181). In para.

13.3 the Commission stated: "We recommend that certain beneficiaries should have a right to occupy the trust land. This right will extend only to beneficiaries with a present, vested interest in the land". A footnote to this sentence explains the thinking of the Law Commission even more clearly: "In other words, those with a purely monetary interest, or with a future or contingent interest, will be excluded. Where the trust is a discretionary one, beneficiaries will only have an interest if and when the trustees have exercised the discretion in their favour".

In respect of trusts of land this distinction operates as follows:

Implied trusts of land. Whenever a trust of land comes into being by operation of law, the beneficiaries of that trust will have an interest in land. This is so whether the trust is an implied, resulting, or constructive trust or a statutory trust coming into effect because land is conveyed to more than one person. This is so because s.35 of the LPA 1925 which imposed upon such trusts the statutory trusts (so that the interests in beneficiaries would be interests in the proceeds of sale) is repealed.

Express trusts of land. Very often the interest of the beneficiary is an interest only in income, *e.g.* where the form of words is that the trustees "stand possessed of the net proceeds of sale and of the net rent and profits until the sale upon the trusts declared". The trust of the income will then be something like "to stand possessed of the income of the trust fund and the net rents and profits of the property until sale upon trust for AB for life and thereafter". In this case AB does not have a possession in land but only in the income of the trust fund. This is so notwithstanding the effect of s.3. The abolition of the doctrine of conversion in respect of trusts for sale means that land held by trustees is to be regarded as land. This does not mean that the interest of the beneficiary is an interest in land—the interest is what it is stated to be, if it is only in income, it is only income. Thus, in the leading case (for tax purposes) on interests in possession, *Pearson v. I.R.C.* [1981] A.C. 753 the concept of an interest in possession involved the present right to immediate enjoyment of that thing. If the trust is that the beneficiary is entitled to income of a fund that is what he is entitled to and in which he has an interest in possession. The definitions in the LPA 1925 are incorporated in this Act (see s.23(2)). There the definition of possession is as follows—"s.205(1)(xix) 'possession' includes receipts of rents and profits or the right to receive the same, if any; and 'income' includes rents and profits;". Where a beneficiary has the right to receive income from a fund (that is the right to immediate enjoyment in the *Pearson* sense) he has an interest in possession in that fund. The land (which may be the sole property in that fund) is vested in the trustees and the rent of that land is paid to them by any tenant because they have the right to receive it. The trustees are in possession of the land and the beneficiaries of the fund.

Abolition of Doctrine of Conversion (see s.3)

It might be thought that the abolition of the doctrine of conversion affects the above analysis. This is not so. The consequence of the abolition of the doctrine of conversion is that the land which is subject to a trust for sale is to be regarded as land. Whether a particular beneficiary is entitled to an interest in possession in land under a trust will depend on the analysis of the nature of their interest. The position is as follows:

In the case of a discretionary trust, no beneficiary has an interest in possession.

In the case of an implied resulting or constructive trust, whenever created, the beneficiaries for whom the land is held via trust will almost always have an interest in possession. This is so whenever the trust comes into being. There is no question of the interest being an interest in income only as the statutory trusts (s.35 of the LPA 1925) have been abolished.

Very rarely the terms of a constructive trust will require successive interests (in circumstances such as *Binions v. Evans* [1972] Ch. 359, and see for discussion (1977) 93 L.Q.R. 561 (HA Hornby)).

Where the terms of the trust make it clear that the only interest of the beneficiary is an interest in income and profits from a fund of money then no right of occupation can arise.

The right of occupation under this section is, in any event, available only if either s.12(1)(a) or (b) is satisfied. These paragraphs are infelicitously drafted.

Subs. (1)(a)

It is not clear here what is meant by the "purpose" of the trust. Are these to be discovered from "purposes" expressed in the trust instrument, or will the court embark upon the kind of speculative journey it has taken in "family home" cases under s.30 of the LPA 1925 (and s.17 of the Married Women's Property Act 1882)? In a string of such cases the court has embarked on an enquiry into the "purpose of the trust"—notably *Dennis v. McDonald* [1982] Fam. 63; *Evers' Trust, Re; Papps v. Evers* [1980] 1 W.L.R. 1327; and setting the scene for three decades of such judicial fiction *Jones v. Challenger* [1961] 1 Q.B. 176. The willingness of the court to manufacture a "purpose" which the parties to an arrangement may or may not ever have had must be an object lesson to settlors. Consideration must be given to making the purpose of the trust explicit in the trust instrument.

Subs. (1)(b)
There is presumably intended to be a difference between this and the former paragraph. It is inconceivable that the legislature can intend the land to be regarded as "so available" if the purposes of the trust are expressly that it is not to be so available. To this extent (a) must take precedence over (b) and the importance of clearly expressed *purposes* be realised by the drafts-person. Where land is not intended to be available for occupation then it might be sensible to say so succinctly in the trust deed. Otherwise this paragraph seems to introduce a simple test of fact.

Subs. (2)
These two factual tests of "unavailability" or "unsuitability" do nothing to make the trustees' role easier. Is a castle unsuitable for a drug-debauched heir apparent? Is a house unavailable because it is presently occupied by retired retainers whom the trustees have the right but not the will to evict? For the managing trustees this right of occupation and the astonishingly vague terms in which it is circumscribed are a considerable nuisance.

Subs. (3)
This simple statement is not without its problems—in particular, the extent to which s.12 can simply be excluded.

Exclusion of s.12
It is not provided for in s.12 that it can be expressly excluded. By subs. (3), s.12 is made subject to s.13. Section 13(6) refers to situations "where the entitlement of any beneficiary to occupy land under s.12 has been excluded or restricted". This, however, probably refers to an exclusion or restriction by the beneficiaries under s.13 rather than one contained in the trust instrument. The safer view is to deal with the question of exclusion by a clear statement that the purposes of the trust do not include occupation by a beneficiary and that the land is unavailable for such purposes.

Exclusion and restriction of right to occupy

13.—(1) Where two or more beneficiaries are (or apart from this subsection would be) entitled under section 12 to occupy land, the trustees of land may exclude or restrict the entitlement of any one or more (but not all) of them.

(2) Trustees may not under subsection (1)—
(a) unreasonably exclude any beneficiary's entitlement to occupy land, or
(b) restrict any such entitlement to an unreasonable extent.

(3) The trustees of land may from time to time impose reasonable conditions on any beneficiary in relation to his occupation of land by reason of his entitlement under section 12.

(4) The matters to which trustees are to have regard in exercising the powers conferred by this section include—
(a) the intentions of the person or persons (if any) who created the trust,
(b) the purposes for which the land is held, and
(c) the circumstances and wishes of each of the beneficiaries who is (or apart from any previous exercise by the trustees of those powers would be) entitled to occupy the land under section 12.

(5) The conditions which may be imposed on a beneficiary under subsection (3) include, in particular, conditions requiring him—
(a) to pay any outgoings or expenses in respect of the land, or
(b) to assume any other obligation in relation to the land or to any activity which is or is proposed to be conducted there.

(6) Where the entitlement of any beneficiary to occupy land under section 12 has been excluded or restricted, the conditions which may be imposed on any other beneficiary under subsection (3) include, in particular, conditions requiring him to—

(a) make payments by way of compensation to the beneficiary whose entitlement has been excluded or restricted, or

(b) forgo any payment or other benefit to which he would otherwise be entitled under the trust so as to benefit that beneficiary.

(7) The powers conferred on trustees by this section may not be exercised—

(a) so as prevent any person who is in occupation of land (whether or not by reason of an entitlement under section 12) from continuing to occupy the land, or

(b) in a manner likely to result in any such person ceasing to occupy the land,

unless he consents or the court has given approval.

(8) The matters to which the court is to have regard in determining whether to give approval under subsection (7) include the matters mentioned in subsection (4)(a) to (c).

DEFINITION
    "beneficiary": s.22.

GENERAL NOTE
    This section is confusing in various aspects of its drafting. It received little attention in its passage through Parliament and when litigated will prove hard to apply. Parts of the section apply only where two or more beneficiaries are entitled under s.12 to occupy land and parts of the section apply to all cases which fall under s.12. The application is as follows:
    Subsection (1) applies if there are two or more beneficiaries entitled.
    Subsection (2) applies only when subs. (1) applies.
    Subsection (6) can only apply if there are two beneficiaries entitled.
    Subsections (3), (4), (5), (7) and (8) appear to apply to all cases which fall under s.12.
    The main difficulty of application, therefore, is with s.13(6), which may refer to a permitted total exclusion of s.12. This is dealt with further in the note on subs. (6). When s.13 is examined as a whole it seems to make most coherent sense if it is assumed that the whole of the section applies only when two or more beneficiaries are entitled to occupy land. Yet, this is clearly not so as there is nothing in subs. (3) and the following subsections, other than subs. (6), to link them to this fundamental requirement in subs. (1).

Subs. (1)
    There is a certain lack of reality about this provision. In numerical terms the trusts that come within this subsection will be overwhelmingly co-ownership trusts of houses. All these, whether bought in joint names or the result of an implied or constructive trust, will be trusts of land and usually have two, and sometimes more, beneficiaries who fall under s.12 as having the right to occupy trust land. However, any dispute between beneficiaries such as these will in reality not be resolved by application of s.13. What will be required is an application to the court under s.14 for the court to apply its very wide jurisdiction under that section. In express trusts set up to provide a long-term vehicle for the tax-efficient management of family assets, it is equally hard to see how this provision will help. For new such trusts it can be envisaged that drafting steps will be taken to circumvent or exclude the right. This is discussed at length in the General Note on s.12.

Subs. (2)
    This is legislation at its most pointless. Trustees must not exclude a beneficiary unreasonably or restrict their right "to an unreasonable extent". No real clue is given as to what is reasonable or unreasonable. In the context of the family home, is it unreasonable to ask somebody to share a house with a person they do not like? In the context of a trust of a landed estate, is it unreasonable to refuse occupation to an heir who is a devotee of free love and new age philosophy? This is, if ever there was one, an area where "one man's meat is another man's poison". Does the trustee have a discretion or not? The answer is yes, so long as this is exercised reasonably. Regrettably, in context, all that the introduction of this concept does is to transfer the discretion to the court. Given the propensity of the court to read into former trusts for sale purposes never averred to by their creators, there is all the more need for draftspersons to express clearly the purposes for which land is held by a trust.

Subs. (3)
    The concept of *reasonableness* has already received comment in the note on subs. (2). It appears possible that that subsection and the remainder of s.13 apply to cases where there is

only one beneficiary entitled. What sort of conditions are reasonable is a matter of open-ended speculation.

Of some interest is the question of whether a beneficiary can be required to pay rent for the land occupied. There are particular circumstances (subs. (6)) where payments akin to rent may be required. Where that does not apply then the wording of this subsection does not exclude a more general condition requiring rent. The court may find some relevance in the previous case law as to payment of rent to non-occupying tenants in common. Of particular interest is *Dennis v. McDonald* [1982] Fam. 63. The relevant principle was expressed by Millet J. in *Pavlou (A Bankrupt), Re* [1993] 1 W.L.R. 1046 as "...a court of equity will order an inquiry and payment of occupation rent, not only in the case where the co-owner in occupation has ousted the other, but in any other case in which it is necessary in order to do equity between the parties that an occupation rent should be paid" (p.959).

Subs. (4)

This is possibly of some help in drafting trust instruments. The factors specified in subs. (4)(a) and (b) may be spelled out in the trust instrument. Where they are not so spelled out (and this will be the case in virtually all trusts existing at the date of the Act) how are these intentions and purposes to be discovered? So far as (c) is concerned there is one small oddity. It says that the circumstances and wishes of each beneficiary entitled to occupy the land are matters to which the trustees must have regard. This cannot, presumably, mean that they are to have no regard to the wishes of other beneficiaries—reversioners or dowagers, for example, who might have strong views on whether the ancestral home should be occupied by a drug addict.

Subs. (5)

Since these conditions are conditions imposed under subs. (3), then the outgoings, expenses or obligations must be reasonable. The matters referred to here are requirements for the beneficiary to take over existing obligations in relation to the land. These vague matters are covered by an over-arching requirement of reasonableness but there can still be difficulties of interpretation. Can conditions be imposed as to future charitable activities on the land? Can the beneficiary be required to house or employ particular retainers? Can requirements about the support or fostering of country sports be included in the list of conditions? Since the examples of types of conditions given in this subsection are only examples of the open-ended class of *reasonable conditions*, all of these it seems may be possible and it is never necessary to test the meaning of any of the particular phrases used in subs. (5). This leads to the conclusion that subs. (5) is otiose.

Subs. (6)

This applies where there were two or more beneficiaries entitled to occupy under s.12 and the entitlement of one or more has been excluded or restricted. Then the trustees may impose reasonable conditions which lead to any beneficiary in occupation making financial contributions to the one or more beneficiaries whose rights have been excluded or restricted.

Subss. (7) and (8)

These subsections give support to the view that s.13 as a whole is not involved with a world of reality. The fetter it imposes on a trustee's discretion is so great that it will be either ignored or litigated. The circumstances where the beneficiaries would wish to litigate will most often be those intractable "family home" cases which would have been resolved (satisfactorily) under s.30 of the LPA 1925.

Powers of court

Applications for order

14.—(1) Any person who is a trustee of land or has an interest in property subject to a trust of land may make an application to the court for an order under this section.

(2) On an application for an order under this section the court may make any such order—

(a) relating to the exercise by the trustees of any of their functions (including an order relieving them of any obligation to obtain the consent of, or to consult, any person in connection with the exercise of any of their functions), or

(b) declaring the nature or extent of a person's interest in property subject to the trust, as the court thinks fit.

(3) The court may not under this section make any order as to the appointment or removal of trustees.

(4) The powers conferred on the court by this section are exercisable on an application whether it is made before or after the commencement of this Act.

DEFINITIONS
"trustee of land": s.17(1).
"trust of land": s.17(2)(3).

GENERAL NOTE
Section 14 enables a trustee of the land, or any person with an interest in the property subject to a trust of land, to apply to the court to order a proposed course of action (subs. (2)(a)). To this extent it mimics s.30 of the LPA 1925. In addition, the court has two powers not available under s.30 of the LPA 1925. Firstly, it can declare the nature or extent of a claimant's interest in the property (subs. (2)(b)). Secondly, the wording of subs. (2)(a) is wide enough to allow it to authorize transactions which would otherwise be a breach of trust. The court has no jurisdiction, however, to make any order as to the appointment or removal of trustees under s.14 (subs. (3)).

The provisions in s.14 come into force on the commencement date, applying to all applications whether made before or after the commencement of the Act (subs. (4)). Section 30 of the LPA 1925 is repealed. The extensive case law setting out the criteria that must be applied in deciding an application under s.30, particularly in relation to ordering a sale, would at first sight appear to have little relevance to applications under s.14. This is because s.15 prescribes the matters that a court must take into account in exercising its discretion in determining applications under s.14. The case law is not entirely redundant though, still having a place in analysing the criteria under s.15 and also s.17 of the Married Women's Property Act 1882 (c. 75). The court still has a discretion under the 1882 Act to order a sale of property owned by spouses, former spouses (s.39 of the Matrimonial Proceedings and Property Act 1970 (c. 45)) and former engaged couples (s.2(2) of the Law Reform (Miscellaneous Provisions) Act 1970 (c. 33)). The discretion under s.17 of the 1882 Act and s.30 of the LPA 1925 was exercised on the same basis (*Jackson v. Jackson* [1971] 1 W.L.R. 1539) and decisions on s.30 of the LPA 1925 will still be relevant in deciding applications under s.17 of the 1882 Act.

Subs. (1)
Power to make applications. Applications can be made by any trustee of land, or by any person with an interest in property subject to a trust of land. This must be read in the light of s.17. The effect of s.17(2) is that the application can be made by a trustee or beneficiary of the proceeds of sale of land (subs. (2)).

"Proceeds of sale of land" includes any "property representing such proceeds" (s.17(3)(b)). There is no requirement that the proceeds have been further invested in land and this would enable application to be made where, for example, shares have been purchased with the proceeds of sale of the land.

The jurisdiction given to the court in subs. (2)(a) to make orders relating to the trustees' functions is very wide, reflecting the Law Commission's view that the "courts should be able to intervene in any dispute relating to a trust of land" (Law Comm. No. 181, para. 12.6). It will frequently involve deciding applications for an order for a sale in a dispute between the trustees (*e.g.* co-owners of the family home) or trustees and beneficiaries or on application by creditors. As the power to dispose of property with successive interests has now passed from the tenant for life under the SLA 1925 to the trustees, this section may be used by beneficiaries in future to prevent dispositions of property by the trustees.

Subs. (2)
The order. The wording specifically refers to orders relieving the trustees of the duty to obtain consents. In addition, the very general words in subs. (2)(a) giving the court jurisdiction to make orders "relating to the exercise of any of their functions" are wide enough to cover any aspect of the trust administration. They would encompass orders authorising other actions which would otherwise be a breach of trust, for example, purchase of the trust property by a trustee.

Paragraph (b) confers jurisdiction on the court to make orders declaring the nature or extent of a person's interest in the property subject to the trust. Usually this will be clearly established by the trust instrument or, in the case of co-owners, a declaration of trust. This means that the provisions will most usually be needed where there is a claim to an interest in property under a resulting or constructive trust. The principles used to decide the outcome of such cases are unaffected by s.15. Recourse will still be had to the case law, to decide whether a claimant has an interest, (see, for example, *Lloyds Bank v. Rosset* [1989] Ch. 350) and the type of interest (see, for example, *Grant v. Edwards* [1986] Ch. 638). Even in cases of recognized co-ownership, the section may occasionally be needed. An example would be the *Huntingford v. Hobbs* [1993] 1 F.L.R. 736 situation where the court had to decide whether the registered proprietors were joint tenants or tenants in common. The section may also be used to settle disputes about the extent of the beneficial interest.

Matters relevant in determining applications

15.—(1) The matters to which the court is to have regard in determining an application for an order under section 14 include—
  (a) the intentions of the person or persons (if any) who created the trust,
  (b) the purposes for which the property subject to the trust is held,
  (c) the welfare of any minor who occupies or might reasonably be expected to occupy any land subject to the trust as his home, and
  (d) the interests of any secured creditor of any beneficiary.
  (2) In the case of an application relating to the exercise in relation to any land of the powers conferred on the trustees by section 13, the matters to which the court is to have regard also include the circumstances and wishes of each of the beneficiaries who is (or apart from any previous exercise by the trustees of those powers would be) entitled to occupy the land under section 12.
  (3) In the case of any other application, other than one relating to the exercise of the power mentioned in section 6(2), the matters to which the court is to have regard also include the circumstances and wishes of any beneficiaries of full age and entitled to an interest in possession in property subject to the trust or (in case of dispute) of the majority (according to the value of their combined interests).
  (4) This section does not apply to an application if section 335A of the Insolvency Act 1986 (which is inserted by Schedule 3 and relates to applications by a trustee of a bankrupt) applies to it.

DEFINITION
    "beneficiary": s.22.

GENERAL NOTE
    Section 14 must be read with s.15 as it sets out the criteria to be applied by the court in determining an application under s.14. It should have regard to the four matters listed in subs. (1)(a)–(d). These are the matters which the court would have applied in considering an application under s.30 of the LPA 1925, the Law Commission's aim here being to consolidate and rationalise. This clear statement of the relevant criteria removing the need to consider the purpose of the trust (*Re Buchanan-Wollaston's Conveyance* [1939] Ch. 738), is to be welcomed. Nevertheless, the case law is merely given statutory force and not made redundant. Its help may be invoked in interpreting the criteria under s.15. More importantly the section provides no order of precedence nor weighting to be attached to the matters it deems relevant and again recourse may be had to the case law (*e.g.* in relation to subs. (1) below).

Subs. (1)
    The criteria. The wording of this provision allows for the possibility of further matters not listed in the section being relevant in the determination of an application. The use of the word "include" shows that the list is not intended to be prescriptive. Of the four matters mentioned in the subsection, paras. (a) and (b) refer respectively to the intentions of the person(s) who created the trust and the purposes for which the property subject to the trust is held. Difficulties in establishing these points could be avoided by appropriate declarations at the time of purchase. For example, although the power of delegation cannot be excluded, a statement by the settlor of why there should be no delegation would be considered by the court on an application by a beneficiary under s.14 to force such a delegation. Paragraph (c) in specifying the welfare of any minor who occupies or might reasonably be expected to occupy the land as his home is a simple reflection of the case law position, whereby the provision of a home for the children can be implicit in the purpose as in *Evers' Trust, Re; Papps v. Evers* [1980] 1 W.L.R. 1327. Making the interests of the children an independent consideration does mean that there is no danger of them being treated as incidental to the beneficial interests and the provision of a matrimonial home, and therefore not within the purpose of the trust (*Holliday (A Bankrupt), Re; ex p. Trustee of the Bankrupt v. Bankrupt, The* [1981] Ch. 405).

This statutory guidance on the matters relevant to deciding applications does remove the uncertainty inherent in deciding applications under s.30 of the LPA 1925, where the court was looking for the collateral or underlying purpose behind the trust for sale. Problems remain with the lack of priority between these matters. What happens where there is a conflict of interest between the welfare of any children, para. (c) and the interests of the second creditors, as specified in para. (d)? Applying the case law, by virtue of s.30 of the LPA 1925 priority will be given to the interests of the creditors, *Citro, Domenico (A Bankrupt), Re*; *Citro, Carmine (A Bankrupt), Re* [1991] Ch. 142. The Law Commission in its report concluded that there is much of value in the existing body of case law (Law Comm. No. 181, para. 12.9).

Subss. (2) and (3)
The beneficiaries' interests. The beneficiaries' circumstances and wishes are matters to which the court must have regard. Where the application relates to occupation rights, the court must consider the beneficiaries who are or would be entitled to occupy the land under s.12 (subs. (2)). Where the application under s.15 concerns any other power, the court must have regard to the circumstances of beneficiaries of full age and entitled to an interest in possession. If there is a dispute, then the interests of the majority in value will prevail (subs. (3)). There is no duty to consider the beneficiaries where the application relates to s.6(2).

Subs. (4)
Where the s.14 application is by a trustee in bankruptcy, s.15 is inapplicable. The trustee applies to the court with jurisdiction over the bankruptcy (Sched. 3, adding a new s.335A to the Insolvency Act 1986 (c. 45)). The criteria to be applied to all applications by a trustee, whether the parties are married or not, are set out in s.335A(2). These reflect the repealed provisions (Sched. 4) in s.336(3) Insolvency Act 1986. As in s.336(5) there is a provision in s.335(A)(3) that, in the absence of exceptional circumstances, on an application a year after the property vests in a trustee in bankruptcy, the interests of the bankrupt's creditors outweigh all other considerations. These rules apply to an application whether it is made before or after the commencement date of the Act (*ibid.* subs. (4)).

Purchaser protection

Protection of purchasers

16.—(1) A purchaser of land which is or has been subject to a trust need not be concerned to see that any requirement imposed on the trustees by section 6(5), 7(3) or 11(1) has been complied with.

(2) Where—
(a) trustees of land who convey land which (immediately before it is conveyed) is subject to the trust contravene section 6(6) or (8), but
(b) the purchaser of the land from the trustees has no actual notice of the contravention,
the contravention does not invalidate the conveyance.

(3) Where the powers of trustees of land are limited by virtue of section 8—
(a) the trustees shall take all reasonable steps to bring the limitation to the notice of any purchaser of the land from them, but
(b) the limitation does not invalidate any conveyance by the trustees to a purchaser who has no actual notice of the limitation.

(4) Where trustees of land convey land which (immediately before it is conveyed) is subject to the trust to persons believed by them to be beneficiaries absolutely entitled to the land under the trust and of full age and capacity—
(a) the trustees shall execute a deed declaring that they are discharged from the trust in relation to that land, and
(b) if they fail to do so, the court may make an order requiring them to do so.

(5) A purchaser of land to which a deed under subsection (4) relates is entitled to assume that, as from the date of the deed, the land is not subject to the trust unless he has actual notice that the trustees were mistaken in their belief that the land was conveyed to beneficiaries absolutely entitled to the land under the trust and of full age and capacity.

(6) Subsections (2) and (3) do not apply to land held on charitable, ecclesiastical or public trusts.

(7) This section does not apply to registered land.

DEFINITION
"purchaser": s.23.

GENERAL NOTE
This section has the purpose of absolving the purchaser from the need to investigate whether there has been a breach of trust in various circumstances.

Subs. (1)
The purchaser does not have to investigate whether the trustees have:
  (a) had regard to the rights of beneficiaries (s.6(5));
  (b) obtained the consent of beneficiaries to a partition (s.7(3));
  (c) consulted the beneficiaries (s.11(1)).
The subsection says that the purchaser "need not be concerned to see" that these matters are complied with. Does this mean that a sale can never be impeached against a seller on these grounds? The answer must be given in stages as follows:
  (i) it is clear from the wording that the first proposition given in this note must be correct; the purchaser has no positive duty to investigate these matters;
  (ii) it also seems tolerably certain from the words used that a purchaser is not affected simply by failure to make enquiries which a reasonably competent purchaser would make;
  (iii) the position cannot be stated with such certainty if the purchaser actually knows of the breach. However, the words are that the purchaser "need not be concerned". This suggests that even actual knowledge does not damnify the purchaser;
  (iv) however, it cannot be that a purchaser who is a party to a breach can escape the consequences. Thus, if the trustees agree to a sale to P and agree with P not to consult the beneficiaries or obtain their consent (when there was a duty to do either) then the sale can be impeached as against P. This obvious application of the principle of equitable fraud cannot be intended to be prevented by Parliament except by the clearest words which are not present. A purchaser from P, however, is protected by principle (iii) unless he is himself a party to the equitable fraud.

Subs. (2)
A purchaser of land from the trustees is protected from a breach of s.6(6) or (8) unless they have actual knowledge of the infringement. This seems to apply to a purchase from trustees which involves a breach of any enactment whatsoever or any rule of law.

Subs. (3)
This is a very odd and wholly ineffectual provision. The trustees are required to take steps to tell a purchaser that their powers are limited. There is no consequence of their failure to do so; they will be in breach of trust in any event and subject to possible action by the beneficiaries. Subsection (3)(b) provides that a conveyance is not invalidated where a purchaser has no actual notice of the limitation but this is inconceivable if the trustees comply with subs. (3)(a) and tell the purchaser of the limitation.

Subss. (4) and (5)
On the face of it, these provisions appear to assist in simplifying conveyancing. There may be an ongoing trust of land and the situation arises that a certain person(s) is/are entitled to the land beneficially. The trustees can convey the land to that person and at the same time (and sensibly in the same deed) execute a declaration that the trust has ended. On this declaration a purchaser may rely. However, the following problems arise:
  (i) Does this provision apply where there is a single trustee? The plural trustees is used through the Act. The Interpretation Act 1978 (c. 30), s.6 provides that the plural includes the singular; as does s.61(c) of the LPA 1925 which is incorporated in this Act by s.23(2). It, thus, appears that a deed of discharge may be executed by one trustee.
  (ii) The position of a purchaser under subs. (5) is not strong. It applies if the purchaser has actual notice that the beneficiaries were either not entitled or not of full age and capacity. If the purchaser is aware of any of these defects then the trustees were mistaken in that regard in their belief and the purchaser has actual notice of that mistaken belief.

Subs. (6)
For a discussion of the meaning of this exception see the note on s.8(3).

Subs. (7)
The non-application to registered land is because a purchaser of registered land can rely upon the state of the register. If it is intended to restrict the trustees' powers or require particular consents, then the settlor will wish to see restriction(s) placed on the register of title.

Supplementary

Application of provisions to trusts of proceeds of sale

17.—(1) Section 6(3) applies in relation to trustees of a trust of proceeds of sale of land as in relation to trustees of land.

(2) Section 14 applies in relation to a trust of proceeds of sale of land and trustees of such a trust as in relation to a trust of land and trustees of land.

(3) In this section "trust of proceeds of sale of land" means (subject to subsection (5)) any trust of property (other than a trust of land) which consists of or includes—

(a) any proceeds of a disposition of land held in trust (including settled land), or

(b) any property representing any such proceeds.

(4) The references in subsection (3) to a trust—

(a) are to any description of trust (whether express, implied, resulting or constructive), including a trust for sale and a bare trust, and

(b) include a trust created, or arising, before the commencement of this Act.

(5) A trust which (despite section 2) is a settlement for the purposes of the Settled Land Act 1925 cannot be a trust of proceeds of sale of land.

(6) In subsection (3)—

(a) "disposition" includes any disposition made, or coming into operation, before the commencement of this Act, and

(b) the reference to settled land includes personal chattels to which section 67(1) of the Settled Land Act 1925 (heirlooms) applies.

GENERAL NOTE
The definition of a trust of land as a trust which has land in it (s.1) has led the draftsperson to see the need to deal separately with trusts which have no land but only the proceeds of land. However, this then requires separate provisions for trusts which have in them the proceeds of settled land—because, while there is land in them, these are not trusts of land.

Subs. (1)
Trustees who have in hand the proceeds of sale of land may use it to purchase a legal estate in land under s.6(3). If the trust falls under the SLA 1925 then land may be purchased pursuant to s.73 of that Act. If it is not an SLA 1925 trust, then this provision applies.

Subs. (2)
The provisions of s.14 allow for application to the court to settle disputes over the shares in a trust or the exercise of the trustee's powers. These apply to a trust of the proceeds of sale.

Subss. (3)–(6)
These four subsections together give the definition of a trust of proceeds of sale. They are drafted with unusual opaqueness but the effect is as follows.

(i) If the trust in question falls under the SLA 1925, then it cannot be a trust of the proceeds of land (subs. (5)). For the circumstances when an existing SLA trust ceases to come under the SLA 1925 see the note on s.2.

(ii) Otherwise there is a trust of the proceeds of sale of land which was formerly held on a trust of land or an SLA settlement so long as it is no longer a trust of land. In the case of trusts other than existing SLA 1925 trusts, this will happen when there is no land left. In the case of a former SLA settlement this may happen pursuant to either s.2(3) or (4).

Application of Part to personal representatives

18.—(1) The provisions of this Part relating to trustees, other than sections 10, 11 and 14, apply to personal representatives, but with appropriate modifications and without prejudice to the functions of personal representatives for the purposes of administration.

(2) The appropriate modifications include—

(a) the substitution of references to persons interested in the due administration of the estate for references to beneficiaries, and

(b) the substitution of references to the will for references to the disposition creating the trust.

(3) Section 3(1) does not apply to personal representatives if the death occurs before the commencement of this Act.

GENERAL NOTE

This mirrors the more elegantly drafted s.33 of the LPA 1925 which is not, of course, repealed since Pt. I of the LPA 1925 remains in force. Section 33 is simply amended by Sched. 3, para. 4(9) so that it applies to trusts of land which fall within that Part.

Subs. (3)

For the treatment of the doctrine of conversion, see s.3(1) above. Where a person has died before the commencement of this Act, then the personal representatives will hold on a trust for sale if a grant of administration is taken out before the commencement of this Act—by virtue of the statutory trusts implied under s.33 of the Administration of Estates Act 1925.

PART II

APPOINTMENT AND RETIREMENT OF TRUSTEES

Appointment and retirement of trustee at instance of beneficiaries

19.—(1) This section applies in the case of a trust where—

(a) there is no person nominated for the purpose of appointing new trustees by the instrument, if any, creating the trust, and

(b) the beneficiaries under the trust are of full age and capacity and (taken together) are absolutely entitled to the property subject to the trust.

(2) The beneficiaries may give a direction or directions of either or both of the following descriptions—

(a) a written direction to a trustee or trustees to retire from the trust, and

(b) a written direction to the trustees or trustee for the time being (or, if there are none, to the personal representative of the last person who was a trustee) to appoint by writing to be a trustee or trustees the person or persons specified in the direction.

(3) Where—

(a) a trustee has been given a direction under subsection (2)(a),

(b) reasonable arrangements have been made for the protection of any rights of his in connection with the trust,

(c) after he has retired there will be either a trust corporation or at least two persons to act as trustees to perform the trust, and

(d) either another person is to be appointed to be a new trustee on his retirement (whether in compliance with a direction under subsection (2)(b) or otherwise) or the continuing trustees by deed consent to his retirement,

he shall make a deed declaring his retirement and shall be deemed to have retired and be discharged from the trust.

(4) Where a trustee retires under subsection (3) he and the continuing trustees (together with any new trustee) shall (subject to any arrangements for the protection of his rights) do anything necessary to vest the trust property in the continuing trustees (or the continuing and new trustees).

(5) This section has effect subject to the restrictions imposed by the Trustee Act 1925 on the number of trustees.

DEFINITION
"beneficiary": s.22.

GENERAL NOTE
This section gives the beneficiaries two rights:
  (i) to direct the trustees to make a particular appointment; and
  (ii) to direct any of the trustees to retire.
Section 19 should be read in conjunction with s.21 which contains further details about the direction and power to exclude the application of these provisions.

Subs. (1)
Appointment and retirement at the instance of the beneficiaries. This makes s.19 inapplicable:
  (a) where "there is" a person nominated by the first instrument for the purpose of appointing new trustees. If that person is dead, there "is" no person so nominated and s.19 applies;
  (b) unless all the beneficiaries under the trust are of full age and capacity and (taken together) are absolutely entitled to the property subject to the trust. Discretionary trusts, charitable trusts and fixed trusts with unborn, infant, mentally incapable beneficiaries, or beneficiaries with a contingent interest, are clearly excluded.

Subss. (2)–(5)
The Direction. Subsection (2) empowers the beneficiaries to give the trustees directions to retire and/or to make the specified appointments of new trustees. The direction must be in writing, but the Act contains no provisions about the timing of it. As the trustees have no duty under the Act to notify beneficiaries of a potential vacancy, the beneficiaries could take advantage of this to give a direction to make an appointment of their choice even before there was a vacancy. It should be noted that:
  (a) the direction to retire is given only to the retiring trustee(s); but
  (b) the direction to make the specified appointment is given to all the trustees for the time being, of if there are none, to the personal representative of the last trustee. This direction must require the appointment to be made in writing (subs. (2)(b)). This follows s.36 of the Trustee Act 1925 (c. 19) requiring appointments to be made in writing with a deed commonly being used for vesting purposes (s.40 of the Trustee Act 1925). Whilst the direction may specify the appointment of additional trustees, it is subject to the restrictions in the number of trustees imposed by the Trustee Act 1925 in ss.34 and 36 (subs. (5)). There is nothing to prevent the beneficiaries from naming one of their number for appointment.
The Act does not define what constitutes giving a written direction to all the trustees. Is a written notice handed to one trustee but addressed to them all sufficient? For safety's sake, it is suggested that a copy of the written direction be sent to each trustee.
The Act contains no provision making it mandatory for the trustees to follow the beneficiaries' directions regarding appointment. This is by contrast with the earlier drafts of the Bill which required the trustees to make the specified appointment. In addition, the comparison with subs. 3(b) which compels the trustee to retire in certain circumstances, might lead to the conclusion that even the use of the word "direction" does not oblige the trustees to appoint the beneficiaries' nominee. It seems, however, more likely that a court would find the word "direction" sufficiently imperative to require compliance with its instructions. The other construction renders pointless the provisions of the Act in relation to the power of beneficiaries to direct an appointment; and for that reason is an untenable view. Nevertheless, the uncertainty on this issue and the consequential possibility of litigation is to be regretted.
Assuming the direction is mandatory, the question remains of the trustees' liability for an unsuitable appointment. It is not apparent whether the following of the beneficiaries' direction absolves trustees from their duty of care. If a resulting unsuitable appointment were construed as a breach of trust, the beneficiaries' direction having been given by them all, would this bar any action for breach of trust?
The direction to retire is mandatory if the conditions specified in s.19(3) are satisfied. Paragraph (b) entitles a trustee to an offer of reasonable arrangements for the protection of his rights

in connection with the trust. Reasonable arrangements would, for example, include unpaid fees and expenses. It would not include protection from liabilities, such as the arrangement of indemnities, where these are not already provided for by the trust instrument. The trustee, in line with s.39 of the Trustee Act 1925, cannot retire unless there will be either a trust corporation or two people left to perform the trust. Furthermore, unless there is to be a substitutional appointment, the continuing trustees must consent by deed to the retirement.

If they are not willing to consent to the retirement, the beneficiaries' wishes will be frustrated and the trustee cannot retire under s.19. In such circumstances, a trustee who felt he had lost the beneficiaries' confidence and wanted to retire would have to rely on the court's assistance (s.19 and also s.36 of the Trustee Act 1925 being unavailable where the co-trustees are refusing to consent to the retirement). The beneficiaries too would be powerless to compel the trustees to follow their directions. The court has no power to make an order under s.14 (see subs. (3)). Only if there is maladministration could the beneficiaries invoke the court's assistance.

Where the conditions are satisfied, retirement is by deed. Subsection (4) gives all the trustees, retiring, continuing and new, a duty to do anything necessary to vest the trust property in the continuing (or continuing and new trustees). There may be a need to make amendment to, for example, company share registers.

Appointment of substitute for incapable trustee

20.—(1) This section applies where—
(a) a trustee is incapable by reason of mental disorder of exercising his functions as trustee,
(b) there is no person who is both entitled and willing and able to appoint a trustee in place of him under section 36(1) of the Trustee Act 1925, and
(c) the beneficiaries under the trust are of full age and capacity and (taken together) are absolutely entitled to the property subject to the trust.
(2) The beneficiaries may give to—
(a) a receiver of the trustee,
(b) an attorney acting for him under the authority of a power of attorney created by an instrument which is registered under section 6 of the Enduring Powers of Attorney Act 1985, or
(c) a person authorised for the purpose by the authority having jurisdiction under Part VII of the Mental Health Act 1983,
a written direction to appoint by writing the person or persons specified in the direction to be a trustee or trustees in place of the incapable trustee.

DEFINITIONS
"beneficiary": s.22.
"disposition": s.17(6).
"mental disorder": s.23(2) and s.205(xiii) of the Law of Property Act 1925.
"receiver": s.23(2) and s.205(xiii) of the Law of Property Act 1925.
"will": s.23(2) and s.205(xxxi) of the Law of Property Act 1925.

GENERAL NOTE
This section provides for the situation where a mentally disordered trustee is incapable of carrying out his functions, and there is no one able and willing to appoint a replacement under s.36(1) of the Trustee Act 1925. Such a trustee cannot deal with the legal estate in the land (s.22(2) of the LPA 1925). Where the trustee also has a beneficial interest, a new appointment cannot be made without the leave of the person with authority under the Mental Health Act 1983 (c. 20) (unless it is made by the person nominated in the first instrument). If no such appointment is made by the other trustees, or there is no one to make it, the beneficiaries can give a *written* direction to appoint a substitute trustee. The applicability of this section will be limited. Normally the other trustees would want to appoint a replacement. Even a sole trustee may have delegated his functions under the Enduring Power of Attorney Act 1985 (c. 29). As with s.19 there are no express provisions compelling the trustees to follow the direction. An earlier provision to this effect was removed by later amendments.

Subs. (1)
Application of s.20. It is applicable whenever there is no one entitled, able and willing to appoint a substitute trustee for the mentally disordered trustee. This means that the beneficiaries can exercise their powers under this section even where there is an express power of appointment, if the person with the express power is unable to or unwilling to exercise it. By

para. (a), s.20 only applies if the trustee's mental disorder means that he is incapable of exercising his functions as a trustee. Mental disorder bears the same definition as in the LPA 1925 (s.23(2)) *i.e.* the meaning assigned to it by the Mental Health Act 1983, s.1.

The power to give a written direction can only be exercised by the beneficiaries where they are of full age and capacity and between them absolutely entitled to the property subject to the trust.

Subs. (2)
   The beneficiaries' direction. The beneficiaries' direction should be given to:
   (a) a receiver of the trustee;
   (b) an attorney for the trustee registered under the Enduring Powers of Attorney Act 1985; or
   (c) a person with authority to act under Pt. VII of the Mental Health Act 1983.
The direction can specify for the appointment of a "person or persons", allowing for the appointment of more than one trustee to replace the mentally disordered trustee. Although not expressly mentioned in s.20, there is no reason why the same restrictions on the number of trustees imposed by the Trustee Act 1925 will not apply.

Supplementary

21.—(1) For the purposes of section 19 or 20 a direction is given by beneficiaries if—
   (a) a single direction is jointly given by all of them, or
   (b) (subject to subsection (2)) a direction is given by each of them (whether solely or jointly with one or more, but not all, of the others),
and none of them by writing withdraws the direction given by him before it has been complied with.
   (2) Where more than one direction is given each must specify for appointment or retirement the same person or persons.
   (3) Subsection (7) of section 36 of the Trustee Act 1925 (powers of trustees appointed under that section) applies to a trustee appointed under section 19 or 20 as if he were appointed under that section.
   (4) A direction under section 19 or 20 must not specify a person or persons for appointment if the appointment of that person or those persons would be in contravention of section 35(1) of the Trustee Act 1925 or section 24(1) of the Law of Property Act 1925 (requirements as to identity of trustees).
   (5) Sections 19 and 20 do not apply in relation to a trust created by a disposition in so far as provision that they do not apply is made by the disposition.
   (6) Sections 19 and 20 do not apply in relation to a trust created before the commencement of this Act by a disposition in so far as provision to the effect that they do not apply is made by a deed executed—
   (a) in a case in which the trust was created by one person and he is of full capacity, by that person, or
   (b) in a case in which the trust was created by more than one person, by such of the persons who created the trust as are alive and of full capacity.
   (7) A deed executed for the purposes of subsection (6) is irrevocable.
   (8) Where a deed is executed for the purposes of subsection (6)—
   (a) it does not affect anything done before its execution to comply with a direction under section 19 or 20, but
   (b) a direction under section 19 or 20 which has been given but not complied with before its execution shall cease to have effect.

GENERAL NOTE
   Section 21 contains supplementary provisions relating to the beneficiaries' directions, and the power to exclude its operation.

Subss. (1) and (2)
   The beneficiaries' direction—Format and withdrawal. These provisions regulate the nature of the direction under ss.19 and 20. Although it physically may take the form of more 'han one

direction from any combination of beneficiaries, it will only be effective if each direction specifies the appointment or retirement of the same person or persons. Withdrawal in writing of the direction by any one of the beneficiaries before it is complied with, will make the direction ineffective (subss. (1) and (2)). There is no indication in the section of whether the withdrawal must be given to all the trustees, but this would be the safest course.

Subss. (3) and (4)
   The effect of appointment and identity of appointee in specific cases. A trustee appointed in pursuance of the beneficiaries' direction has the benefit of s.36(7) of the Trustee Act 1925, having all the powers of a trustee appointed by the trust instrument (sub. (3)). Subsection (4) makes s.35(1) of the Trustee Act 1925 and s.24(1) of the LPA 1925 applicable to a direction under ss.19 or 20, *i.e.* trustees of conveyances on trust for sale and of the settlement of the proceeds of sale must be the same persons, but appointed by separate instruments. This will occur where a separate document has been used to keep the trusts of the proceeds of sale off the title.

Subss. (5)–(8)
   Exclusion of power to give directions. These provisions regulate the exclusion of the beneficiaries' power of giving directions. For trusts, whether *inter vivos*, or by will, created after the commencement of the Act an express provision can be used to exclude ss.19 and 20 (subs. (5)). Whilst there may be a standard exclusion clause in express trusts, such exclusion will never apply to implied, resulting and constructive trusts. The sections will apply to wills made before the commencement of the Act, but can be excluded from existing trusts by deed. The settlor, or where there was more than one, the surviving settlors (being of full capacity) must execute a deed declaring that they shall not so apply (subs. (6)(a)(b)). Such a deed is irrevocable (subs. (7)), to prevent a settlor opting in and out. Any appointment pursuant to a beneficiaries' direction before the execution of such a deed would not be invalidated (subs. (7)(a)) but the direction could not be complied with after the deed has been executed (subs. (7)(b)).

PART III

SUPPLEMENTARY

Meaning of "beneficiary"

22.—(1) In this Act "beneficiary", in relation to a trust, means any person who under the trust has an interest in property subject to the trust (including a person who has such an interest as a trustee or a personal representative).

   (2) In this Act references to a beneficiary who is beneficially entitled do not include a beneficiary who has an interest in property subject to the trust only by reason of being a trustee or personal representative.

   (3) For the purposes of this Act a person who is a beneficiary only by reason of being an annuitant is not to be regarded as entitled to an interest in possession in land subject to the trust.

GENERAL NOTE
   This section gives a broad definition of beneficiary to include any person with an interest in the property subject to the trust. This brings within its scope a mortgagee or trustee in bankruptcy of one of two co-owners, whether the trust was created expressly or by implication.
   Those with interests as trustees or personal representative are expressly included in the definition of beneficiary by subs. (1). However, this is severely limited by subs. (2) which provides that references to a beneficiary do not include a trustee or a personal representative who is interested only in that capacity whenever there is a reference to a beneficiary who is "beneficially entitled". This makes the delegation, occupation and appointment and retirement provisions (ss.9, 12, 19 and 20) indubitably inapplicable to trustees and personal representatives as such although it will apply to them if they have a beneficial interest.
   Finally, subs. (3) makes it clear that a person with an interest under the trust as an annuitant is not to be regarded as entitled to an interest in possession in the land.
   Recourse to this definition in s.22 will be infrequent. The applicability of most sections is clear, without using s.22. Section 14, for example, makes it clear that a trustee, or any person with an interest in land can apply to court for an order.

Other interpretation provisions

23.—(1) In this Act "purchaser" has the same meaning as in Part I of the Law of Property Act 1925.

(2) Subject to that, where an expression used in this Act is given a meaning by the Law of Property Act 1925 it has the same meaning as in that Act unless the context otherwise requires.

(3) In this Act "the court" means—

(a) the High Court, or

(b) a county court.

GENERAL NOTE

Section 23 contains further definitions.

Subs. (1)

Purchaser. Purchaser is defined by reference to the definition for the purposes of Pt. I of the LPA 1925, which is: "a person who acquires an interest in or charge on property for money or money's worth; and in reference to a legal estate includes a chargee by way of legal mortgage" (s.205(xxi) of the LPA 1925).

Subs. (2)

Other Words. Other expressions have the same meaning as in the LPA 1925 unless the context otherwise requires. This includes *land* (s.205(ix) of the LPA 1925) although Sched. 4 of this Act repeals the words which remove tenancies in common from the definition of "Land". The repealed expressions are: "but not an undivided share in Land" and the words "but not an undivided share thereof". The reason is that with the substitution under the Act of the trust of land for the automatic trust for sale and the abolition of the doctrine of conversion, tenancies in common of land are bound to be interests in land.

Subs. (3)

The court—means either the High Court (para. (a)) or the county court (para. (b)) as appropriate.

Application to Crown

24.—(1) Subject to subsection (2), this Act binds the Crown.

(2) This Act (except so far as it relates to undivided shares and joint ownership) does not affect or alter the descent, devolution or nature of the estates and interests of or in—

(a) land for the time being vested in Her Majesty in right of the Crown or of the Duchy of Lancaster, or

(b) land for the time being belonging to the Duchy of Cornwall and held in right or respect of the Duchy.

Amendments, repeals, etc.

25.—(1) The enactments mentioned in Schedule 3 have effect subject to the amendments specified in that Schedule (which are minor or consequential on other provisions of this Act).

(2) The enactments mentioned in Schedule 4 are repealed to the extent specified in the third column of that Schedule.

(3) Neither section 2(5) nor the repeal by this Act of section 29 of the Settled Land Act 1925 applies in relation to the deed of settlement set out in the Schedule to the Chequers Estate Act 1917 or the trust instrument set out in the Schedule to the Chevening Estate Act 1959.

(4) The amendments and repeals made by this Act do not affect any entailed interest created before the commencement of this Act.

(5) The amendments and repeals made by this Act in consequence of section 3—

(a) do not affect a trust created by a will if the testator died before the commencement of this Act, and

(b) do not affect personal representatives of a person who died before that commencement;

and the repeal of section 22 of the Partnership Act 1890 does not apply in any circumstances involving the personal representatives of a partner who died before that commencement.

GENERAL NOTE
Section 25 gives force to the repeals and amendments set out in Scheds. 3 and 4.

Subs. (5)
 The Doctrine of Conversion. This subsection, in para. (a), provides that the abolition of the doctrine of conversion, and the consequential repeals and amendments, do not affect trusts created by will where the testator died before the commencement date (repeating s.3(2)). Trustees of such trusts are not affected by the abolition of this doctrine. Nor are the personal representatives of a person dying before the commencement date (para. (b)). Finally, the repeal of s.22 of the Partnership Act 1890 (c. 39) (which applied the doctrine of conversion to partnership land) will not affect the distribution of the estate of a partner who died before the commencement. Partnership shares in land are still to be treated as personalty in respect of such deaths. For deaths after the Act comes into force, such a share is a share in realty.

Power to make consequential provision

26.—(1) The Lord Chancellor may by order made by statutory instrument make any such supplementary, transitional or incidental provision as appears to him to be appropriate for any of the purposes of this Act or in consequence of any of the provisions of this Act.
 (2) An order under subsection (1) may, in particular, include provision modifying any enactment contained in a public general or local Act which is passed before, or in the same Session as, this Act.
 (3) A statutory instrument made in the exercise of the power conferred by this section is subject to annulment in pursuance of a resolution of either House of Parliament.

GENERAL NOTE
 The power given to vary legislation made in order to tidy up the effect of this Act is not a power that was found necessary in the remarkably well-drafted 1925 legislation. The problem with piecemeal "reform" such as that exemplified by this Act is that it tends to create as many problems as it solves. The Act, thus, provides an *ad hoc* solution to the problems it spawns.

Short title, commencement and extent

27.—(1) This Act may be cited as the Trusts of Land and Appointment of Trustees Act 1996.
 (2) This Act comes into force on such day as the Lord Chancellor appoints by order made by statutory instrument.
 (3) Subject to subsection (4), the provisions of this Act extend only to England and Wales.
 (4) The repeal in section 30(2) of the Agriculture Act 1970 extends only to Northern Ireland.

GENERAL NOTE
 The Act is to be brought in force as whole by a single appointed day order. The expected day is January 1, 1997.

SCHEDULES

Section 2   SCHEDULE 1

Minors

1.—(1) Where after the commencement of this Act a person purports to convey a legal estate in land to a minor, or two or more minors, alone, the conveyance—
 (a) is not effective to pass the legal estate, but
 (b) operates as a declaration that the land is held in trust for the minor or minors (or if he purports to convey it to the minor or minors in trust for any persons, for those persons).
 (2) Where after the commencement of this Act a person purports to convey a legal estate in land to—

(a) a minor or two or more minors, and

(b) another person who is, or other persons who are, of full age,

the conveyance operates to vest the land in the other person or persons in trust for the minor or minors and the other person or persons (or if he purports to convey it to them in trust for any persons, for those persons).

(3) Where immediately before the commencement of this Act a conveyance is operating (by virtue of section 27 of the Settled Land Act 1925) as an agreement to execute a settlement in favour of a minor or minors—

(a) the agreement ceases to have effect on the commencement of this Act, and

(b) the conveyance subsequently operates instead as a declaration that the land is held in trust for the minor or minors.

2. Where after the commencement of this Act a legal estate in land would, by reason of intestacy or in any other circumstances not dealt with in paragraph 1, vest in a person who is a minor if he were a person of full age, the land is held in trust for the minor.

Family charges

3. Where, by virtue of an instrument coming into operation after the commencement of this Act, land becomes charged voluntarily (or in consideration of marriage) or by way of family arrangement, whether immediately or after an interval, with the payment of—

(a) a rentcharge for the life of a person or a shorter period, or

(b) capital, annual or periodical sums for the benefit of a person,

the instrument operates as a declaration that the land is held in trust for giving effect to the charge.

Charitable, ecclesiastical and public trusts

4.—(1) This paragraph applies in the case of land held on charitable, ecclesiastical or public trusts (other than land to which the Universities and College Estates Act 1925 applies).

(2) Where there is a conveyance of such land—

(a) if neither section 37(1) nor section 39(1) of the Charities Act 1993 applies to the conveyance, it shall state that the land is held on such trusts, and

(b) if neither section 37(2) nor section 39(2) of that Act has been complied with in relation to the conveyance and a purchaser has notice that the land is held on such trusts, he must see that any consents or orders necessary to authorise the transaction have been obtained.

(3) Where any trustees or the majority of any set of trustees have power to transfer or create any legal estate in the land, the estate shall be transferred or created by them in the names and on behalf of the persons in whom it is vested.

Entailed interests

5.—(1) Where a person purports by an instrument coming into operation after the commencement of this Act to grant to another person an entailed interest in real or personal property, the instrument—

(a) is not effective to grant an entailed interest, but

(b) operates instead as a declaration that the property is held in trust absolutely for the person to whom an entailed interest in the property was purportedly granted.

(2) Where a person purports by an instrument coming into operation after the commencement of this Act to declare himself a tenant in tail of real or personal property, the instrument is not effective to create an entailed interest.

Property held on settlement ceasing to exist

6. Where a settlement ceases to be a settlement for the purposes of the Settled Land Act 1925 because no relevant property (within the meaning of section 2(4)) is, or is deemed to be, subject to the settlement, any property which is or later becomes subject to the settlement is held in trust for the persons interested under the settlement.

PROVISIONS CONSEQUENTIAL ON SECTION 2

GENERAL NOTE

This schedule contains a variety of provisions expressed to be consequential on s.2 of the Act which deals with the abolition of new SLA settlements.

para. 1(1)
   A conveyance of a legal estate to a minor takes effect as a declaration of trust. If there are two or more minors, it is a declaration of trust for them together. If the intention was that the minors should hold the land as trustees then it operates as a declaration of trust for the beneficiaries of that trust. The words of the section refer to a conveyance to the minor(s) "in trust for any person". However, the same result is presumably intended where the trust is for a valid purpose, *e.g.* a charitable trust? (but see the comment on para. 2 below).

para. 1(2)
   Where there is conveyance to minor(s) and person(s) of full age, then the land is vested in the person(s) of full age. The same comment applies on the use of the words "for any persons" as in para. 1(1).
   If the land is registered land, then the conveyance to the adult person(s) will be given effect to on the register of title.

para. 1(3)
   This will be an academic curiosity. There may be cases where, before this new Act, a conveyance to a minor or minors took effect by virtue of s.27, SLA 1925. Such a conveyance took effect as if it were an agreement for valuable consideration to execute a settlement in favour of the infant(s). The intention of the Act is that there should be no new strict settlements, instead the conveyance is to operate as if it were a declaration of trust in favour of the minors.

para. 2
   This is intended as "belt and braces" legislation but has an unexpected twist. Whenever, by any circumstances, a legal estate would vest in a minor, instead the land is to be held in trust for the minor. Suppose land is conveyed to a person who is a minor but on charitable trusts. On their strict wording neither para. 1(1) nor para. 1(2) apply (because there is no trust for persons); consequently para. 2 applies and the land is held in trust for the minor beneficially. This is an unexpectedly bizarre result.

para. 4
   This is consequential upon the repeal of s.29 of the SLA 1925.

para. 5
   This paragraph has the rather petty aim of preventing the creation of any more entailed interests. The technical words of limitation to create freehold estates and interests are one of the great studies of English land law. Much of the past was laid to rest on January 1, 1926 with the coming into effect of the 1925 legislation. In particular s.60(1) abolished the need for strict words, or indeed any words of limitation, to create a fee simple estate. So far as entails were concerned they could (by deed) be created from January 1, 1882 only by strict words of limitation (using the words "in tail" or "A and the heirs of his body"). This requirement for strict words of limitation was extended to wills by s.130 of the LPA 1925. Thus, at the time of the present Act an entail could be created only by strict words of limitation either "entail" or by the use of the expression "heirs" and not by alternative words of procreation. Oddly, the draftsperson in para. 5 refers to words which "purport ... to grant an entail". This must have been intended to mean words which would immediately before this Act came into force have created an entail although it does not quite say that. Literally it could quite easily be taken to mean grants where only the word "entail" is used. More oddly would be cases where the draftsman appears to try to create an entail but used the wrong words of procreation, *e.g.* to A and his successors. These cases were covered by s.130(2) of the LPA 1925 which is repealed. The repeal of parts of s.130 raised the spectre that we first have to return to the pre-1926 law in order to apply para. 5, but its net effect may best be realised by reading it with the following meaning "where the purport of any grant might be to create an entailed interest then para. (1)(b) takes effect". This means that any limitation on trust which has the effect that the donee's interest is equivalent in extent to an entailed interest is avoided.

para. 5(2)
   This was added in the passage of the Bill. Its aim is to prevent the creation of new entails by a settlor settling property on himself in tail. It says such a gift is not effective to create an entailed interest. The intention must be, though it is not expressed, that the settlor remains absolutely entitled; although by leaving this unsaid it is left open to argue the construction that the settlor has settled property on himself for life with appropriate remainders.

para. 6
   In the light of s.2(4), the meaning of which is perfectly clear, this paragraph seems superfluous. Imagine a strict settlement on the Earl of Cumbria of all the land in the Lake District National Park, if all the land is sold to the state, the resulting money is held on the same trusts as the land was formerly held. There is no longer an SLA 1925 settlement.

Section 5   SCHEDULE 2

AMENDMENTS OF STATUTORY PROVISIONS IMPOSING TRUST FOR SALE

Mortgaged property held by trustees after redemption barred

1.—(1) Section 31 of the Law of Property Act 1925 (implied trust for sale of mortgaged property where right of redemption is barred) is amended as follows.

(2) In subsection (1), for the words "on trust for sale." substitute "in trust—

    (a) to apply the income from the property in the same manner as interest paid on the mortgage debt would have been applicable; and

    (b) if the property is sold, to apply the net proceeds of sale, after payment of costs and expenses, in the same manner as repayment of the mortgage debt would have been applicable."

(3) In subsection (2), for the words from the beginning to "this subsection" substitute—
"(2) Subsection (1) of this section".

(4) Omit subsection (3).

(5) For subsection (4) substitute—
"(4) Where—

    (a) the mortgage money is capital money for the purposes of the Settled Land Act 1925;

    (b) land other than any forming the whole or part of the property mentioned in subsection (1) of this section is, or is deemed to be, subject to the settlement; and

    (c) the tenant for life or statutory owner requires the trustees to execute with respect to land forming the whole or part of that property a vesting deed such as would have been required in relation to the land if it had been acquired on a purchase with capital money,

the trustees shall execute such a vesting deed."

(6) In accordance with the amendments made by sub-paragraphs (2) to (5), in the sidenote of section 31 for the words "Trust for sale" substitute "Trust".

(7) The amendments made by this paragraph—

    (a) apply whether the right of redemption is discharged before or after the commencement of this Act, but

    (b) are without prejudice to any dealings or arrangements made before the commencement of this Act.

Land purchased by trustees of personal property etc.

2.—(1) Section 32 of the Law of Property Act 1925 (implied trust for sale of land acquired by trustees of personal property or of land held on trust for sale) is omitted.

(2) The repeal made by this paragraph applies in relation to land purchased after the commencement of this Act whether the trust or will in pursuance of which it is purchased comes into operation before or after the commencement of this Act.

Dispositions to tenants in common

3.—(1) Section 34 of the Law of Property Act 1925 is amended as follows.

(2) In subsection (2) (conveyance of land in undivided shares to operate as conveyance to grantees on trust for sale), for the words from "upon the statutory trusts" to "those shares" substitute "in trust for the persons interested in the land".

(3) In subsection (3) (devise etc. of land in undivided shares to operate as devise etc. to trustees of will etc. on trust for sale)—

    (a) omit the words from "the trustees (if any)" to "then to" and the words "in each case", and

    (b) for the words "upon the statutory trusts hereinafter mentioned" substitute "in trust for the persons interested in the land".

(4) After that subsection insert—

    "(3A) In subsections (2) and (3) of this section references to the persons interested in the land include persons interested as trustees or personal representatives (as well as persons beneficially interested)."

(5) Omit subsection (4) (settlement of undivided shares in land to operate only as settlement of share of profits of sale and rents and profits).

(6) The amendments made by this paragraph apply whether the disposition is made, or comes into operation, before or after the commencement of this Act.

Joint tenancies

4.—(1) Section 36 of the Law of Property Act 1925 is amended as follows.

(2) In subsection (1) (implied trust for sale applicable to land held for persons as joint tenants), for the words "on trust for sale" substitute "in trust".

(3) In subsection (2) (severance of beneficial joint tenancy)—

(a) in the proviso, for the words "under the trust for sale affecting the land the net proceeds of sale, and the net rents and profits until sale, shall be held upon the trusts" substitute "the land shall be held in trust on terms", and

(b) in the final sentence, for the words "on trust for sale" substitute "in trust".

(4) The amendments made by this paragraph apply whether the legal estate is limited, or becomes held in trust, before or after the commencement of this Act.

Intestacy

5.—(1) Section 33 of the Administration of Estates Act 1925 (implied trust for sale on intestacy) is amended as follows.

(2) For subsection (1) substitute—

"(1) On the death of a person intestate as to any real or personal estate, that estate shall be held in trust by his personal representatives with the power to sell it."

(3) In subsection (2), for the words from the beginning to "pay all" substitute—

"(2) The personal representatives shall pay out of—

(a) the ready money of the deceased (so far as not disposed of by his will, if any); and

(b) any net money arising from disposing of any other part of his estate (after payment of costs),

all".

(4) In subsection (4), for the words from "including" to "retained" substitute "and any part of the estate of the deceased which remains".

(5) The amendments made by this paragraph apply whether the death occurs before or after the commencement of this Act.

Reverter of sites

6.—(1) Section 1 of the Reverter of Sites Act 1987 (right of reverter replaced by trust for sale) is amended as follows.

(2) In subsection (2)—

(a) after "a trust" insert "for the persons who (but for this Act) would from time to time be entitled to the ownership of the land by virtue of its reverter with a power, without consulting them,", and

(b) for the words "upon trust" onwards substitute "in trust for those persons; but they shall not be entitled by reason of their interest to occupy the land."

(3) In subsection (3), for the words "trustees for sale" substitute "trustees".

(4) In subsection (4), for the words "on trust for sale" substitute "in trust".

(5) In accordance with the amendments made by this paragraph, in the sidenote, for "trust for sale" substitute "trust".

(6) The amendments made by this paragraph apply whether the trust arises before or after the commencement of this Act.

Trusts deemed to arise in 1926

7. Where at the commencement of this Act any land is held on trust for sale, or on the statutory trusts, by virtue of Schedule 1 to the Law of Property Act 1925 (transitional provisions), it shall after that commencement be held in trust for the persons interested in the land; and references in that Schedule to trusts for sale or trustees for sale or to the statutory trusts shall be construed accordingly.

GENERAL NOTE

The various paragraphs of this Schedule all deal with cases where the 1925 legislation imposed a trust for sale. For the sake of conformity, these have to be converted to trusts of land. That is the result of the numerous amendments made by this schedule.

para. 1

Trustees may have power to lend money upon the security of a mortgage. The borrower may lose the benefit of the equity of redemption by foreclosure, by limitation of title, by disclaimer or surrender. In such a case s.31 of the LPA 1925 provided that the trustees held the land upon trust for sale. This paragraph changes any existing such trust for sale into a trust of land and provides that in future cases the trustees will hold the land on a trust of land.

para. 1(5)

The new s.31(4) has the following purpose: first, it must be recalled that an existing strict settlement is no longer dealt with under the SLA 1925, once there is no land in the settlement (s.2(4) of this Act). The new provisions make sense only on the basis that where trustees of settled land lend money on a mortgage, the estate vested in them (as mortgagees) is not regarded as settled land. This seems to be implicit in the former s.31(4), now repealed, which assumes that the mortgage was held by the trustees and not vested in the tenant for life under s.10 of the SLA 1925. This view means that once there is no land (except the mortgage) forming part of the settlement then s.2(4) does apply and there is no longer an SLA 1925 settlement. If there is any other land in the settlement when the equity of redemption is lost then the tenant for life or statutory owner can require the formerly mortgaged land to be vested in him by a vesting deed.

para. 1(7)

These new rules are retrospective, except in so far as steps have been taken to apply the former rules.

para. 2

Section 32 of the LPA 1925 implied a trust for sale where trustees of personal property or of a trust for sale purchased land. This is unnecessary as in such cases there will now be a trust of land (by virtue of s.1 of this Act). Accordingly, s.32, LPA 1925 is repealed. However, para. 2(2) of that section still applies to any purchase made before this Act and after December 31, 1911 (LPA 1925, s.32(2)) but, all trusts for sale so created are turned into trusts of land by s.1 of the present Act.

The amendments to s.34, LPA 1925 have little practical effect. There can still be no conveyance of a legal estate to tenants in common (s.34(1), LPA 1925).

Wherever land is, or was, expressed to be conveyed to persons as tenants in common, then the conveyance takes effect as a conveyance to them (or the first four names) as joint tenants upon a trust of land for themselves as tenants in common (s.34(2), as amended).

para. 4

These amendments to s.36 LPA 1925 have no practical significance. Where land is, or was, conveyed to joint tenants then they hold upon a trust of land. The rules for severance are unaffected. A legal joint tenancy cannot be severed. When a joint tenancy in equity is severed, then the equitable interests are held on a trust of land.

para. 5

Section 33 of the Administration of Estates Act 1925 imposed an implied trust for sale on any land or personal property in an intestate estate. Instead, whenever the death occurred or occurs the trustees hold the land on trust with a power of sale. If there is land in the estate, this is held on a trust of land.

para. 6

This amendment to the well known provisions of s.1 of the Reverter of Sites Act 1987 (c. 15) has some practical significance. In the case of a reverter to which that Act applies, the land was held on a trust for sale. Now, whenever that reverter occurred or occurs, the land is held on trust for the person to whom it would revert. This trust is one that gains them no right to occupy the land (para. 6(2)(b)). They may, however, have an interest in possession and the provisions of s.11 of the Act appear to apply to them, but s.1(2) of the 1987 Act is amended so that they have no right to be consulted.

Section 25(1)   SCHEDULE 3

MINOR AND CONSEQUENTIAL AMENDMENTS

The Law of Property Act 1922 (c. 16)

1. In paragraph 17(3) and (4) of Schedule 15 to the Law of Property Act 1922, for the words "held on trust for sale" substitute "subject to a trust of land".

The Settled Land Act 1925 (c. 18)

2.—(1) The Settled Land Act 1925 is amended as follows.

(2) In section 1(1)(ii)(c), after the word "fee" insert "(other than a fee which is a fee simple absolute by virtue of section 7 of the Law of Property Act 1925)".

(3) In section 3, for the words "not held upon trust for sale which has been subject to a settlement" substitute "which has been subject to a settlement which is a settlement for the purposes of this Act".

(4) In section 7(5), for the words "trustee for sale" substitute "trustee of land".

(5) In section 12(1), for the words "trustee for sale" substitute "trustee of land".

(6) In section 17—

(a) in subsection (1)—
     (i) for the words "trust for sale", in the first three places, substitute "trust of land", and
     (ii) for the words "held on trust for sale" substitute "subject to a trust of land",

(b) in subsection (2)(c), for the words "a conveyance on trust for sale" substitute "land", and

(c) in subsection (3), for the words "any trust for sale" substitute "a trust of land".

(7) In section 18(2)(b), for the words "trustee for sale" substitute "trustee of land".

(8) In section 20(1)(viii), for the words "an immediate binding trust for sale" substitute "a trust of land".

(9) In section 30(1)—

(a) in paragraph (iii), for the words "power of or upon trust for sale of" substitute "a power or duty to sell", and

(b) in paragraph (iv)—
     (i) for the words "future power of sale, or under a future trust for sale of" substitute "a future power or duty to sell", and
     (ii) for the words "or trust" substitute "or duty".

(10) In section 33(1), for the words "any power of sale, or trust for sale" substitute "a power or duty to sell".

(11) In section 36—

(a) for the words—
     (i) "upon the statutory trusts" in subsection (2), and
     (ii) "on the statutory trusts" in subsection (3),
substitute "in trust for the persons interested in the land",

(b) in subsection (4), for the words "trust for sale" substitute "trust of land",

(c) for subsection (6) substitute—
    "(6) In subsections (2) and (3) of this section references to the persons interested in the land include persons interested as trustees or personal representatives (as well as persons beneficially interested).", and

(d) in accordance with the amendments made by paragraphs (a) to (c), in the sidenote, for the words "trust for sale of the land" substitute "trust of land".

(12) In section 110(5), for the words "trustee for sale" substitute "trustee of land".

(13) In section 117(1)—

(a) in paragraph (ix), for the words "not being" substitute ", but does not (except in the phrase "trust of land") include", and

(b) in paragraph (xxx), for the words " "trustees for sale" and "power to postpone a sale" have the same meanings" substitute "has the same meaning".

The Trustee Act 1925 (c. 19)

3.—(1) The Trustee Act 1925 is amended as follows.

(2) In section 12—

(a) in subsection (1), for the words "a trust for sale or a power of sale of property is vested in a trustee" substitute "a trustee has a duty or power to sell property", and

(b) in subsection (2), for the word "trust", in both places, substitute "duty".

(3) In section 14(2), for paragraph (a) substitute—
    "(a) proceeds of sale or other capital money arising under a trust of land;".

(4) In section 19—

(a) in subsection (1), for the words "against loss or damage by fire any building or other insurable property" substitute "any personal property against loss or damage", and

(b) in subsection (2), for the words "building or" substitute "personal".

(5) In section 20(3)(c), for the words "property held upon trust for sale" substitute "land subject to a trust of land or personal property held on trust for sale".

(6) In section 24—

(a) for the words "the proceeds of sale of land directed to be sold, or in any other" substitute "any",

(b) for the words "trust for sale" substitute "trust",

(c) for the words "trustees for sale" substitute "trustees", and

(d) for the words "trust or" substitute "duty or".

(7) In section 27(1), for the words "or of a disposition on trust for sale" substitute ", trustees of land, trustees for sale of personal property".

(8) In section 32, for subsection (2) substitute—

"(2) This section does not apply to capital money arising under the Settled Land Act 1925."

(9) In section 34(2), for the words "on trust for sale of land" substitute "creating trusts of land".

(10) In section 35—

(a) for subsection (1) substitute—

"(1) Appointments of new trustees of land and of new trustees of any trust of the proceeds of sale of the land shall, subject to any order of the court, be effected by separate instruments, but in such manner as to secure that the same persons become trustees of land and trustees of the trust of the proceeds of sale.",

(b) for subsection (3) substitute—

"(3) Where new trustees of land are appointed, a memorandum of the persons who are for the time being the trustees of the land shall be endorsed on or annexed to the conveyance by which the land was vested in trustees of land; and that conveyance shall be produced to the persons who are for the time being the trustees of the land by the person in possession of it in order for that to be done when the trustees require its production.", and

(c) in accordance with the amendments made by paragraphs (a) and (b), in the sidenote, for the words "dispositions on trust for sale of land" substitute "and trustees of land".

(11) In section 36(6), for the words before paragraph (a) substitute—

"(6) Where, in the case of any trust, there are not more than three trustees—".

(12) In section 37(1)(c), for the word "individuals" substitute "persons".

(13) In section 39(1), for the word "individuals" substitute "persons".

(14) In section 40(2), for the words "the statutory power" substitute "section 39 of this Act or section 19 of the Trusts of Land and Appointment of Trustees Act 1996".

The Law of Property Act 1925 (c. 20)

4.—(1) The Law of Property Act 1925 is amended as follows.

(2) In section 2—

(a) in subsection (1), in paragraph (ii)—

(i) for the words "trustees for sale" substitute "trustees of land", and

(ii) for the words "the statutory requirements respecting the payment of capital money arising under a disposition upon trust for sale" substitute "the requirements of section 27 of this Act respecting the payment of capital money arising on such a conveyance",

(b) after that subsection insert—

"(1A) An equitable interest in land subject to a trust of land which remains in, or is to revert to, the settlor shall (subject to any contrary intention) be overreached by the conveyance if it would be so overreached were it an interest under the trust.", and

(c) in subsection (2)—

(i) for the words "a trust for sale" substitute "a trust of land",

(ii) for the words "under the trust for sale or the powers conferred on the trustees for sale" substitute "by the trustees", and

(iii) for the words "to the trust for sale" substitute "to the trust".

(3) In section 3(1)(c), for the words "Where the legal estate affected is neither settled land nor vested in trustees for sale" substitute "In any other case".

(4) In section 16—

(a) in subsection (2), for the words "pursuant to a trust for sale" substitute "by trustees of land", and

(b) in subsection (6), for the words "trustee for sale" substitute "trustee of land".

(5) In section 18—

(a) in subsection (1)—

(i) after the word "settled" insert "or held subject to a trust of land", and

(ii) for the words "trustee for sale" substitute "trustee of land", and

(b) in subsection (2)(b), for the words "of the land or of the proceeds of sale" substitute "or trust".

(6) In section 22(2)—

(a) for the words "held on trust for sale" substitute "subject to a trust of land", and

(b) for the words "under the trust for sale or under the powers vested in the trustees for sale" substitute "by the trustees",

and, in accordance with the amendments made by paragraphs (a) and (b), in the sidenote of section 22, for the words "on trust for sale" substitute "in trust".

(7) For section 24 substitute—

"Trusts of land

Appointment of trustees of land

24.—(1) The persons having power to appoint new trustees of land shall be bound to appoint the same persons (if any) who are for the time being trustees of any trust of the proceeds of sale of the land.

(2) A purchaser shall not be concerned to see that subsection (1) of this section has been complied with.

(3) This section applies whether the trust of land and the trust of proceeds of sale are created, or arise, before or after the commencement of this Act."

(8) In section 27—

(a) for subsection (1) substitute—

"(1) A purchaser of a legal estate from trustees of land shall not be concerned with the trusts affecting the land, the net income of the land or the proceeds of sale of the land whether or not those trusts are declared by the same instrument as that by which the trust of land is created.", and

(b) in subsection (2)—

(i) for the words "trust for sale" substitute "trust",

(ii) for the words "the settlement of the net proceeds" substitute "any trust affecting the net proceeds of sale of the land if it is sold", and

(iii) for the words "trustees for sale" substitute "trustees".

(9) In section 33—

(a) for the words "trustees for sale" substitute "trustees of land", and

(b) for the words "on trust for sale" substitute "land in trust".

(10) In section 39(4), for the words "trusts for sale" substitute "trusts".

(11) In section 42—

(a) in subsection (1)(a), for the words "trust for sale" substitute "trust of land", and

(b) in subsection (2)—

(i) in paragraph (a), for the words "a conveyance on trust for sale" substitute "land", and

(ii) in paragraph (b), for the words "on trust for sale" substitute "in trust".

(12) In section 66(2), for the words "trustee for sale" substitute "trustee of land".

(13) In section 102(1)—

(a) for the words "share in the proceeds of sale of the land and in the rents and profits thereof until sale" substitute "interest under the trust to which the land is subject", and

(b) for the words "trustees for sale" substitute "trustees".

(14) In section 131, after the words "but for this section" insert "(and paragraph 5 of Schedule 1 to the Trusts of Land and Appointment of Trustees Act 1996)".

(15) In section 137—

(a) in subsection (2)(ii), for the words "the proceeds of sale of land" onwards substitute "land subject to a trust of land, or the proceeds of the sale of such land, the persons to be served with notice shall be the trustees.", and

(b) in subsection (5), for the words "held on trust for sale" substitute "subject to a trust of land".

(16) In section 153(6)(ii), for the words "in trust for sale" substitute "as a trustee of land".

The Land Registration Act 1925 (c. 21)

5.—(1) The Land Registration Act 1925 is amended as follows.

(2) In section 3(xv)(a)—

(a) for the words "held on trust for sale" substitute "subject to a trust of land", and

(b) for the words "trustees for sale" substitute "trustees".

(3) In section 4, for the words "trustee for sale" substitute "trustee of land".

(4) In section 8(1), for the words "trustee for sale" substitute "trustee of land".

(5) In section 49—

(a) in subsection (1)(d)—

(i) for the words "the proceeds of sale of land held on trust for sale" substitute "land subject to a trust of land", and

(ii) for the words "disposition on trust for sale or of the" substitute "trust or",

(b) in subsection (2), for the words "trust for sale" substitute "trust of land",

(c) in the proviso to that subsection, for the words "a disposition on trust for sale or" substitute "land, or trustees of", and

(d) in subsection (3), for the words "on trust for sale" substitute "subject to a trust of land".

(6) In section 78(4), at the end insert "registered at the commencement of this Act".

(7) In section 83, in paragraph (b) of the proviso to subsection (11), for the words "held on trust for sale" substitute "subject to a trust of land".

(8) In section 94—

(a) for subsection (1) substitute—

"(1) Where registered land is subject to a trust of land, the land shall be registered in the names of the trustees.",

(b) in subsection (3), for the words "trust for sale, the trustees for sale" substitute "trust of land, the trustees",

(c) after that subsection insert—

"(4) There shall also be entered on the register such restrictions as may be prescribed, or may be expedient, for the protection of the rights of the persons beneficially interested in the land.

(5) Where a deed has been executed under section 16(4) of the Trusts of Land and Appointment of Trustees Act 1996 by trustees of land the registrar is entitled to assume that, as from the date of the deed, the land to which the deed relates is not subject to the trust unless he has actual notice that the trustees were mistaken in their belief that the land was conveyed to beneficiaries absolutely entitled to the land under the trust and of full age and capacity.", and

(d) in accordance with the amendments made by paragraphs (a) to (c), in the sidenote, for the words "on trust for sale" substitute "in trust".

(9) In section 95, for the words "on trust for sale" substitute "subject to a trust of land".

(10) In paragraph (b) of the proviso to section 103(1)—

(a) for the words "on trust for sale" substitute "subject to a trust of land", and

(b) for the words "the execution of the trust for sale" substitute "a sale of the land by the trustees".

(11) In section 111(1), for the words "trustees for sale" substitute "trustees of land".

The Administration of Estates Act 1925 (c. 23)

6.—(1) The Administration of Estates Act 1925 is amended as follows.

(2) In section 39(1)—

(a) in paragraph (i), at the beginning insert "as respects the personal estate,",

(b) for paragraph (ii) substitute—

"(ii) as respects the real estate, all the functions conferred on them by Part I of the Trusts of Land and Appointment of Trustees Act 1996;", and

(c) in paragraph (iii), for the words "conferred by statute on trustees for sale, and" substitute "necessary".

(3) In section 41(6), for the words "trusts for sale" substitute "trusts".

(4) In section 51(3)—

(a) after the word "married" insert "and without issue",

(b) before the word "settlement", in both places, insert "trust or", and

(c) for the words "an entailed interest" substitute "a life interest".

(5) In section 55(1), after paragraph (vi) insert—

"(via) "Land" has the same meaning as in the Law of Property Act 1925;".

The Green Belt (London and Home Counties) Act 1938 (c. xciii)

7. In section 19(1) of the Green Belt (London and Home Counties) Act 1938—

(a) for the words "trustee for sale within the meaning of the Law of Property Act 1925" substitute "trustee of land", and

(b) for the words "of a trustee for sale" substitute "of a trustee of land".

The Settled Land and Trustee Acts (Court's General Powers) Act 1943 (c. 25)

8. In section 1 of the Settled Land and Trustee Acts (Court's General Powers) Act 1943—

(a) in subsection (1)—

(i) for the words "trustees for sale of land" substitute "trustees of land", and
(ii) for the words "land held on trust for sale" substitute "land subject to a trust of land", and
(b) in subsections (2) and (3), for the words "trust for sale" substitute "trust of land".

The Historic Buildings and Ancient Monuments Act 1953 (c. 49)

9. In sections 8(3), 8A(3) and 8B(3) of the Historic Buildings and Ancient Monuments Act 1953, for the words from "held on" to "thereof" substitute "subject to a trust of land, are conferred by law on the trustees of land in relation to the land and to the proceeds of its sale".

The Leasehold Reform Act 1967 (c. 88)

10. In the Leasehold Reform Act 1967—
(a) in section 6(1), for the words "the statutory trusts arising by virtue of sections 34 to 36" substitute "a trust arising under section 34 or section 36",
(b) in section 24(1)(a), for the words "held on trust for sale" substitute "subject to a trust of land", and
(c) in paragraph 7 of Schedule 2—
(i) in sub-paragraph (1), for the words "a disposition on trust for sale" substitute "trust of land", and
(ii) in sub-paragraph (3), for the words "held on trust for sale" substitute "subject to a trust of land".

The Agriculture Act 1970 (c. 40)

11. In section 33(2) of the Agriculture Act 1970—
(a) for the words "held under a trust for sale" substitute "subject to a trust of land", and
(b) for the words "the trustees for sale" substitute "the trustees of land".

The Land Charges Act 1972 (c. 61)

12.—(1) The Land Charges Act 1972 is amended as follows.
(2) In section 2(4)(iii)(b), for the words "trust for sale" substitute "trust of land".
(3) In section 6, after subsection (1) insert—
"(1A) No writ or order affecting an interest under a trust of land may be registered under subsection (1) above."

The Land Compensation Act 1973 (c. 26)

13. In subsection (2) of section 10 of the Land Compensation Act 1973, for the words "held on trust for sale" substitute "subject to a trust of land" and, in accordance with that amendment, in the sidenote of that section, for the words "trusts for sale" substitute "trusts of land".

The Local Land Charges Act 1975 (c. 76)

14. In section 11(2) of the Local Land Charges Act 1975, for the words "held on trust for sale" substitute "subject to a trust of land".

The Rentcharges Act 1977 (c. 30)

15.—(1) The Rentcharges Act 1977 is amended as follows.
(2) In section 2(3), for paragraphs (a) and (b) substitute—
"(a) in the case of which paragraph 3 of Schedule 1 to the Trusts of Land and Appointment of Trustees Act 1996 (trust in case of family charge) applies to the land on which the rent is charged;
(b) in the case of which paragraph (a) above would have effect but for the fact that the land on which the rent is charged is settled land or subject to a trust of land;".
(3) In section 10(2)(b), for the words "trust for sale" substitute "trust of land".

The Interpretation Act 1978 (c. 30)

16. In Schedule 1 to the Interpretation Act 1978, after the definition of "The Treasury" insert—
" "Trust of land" and "trustees of land", in relation to England and Wales, have the same meanings as in the Trusts of Land and Appointment of Trustees Act 1996."

The Ancient Monuments and Archaeological Areas Act 1979 (c. 46)

17. In the Ancient Monuments and Archaeological Areas Act 1979—
(a) in section 12(3), for the words "trust for sale" substitute "trust of land", and

(b) in section 18(4), for paragraph (b) substitute—
"(b) as trustees of land;".

The Limitation Act 1980 (c. 58)

18. In paragraph 9 of Schedule 1 to the Limitation Act 1980, for the words "held on trust for sale" substitute "subject to a trust of land".

The Highways Act 1980 (c. 66)

19. In section 87(4)(b) of the Highways Act 1980, for the words from "and section 28" to "apply" substitute "applies".

The Wildlife and Countryside Act 1981 (c. 69)

20. In section 30(4)(c) of the Wildlife and Countryside Act 1981, for the words "trusts for sale" substitute "trusts of land".

The Health and Social Services and Social Security Adjudications Act 1983 (c. 41)

21. In section 22 of the Health and Social Services and Social Security Adjudications Act 1983—
(a) in subsection (5)—
(i) for the words "a joint tenant in the proceeds of sale of land held upon trust for sale" substitute "an equitable joint tenant in land", and
(ii) for the words "those proceeds" substitute "the land",
(b) in subsection (6)—
(i) for the words "a joint tenant in the proceeds of sale of land held upon trust for sale" substitute "an equitable joint tenant in land",
(ii) for the words "proceeds is" substitute "land is", and
(iii) for the words "interests in the proceeds" substitute "interests in the land", and
(c) in subsection (8), for the words "an interest in the proceeds of sale of land" substitute "the interest of an equitable joint tenant in land".

The Telecommunications Act 1984 (c. 12)

22. In paragraph 4(10) of Schedule 2 to the Telecommunications Act 1984, for the words "trusts for sale" substitute "trusts of land".

The Insolvency Act 1986 (c. 45)

23. At the beginning of Chapter V of Part IX of the Insolvency Act 1986 insert—

"Rights under trusts of land
Rights under trusts of land
335A.—(1) Any application by a trustee of a bankrupt's estate under section 14 of the Trusts of Land and Appointment of Trustees Act 1996 (powers of court in relation to trusts of land) for an order under that section for the sale of land shall be made to the court having jurisdiction in relation to the bankruptcy.
(2) On such an application the court shall make such order as it thinks just and reasonable having regard to—
(a) the interests of the bankrupt's creditors;
(b) where the application is made in respect of land which includes a dwelling house which is or has been the home of the bankrupt or the bankrupt's spouse or former spouse—
(i) the conduct of the spouse or former spouse, so far as contributing to the bankruptcy,
(ii) the needs and financial resources of the spouse or former spouse, and
(iii) the needs of any children; and
(c) all the circumstances of the case other than the needs of the bankrupt.
(3) Where such an application is made after the end of the period of one year beginning with the first vesting under Chapter IV of this Part of the bankrupt's estate in a trustee, the

court shall assume, unless the circumstances of the case are exceptional, that the interests of the bankrupt's creditors outweigh all other considerations.

(4) The powers conferred on the court by this section are exercisable on an application whether it is made before or after the commencement of this section."

The Patronage (Benifices) Measure 1986 (No. 3)

24. In section 33 of the Patronage (Benifices) Measure 1986—
(a) in subsection (1), for the words from "held by any trustee" to "capable of sale" substitute "subject to a trust of land", and
(b) in subsection (2), for the words "section 26(1) and (2) of the Law of Property Act 1925 (consents to the execution of a trust for sale)" substitute "section 10 of the Trusts of Land and Appointment of Trustees Act 1996 (consents)".

The Family Law Reform Act 1987 (c. 42)

25. In section 19(2) of the Family Law Reform Act 1987, for the words "which is used to create" substitute "purporting to create".

The Charities Act 1993 (c. 10)

26. In section 23 of the Charities Act 1993—
(a) in subsection (1)(b), for the words "trust for sale" substitute "trust",
(b) in subsection (5), for the words "trustee for sale" substitute "trustee".
(c) in subsection (7), for the words "trustees for sale" substitute "trustees", and
(d) in subsection (9), for the words "trust for sale" substitute "trust".

The Leasehold Reform, Housing and Urban Development Act 1993 (c. 28)

27.—(1) The Leasehold Reform, Housing and Urban Development Act 1993 is amended as follows.
(2) In Schedule 2—
(a) in paragraph 5(1) and (2), for the words "held on trust for sale" substitute "subject to a trust of land" (and, accordingly, in the heading immediately preceding paragraph 5 for the words "on trust for sale" substitute "in trust"),
(b) in paragraph 6, for the words "as mentioned in paragraph 5(2)(b) above" substitute "by the landlord on the termination of a new lease granted under Chapter II or section 93(4) (whether the payment is made in pursuance of an order under section 61 or in pursuance of an agreement made in conformity with paragraph 5 of Schedule 14 without an application having been made under that section)", and
(c) in paragraphs 7(2)(b) and 8(3)(b) and (4)(c), for "5(2)(b)" substitute "6".
(3) In Schedule 14—
(a) in paragraph 7(1), for the words "disposition on trust for sale" substitute "trust of land", and
(b) in paragraph 9(a), for the words "held on trust for sale" substitute "subject to a trust of land".

Section 25(2)   SCHEDULE 4

REPEALS

Chapter	Short title	Extent of repeal
3 & 4 Will. 4 c. 74.	The Fines and Recoveries Act 1833.	In section 1, the words ", and any undivided share thereof", in both places.
7 Will. 4 & 1 Vict. c. 26.	The Wills Act 1837.	In section 1, the words "and to any undivided share thereof,". Section 32.
53 & 54 Vict. c. 39.	The Partnership Act 1890.	Section 22.
12 & 13 Geo. 5 c. 16.	The Law of Property Act 1922.	In section 188— in subsection (1), the words "but not an undivided share in land;" and the words "but not an undivided share thereof", and subsection (30).

Chapter	Short title	Extent of repeal
15 & 16 Geo. 5 c. 18.	The Settled Land Act 1925.	Section 27. Section 29.
15 & 16 Geo. 5 c. 19.	The Trustee Act 1925.	In section 10(2)— in the first paragraph, the words "by trustees or" and the words "the trustees, or" and in the second paragraph, the words from the beginning to "mortgage; and". In section 19(1), the words "building or", in the second place. In section 68— in subsection (6), the words ", but not an undivided share in land" and the words ", but not an undivided share thereof", and in subsection (19), the word "binding", the words ", and with or without power at discretion to postpone the sale" and the definition of "trustees for sale".
15 & 16 Geo. 5 c. 20.	The Law of Property Act 1925.	In section 3— subsections (1)(b) and (2), and in subsection (5), the words "trustees for sale or other". In section 7(3), the second paragraph. In section 18— in subsection (1), the words from ", and personal estate" to "payable", in the second place, and the words "or is capable of being" and in subsection (2), the words "of the settlement or the trustees for sale", in both places. Section 19. Section 23 (and the heading immediately preceding it). Sections 25 and 26. Sections 28 to 30. Section 31(3). Section 32. In section 34— in subsection (3), the words from "the trustees (if any)" to "then to" and the words "in each case", and subsection (4). Section 35. Section 42(6). In section 60, paragraphs (b) and (c) of the proviso to subsection (4). In section 130, subsections (1) to (3) and (6) (and the words "Creation of" in the side-note). Section 201(3). In section 205(1)— in paragraph (ix), the words "but not an undivided share in land;" and the words "but not an undivided share thereof", in paragraph (x), the words "or in the proceeds of sale thereof", and in paragraph (xxix), the word "binding", the words ", and with or without a power at discretion to postpone the sale" and the words "and "power" onwards.

Chapter	Short title	Extent of repeal
15 & 16 Geo c. 21.	The Land Registration Act 1925.	In section 3— in paragraph (viii), the words "but not an undivided share in land;", in paragraph (xi), the words "or in the proceeds of sale thereof", in paragraph (xiv), the words ", but not an undivided share thereof", and paragraphs (xxviii) and (xxix).
15 & 16 Geo. 5 c. 23.	The Administration of Estates Act 1925.	In section 3(1)(ii), the words "money to arise under a trust for sale of land, nor". In section 39(1)(i), the words from ", and such power" to "legal mortgage". In section 51— in subsection (3), the word "settled", and subsection (4). In section 55(1)— in paragraph (vii), the words "or in the proceeds of sale thereof", in paragraph (xxiv), the word " "land" ", and paragraph (xxvii).
15 & 16 Geo. 5 c. 24.	The Universities and College Estates Act 1925.	In section 43(iv), the words ", but not an undivided share in land".
16 & 17 Geo. c. 11.	The Law of Property (Amendment) Act 1926.	In the Schedule, the entries relating to section 3 of the Settled Land Act 1925 and sections 26, 28 and 35 of the Law of Property Act 1925.
17 & 18 Geo. 5 c. 36.	The Landlord and Tenant Act 1927.	In section 13— in subsection (1), the words from "(either" to "Property Act, 1925)", in subsection (2), the words ", trustee for sale, or personal representative", and in subsection (3), the words ", and "settled land" " onwards.
22 & 23 Geo. 5 c. 27.	The Law of Property (Entailed Interests) Act 1932.	Section 1.
2 & 3 Geo. 6 c. 72.	The Landlord and Tenant (War Damage) Act 1939.	Section 3(c).
9 & 10 Geo. 6 c. 73.	The Hill Farming Act 1946.	Section 11(2).
12 & 13 Geo. 6 c. 74.	The Coast Protection Act 1949.	In section 11(2)(a)— the words ", by that section as applied by section twenty-eight of the Law of Property Act, 1925, in relation to trusts for sale,", and the words ", by that section as applied as aforesaid,".
2 & 3 Eliz. 2 c. 56.	The Landlord and Tenant Act 1954.	In the Second Schedule, in paragraph 6— the words ", by that section as applied by section twenty-eight of the Law of Property Act, 1925, in relation to trusts for sale,", and the words ", by that section as applied as aforesaid,".
7 & 8 Eliz. 2 c. 72.	The Mental Health Act 1959.	In Schedule 7, in Part I, the entries relating to sections 26 and 28 of the Law of Property Act 1925.

Chapter	Short title	Extent of repeal
1964 No. 2.	The Incumbents and Churchwardens (Trusts) Measure 1964.	In section 1, in the definition of "land", the words "nor an undivided share in land".
1967 c. 10.	The Forestry Act 1967.	In Schedule 2, paragraph 1(4).
1967 c. 88.	The Leasehold Reform Act 1967.	In section 6(5)— the words ", or by that section as applied by section 28 of the Law of Property Act 1925 in relation to trusts for sale,", the words "or by that section as applied as aforesaid", and the words "or by trustees for sale". In Schedule 2, in paragraph 9(1)— the words ", or by that section as applied by section 28 of the Law of Property Act 1925 in relation to trusts for sale, and the words "or by that section as applied as aforesaid".
1969 c. 10.	The Mines and Quarries (Tips) Act 1969.	In section 32(2)(a) and (b), the words ", by that section as applied by section 28 of the Law of Property Act 1925 in relation to trusts for sale".
1970 c. 40.	The Agriculture Act 1970.	In section 30— in subsection (1), the words "(including those provisions as extended to trusts for sale by section 28 of the Law of Property Act 1925)", and in subsection (2), the words "the words from "(including those provisions" to "Law of Property Act 1925)" and".
1972 c. 61.	The Land Charges Act 1972.	In section 17(1), the definition of "trust for sale".
1976 c. 31.	The Legitimacy Act 1976.	Section 10(4).
1976 c. 36.	The Adoption Act 1976.	Section 46(5).
1977 c. 42.	The Rent Act 1977.	In Schedule 2, in Part I, in paragraph 2(b), the words "or, if it is held on trust for sale, the proceeds of its sale are".
1980 c. 58.	The Limitation Act 1980.	In section 18— in subsection (1), the words ", including interests in the proceeds of the sale of land held upon trust for sale,", and in subsections (3) and (4), the words "(including a trust for sale)" and the words "or in the proceeds of sale". In section 38(1)— in the definition of "land", the words ", including an interest in the proceeds of the sale of land held upon trust for sale,", and the definition of "trust for sale". In Schedule 1, in Part I, in paragraph 9— the words "or in the proceeds of sale", the words "or the proceeds", and the words "or the proceeds of sale".
1981 c. 54.	The Supreme Court Act 1981.	In section 128, in the definition of "real estate", in paragraph (b), the words "money to arise under a trust for sale of land, nor".
1983 c. 41.	The Health and Social Services and Social Security Adjudications Act 1983.	Section 22(3).

Chapter	Short title	Extent of repeal
1984 c. 28.	The County Courts Act 1984.	In Schedule 2, in Part II, in paragraph 2— in sub-paragraph (1), the entry relating to section 30 of the Law of Property Act 1925, sub-paragraph (2), and in sub-paragraph (3), "30(2),".
1984 c. 51.	The Inheritance Tax Act 1984.	In section 237(3), the words "and undivided shares in land held on trust for sale, whether statutory or not,".
1986 c. 5.	The Agricultural Holdings Act 1986.	In section 89(1), the words "or the Law of Property Act 1925".
1986 c. 45.	The Insolvency Act 1986.	In section 336— subsection (3), and in subsection (4), the words "or (3)" and the words "or section 30 of the Act of 1925".
1988 c. 50.	The Housing Act 1988.	In Schedule 1, in Part III, in paragraph 18(1)(b), the words "or, if it is held on trust for sale, the proceeds of its sale are".
1989 c. 34.	The Law of Property (Miscellaneous Provisions) Act 1989.	In sections 1(6) and 2(6), the words "or in or over the proceeds of sale of land".
1990 c. 8.	The Town and Country Planning Act 1990.	In section 328— in subsection (1)(a), the words "and by that section as applied by section 28 of the Law of Property Act 1925 in relation to trusts for sale", and in subsection (2)(a), the words "and by that section as so applied".
1991 c. 31.	The Finance Act 1991.	Section 110(5)(b).
1993 c. 10.	The Charities Act 1993.	Section 37(6). Section 39(5).
1993 c. 28.	The Leasehold Reform, Housing and Urban Development Act 1993.	In section 93A(4)— the words ", or by that section as applied by section 28 of the Law of Property Act 1925 in relation to trusts for sale", the words ", or by that section as so applied,", and the words "or by trustees for sale". In Schedule 2, paragraph 5(2)(b) and the word "and" immediately preceding it.
1994 c. 36.	The Law of Property (Miscellaneous Provisions) Act 1994.	In section 16— subsection (2), and in subsection (3), the words "; and subsection (2)" onwards.
1995 c. 8.	The Agricultural Tenancies Act 1995.	In section 33— in subsections (1) and (2), the words from "(either" to "Property Act 1925)", and in subsection (4), the definition of "settled land" and the word "and" immediately preceding it.
1996 c. 53.	The Housing Grants, Construction and Regeneration Act 1996.	Section 55(4)(b). Section 73(3)(b). In section 98(2)(a), the words "or to the proceeds of sale of the dwelling".

PART II: THE ACT IN PRACTICE

1. The End of the Trust for Sale

The fundamental change made by the 1996 Act to English property law is that there will be only one kind of trust for land. The following paragraphs will look at how detailed changes in the Act affect the conveyancer. The change of name to trusts of land is, however, curiously insignificant. To lawyers brought up in the 1925 legislation (as all in practice have been) it seems a portentous change but in itself it does nothing. The fine print of a great deal of (well loved?) legislation is altered by replacing the term "trust for sale" with the term "trust of land". The most astonishing thing is that the basic structure derived by the draftsmen of the Law of Property Act 1925 (c. 20) out of the debris of medieval property law survives so well. The conceptual framework of the 1925 legislation is so sound that the many amendments (some purely of nomenclature, some nonsensical, some petty and none of pressing necessity) made by this Act will readily be taken in their stride by the legal professions.

The effect of the new system—a unified trust of land—is this: equitable co-ownership in its division into joint tenants and tenants in common is unaltered; some small simplifications are possible to conveyances and transfers to co-owners; some considerable redrafting must be considered for express trusts of land and for wills; and strict settlements and entails will eventually disappear into the limbo of legal history.

2. Strict Settlements

For decades land law teachers have conspired with students to remove settled land from the world. In truth very large areas of England and Wales are still covered by settlements under the Settled Land Act 1925 (c. 18). Despite the fact that fewer and fewer solicitors have been taught the very simple machinery needed for a settlement of land, conveyancing under this Act is remarkably straightforward and, for those who handle it in practice, as trouble-free as any area of conveyancing. Parliament's decision to prevent further strict settlements (s.2) has as its only sensible justification the prevention of difficulties caused by persons creating inadvertent strict settlements.[1]

For purposes involved with the management of strict settlements the crucial practical difference from other trusts was the vesting of the legal estate in the tenant for life and the consequence that the tenant for life managed the land. This will now no longer be the case. It will be possible to delegate management to a beneficiary (see s.9, and para. 12.1 below). This new power of delegation is a complex device as explained below and will be little used in practice.

2.1 Variation of Strict Settlements

Existing strict settlements may be varied under s.2(2) of the 1996 Act and remain as strict settlements under the SLA 1925. A typical case where this occurs will be a resettlement under a power contained in the original settlement. Under s.2(3) of the 1996 Act it is possible for a settlement which falls within s.2(3) to be a trust of land instead of a strict settlement if express provision is made to that effect (see p. 47–5). This might be a desirable step to take because if the resettlement becomes a trust of land then the trustees will have the extended powers of management conferred by s.6 of the 1996 Act

---

[1] Not so much in the constructive trust/proprietory estoppel cases such as *Binions v. Evans* [1972] Ch. 359; *Bannister v. Bannister* [1948] 2 All E.R. 133. The courts in these cases decisively side-stepped the possibility of the Settled Land Act 1925 being brought accidentally into play; a more realistic problem could have been inadvertent strict settlement in wills, especially holograph wills. If errors in such were common, which can be doubted, the problem could have been solved by requiring precise words to create a Settled Land Act settlement. But that is now history. Parliament instead opted for petty-minded abolition.

instead of the restricted powers of management contained in the SLA 1925. A further reason for opting for a trust of land is where it is desirable for the powers of management to be exercised by the trustees and not the tenant for life. Thus a declaration that on a resettlement a trust of land comes into being may appeal to professional trustees who have become irritated by the tenant for life.

2.2 Compound and Referential Settlements

Referential settlements are dealt with by s.32 of the SLA 1925. The expression means a settlement which refers to an earlier settlement. Thus, Lord A may settle the Whiteacre estate "on the same trusts as those on which Blackacre is settled". By virtue of s.2 of the 1996 Act such a referential settlement will be a trust of land, because it is essentially a new settlement, not a variation of an existing settlement.

A compound settlement is "the term used to describe the state of affairs when the trusts affecting the land are created by two or more instruments, as where a settlement is followed by a resettlement" (Megarry & Wade, *The Law of Real Property*, 5th ed. (1984) p. 357). A compound settlement may be a settlement created on an alteration of a settlement or on the occasion of a person becoming entitled under the settlement. If this is the case the compound settlement will be within the SLA 1925 and s.31 of the SLA 1925 will apply so that the trustees of the original settlement, if it still exists, will be the trustees of the compound settlement. (If the compound settlement does not fall within s.2(2) of the 1996 Act then it will be a trust of land). Where the compound settlement is created by a disposition and falls within s.2(2) of the 1996 Act as a variation of an existing settlement then the opportunity may be taken to declare that the new settlement is a trust of land (s.23).

2.3 The End of Strict Settlements

Under s.2(4) of the 1996 Act a settlement ceases to be a SLA 1925 settlement if at any time there is no land and no heirlooms held in the settlement. So long as there is either land or heirlooms then s.17, which applies the provisions of the 1996 Act to trusts of proceeds of sale of land, does not apply in this way to the continuing strict settlement.

Once a settlement has ceased to be a strict settlement under s.2(4) it is possible for further land to be acquired. This should be conveyed to the trustees of the settlement on a trust of land (see Sched. 1, para. 6). A purchaser from the trustees will be entitled to rely upon ss.2 and 27 of the LPA 1925 to overreach the interests under the trust. If a mistake is made and the trustees assume that s.2(4) applies when there is in fact relevant property remaining in the settlement, the position is as follows. Suppose under a settlement X and Y are the trustees and Z the tenant for life. Upon certain events Whiteacre falls to be transferred to the settlement but X and Y wrongly assume that s.2(4) applies and take a conveyance to themselves as trustees of land of Whiteacre. The land is in fact vested in X and Y upon a trust of land (although it should have been vested in Z as tenant for life). A purchaser from X and Y is still protected by s.27 of the LPA and not concerned with the trusts affecting the land. If this view were not taken by the courts then X and Y could not convey the legal estate because of the paralysing effect of s.13 of the SLA 1925 (no legal estate to be conveyed until there is a vesting instrument in Z's favour). Perhaps this conundrum may never fall to be resolved by the courts.

3. Entails

The Act (Sched. 1, para. 5) is a very contrived provision which purports to prevent the creation of any future entailed interests. In practice this can cause little excitement. The main concern for the practitioner is the possibility of using words in a trust apposite to create a fee tail with the result that the intended tenant in tail takes absolutely. The most likely circumstance in which this provision may cause problems is where a settlement is varied but is intended, within s.2(2) of the 1996 Act to remain a strict settlement covered by the SLA 1925. Even in this case Sched. 1, para. 5, will operate to turn any entailed interest intended to be so created into an absolute interest.

4. Doctrine of Conversion

Section 3 with its curiously inaccurate marginal note ("abolition of doctrine of conversion") has a very limited practical effect.

In drafting testamentary gifts, solicitors must remember that land held on a trust for sale is land, and money held on trust to be invested in land is money. They must never be lulled into thinking that the doctrine of conversion has been abolished. An interesting note on *Neville v. Wilson* [1996] Conv. 25, 26 provides, for example, illustration "of the difficulties that the doctrine of conversion can create when one is considering the position of the parties under an uncompleted sale of land" (*Thompson*). These difficulties, are, of course, unaffected by s.3 of the 1996 Act.

In practice the only significance of the change is in drafting of wills or trusts. Should the draftsperson desire to include references to land, realty or the technical expression "devise" then there will be included in this, interests in land held on trust for sale. Similarly such interests will not be included if the reference is to personalty or the technical expression "bequeath" is used.

It will be noted that this change does not apply to interests in land subject to a contract of sale or where an option is exercised, see, for example, *Sweeting, Re* [1988] 1 All E.R. 1016; *Laukes v. Bennett* (1785) 1 Cox Eq 167.

The doctrine of conversion is also abolished in its special application in respect of partnership property by the repeal of s.22 of the Partnership Act 1890 (c. 39) (see further para. 11, below).

5. Co-Ownership in Conveyancing

5.1 The Beneficial Interests

The interests of the beneficiaries under a trust of land are described by the trust instrument. In the case of a routine conveyancing transaction it has long been customary to state in the conveyance that the parties are joint tenants or tenants in common.

No conveyance or transfer need now contain an extension of the trustees' powers. So far as trusts for sale existing at the date of commencement are concerned, the full powers of management implied by s.6 are implied in these cases also. The operation of the Act is retrospective to that extent. It does not cure defects of title arising where the transaction in question took place before the commencement date. The retrospective effect of the Act confers the statutory power upon all existing trusts of land, it does not have the effect that these powers are deemed to have existed in the past. Thus, an unregistered title may contain a mortgage by co-owners which is not within the power of mortgaging conferred on trustees for sale by the SLA 1925. An example is a mortgage to raise the purchase price. If there has been such a mortgage before the 1996 Act comes into force then there is a patent defect of title unless the powers of management of the trustees have been extended. However, from the time the Act came into force the trustees had the extended powers of management conferred by s.6 of the 1996 Act and the absence of a clause extending their powers of management is intended by the legislature to be of no consequence (but as to the full effect of this on the power of mortgaging, see para. 7.2.2).

5.2 Declaration of Trust

A declaration of trust should still be included in any transfer or convey-ance to co-owners. Instructions as to the manner in which the co-owners wish to hold the beneficial interest should be taken and given effect to in an express declaration of trust in the conveyance or transfer and this should be executed by the co-owners.

The following statement (from Sweet & Maxwell's *Conveyancing Practice*) was reproduced in the Law Society's *Gazette*, September 22, 1993, advis-ing on this point.

Drafting Form 19(JP)

Two cases, *Huntingford v. Hobbs* [1992] EGCS 38 and *Springette v. Defoe* [1992] Fam. Law 489, require a revision of a small area of practice. When land is transferred to co-owners, Form 19(JP) requires it to be stated in the transfer whether the *survivor can/cannot give a good receipt* for purchase monies. If the purchasers are tenants in common, *can* is deleted. If the purchasers are joint tenants, *cannot* is deleted. These two cases both suggest that if the form is used in this way then the statement that the survivor can give good receipt is not decisive between the pur-chasers as to their interest in the property. The cases are distinguished from *Gorman, Re* [1990] 1 All E.R. 717 which appeared to suggest the contrary on the ground that in that case the *survivor* clause included the word "declare" and could thus be treated as a declaration of trust by the transferees.

Note

1. It is essential to take instructions from the transferees as to whether they wish to be joint tenants or tenants in common.
2. If they wish to be tenants in common the nature of their beneficial interests will presumably be recorded in a separate declaration of trust which will be retained with the Land Certificate when that is returned from the Land Registry.
3. If the transferees are joint tenants then words such as "and the transferees declare that they are beneficial joint tenants" should be add-ed to the *survivor* clause in the transfer and a copy of the completed transfer retained to place with the Land or Charge Certificate.

This is unaffected by the new legislation and specific instructions should be taken as to the interests of co-owners and given effect to in the disposition to them.

5.3 Non-Severable Beneficial Joint Tenancy

Co-parcenary is a form of co-ownership long fallen into desuetude. Exist-ing between husband and wife, it was a joint tenancy without possibility of severance. It cannot exist in law since 1925. It is, however, a possibility that should be considered for ownership of the equitable interest. Some couples may prefer a beneficial "co-parcenary" to the joint tenancy with a right of severance. A form which achieves this result (notwithstanding the 1925 legis-lation) is: "this land is conveyed (transferred) to A & B on a trust of land as joint tenants to the intent that their joint tenancy in equity is unseverable by act of the parties".

This form of words does not, of course, create a technical co-parcenary. However, it has the effect that as between A & B the joint tenancy (and the consequence of survivorship) cannot be unilaterally severed. It had been suggested by Lord Denning M.R. in *Bedson v. Bedson* [1965] 2 Q.B. 666 that severance of a joint tenancy held by husband or wife was not possible. This was clearly wrong (see for example Megarry in 82 L.Q.R. 29). Nevertheless, it may be a desirable result to achieve and there is nothing in s.36 of the LPA 1925 which compels all joint tenancies to be severable in equity if expressed to be otherwise. The form of words used cannot prevent a severance occurring by operation of law upon the bankruptcy of a joint tenant or the homicide by one joint tenant of another (see *Morgan v. Marquis* (1853) 9 Exch. 145 on bankruptcy; *Schobelt v. Barber* [1967] 1 Q.R. on murder).

5.4 Succession Amongst Co-Owners

A common title problem occurs where one beneficial tenant in common leaves their share to a sole survivor. Thus, on W's death W's share of land purchased by H and W as beneficial tenants in common, whether by will or intestacy, passes to H. H will, in order to make a good title, have to appoint another trustee or deduce title by showing the transfer of W's equitable interest.

Instead advantage can be taken of a new provision in s.16(4) of the 1996 Act. A precedent which allows the survivor to make title by relying on s.16(4) of the 1996 Act is found at p. 47–22.

A more obvious use for this provision is circumstances under a trust of land where one beneficiary has become absolutely entitled. For example, property may be held on a trust of land for a widow *dum casta* for life. Upon her marriage the property passes absolutely to the deceased's son. Upon the widow's marriage the trustees may convey the land to the son and execute a deed of discharge under s.16. Instead, of course, the trustees may still sell the land as trustees (at the direction of the son).

5.5 Purchaser—Reliance on Deed of Discharge

A deed of discharge is executed under s.16(4) when trustees of a trust of land convey land to a beneficiary or beneficiaries of full age absolutely entitled thereto. A purchaser may assume where there is a deed of discharge that the land is free of the trust unless he has actual notice that the trustees were mistaken in their belief that the land was conveyed to beneficiaries absolutely entitled and of full age (s.16(5): this provision does not apply to registered land s.16(7)). Where the land is already registered and the trustees convey to a beneficiary so entitled then the beneficiary will be entered as proprietor upon proof to the Land Registry that he is so entitled. Where a deed of discharge is included in a title sent to the Land Registry the situation is dealt with by a new s.94(5) of the LRA 1925 (added by the 1996 Act, Sched. 3, para. 5(8)(c)). This provides that the Registrar is entitled to rely upon the deed unless he has actual notice that the trustees were mistaken in their belief that the land was conveyed to beneficiaries absolutely entitled to the land and of full age and capacity.

The example has already been given of a surviving tenant in common. Suppose a house has been conveyed to David and Bronwen Jones in circumstances where they are tenants in common of the entire beneficial interest. Bronwen has died and David is entitled absolutely to her share. Now there is a case for applying s.16(4). The land under the trust is absolutely owned in equity by David who is of full age and capacity. It seems clear that s.16(4) applies to a conveyance by a sole trustee (see p. 47–23). David can execute a deed declaring that he is discharged from the trust and convey the land to himself as beneficial owner. He can then sell as beneficial owner. These different steps can be achieved in one document which gives the purchaser the benefit of s.16(4) (see Precedent 1 on p. 47–71). This is irrelevant in the case of registered land (s.16(7)) because the purchaser can rely upon the state of the register.

5.6 Co-Ownership Purchases: Advice to Purchasers

The most typical conveyancing transaction is a purchase by a couple of a house. The main reason put forward by the Law Commission for the change from "trusts for sale" to "trusts of land" was that the latter would be easier to explain to the lay client than the former. This may be so. It must be doubted, though, whether any explanation of the trust aspect of their land-holding is of practical interest to the lay person. Whether their young married clients wish to know that they hold as co-owners under a trust of land is a matter for each conveyancer to decide.

Beyond the technicality that the nature of the trust implied by law has changed, the position of co-owners is remarkably similar. They may still hold the land purchased beneficially as either tenants in common or joint tenants. So far as the beneficial holding is concerned these two well-known expressions are mere shorthand for the terms of the trust between the parties and may be varied freely by them. Conveyancers may consider even the possibility of non-severable beneficial joint tenancies (see para. 5.3).

5.7 Purchase from Co-Owners

5.7.1 Overreaching

The fundamental mechanism of overreaching under ss.2 and 27 of the LPA 1925 still applies. When passed in 1925, s.27(1) was "declaratory of the existing law" (Wolstenholme and Cherry, *Conveyancing Statutes*, Vol. 1 (13th ed., p. 72)). A purchaser from a trustee of land is not concerned with the trusts applicable to the purchase money. For this purpose a purchaser means a purchaser of a legal estate for money or money's worth (s.205(1)(xxi) of the LPA 1925 applied to the 1996 Act by s.23(1) of that Act). If capital money arises on the purchase then overreaching will not take place unless it is paid to two trustees or a trust corporation in accordance with s.27(2) of the LPA 1925.

The reform made by s.1 of the 1996 Act, including all trusts in trusts of land, and the consequential amendments made to ss.2 and 27 of the LPA 1925, makes it clear that overreaching applies in the same way in every case where there is a trust of land. A misconception might arise in future as to the consequences for the application of overreaching of the abolition in respect of trusts for sale of the doctrine of conversion (s.3 of the 1996 Act). This has no effect whatsoever on the operation of overreaching which is a statutory mechanism and in no way a consequence of the doctrine of conversion (see Harpum (1990) 49 CLJ 278).

The trusts capable of being overreaching by s.27(1) are "the trusts affecting the land, the net income of the land or the proceeds of sale". Trustees of a bare trust are now able to overreach the beneficial interests.

5.7.2 Overreaching interests—Reverter to the Settlor

There are two cases to consider. The first is not contained in the original LPA 1925. The 1996 Act introduces (by Sched. 3, para. 4(2)(b)) a new s.2(1A) into the LPA 1925. This reads: "(1A) An equitable interest in land subject to a trust of land which remains in, or is to revert to, the settlor shall (subject to any contrary intention) be overreached by the conveyance if it would be so overreached were it an interest under the trust". This deals with cases in which a person has conveyed land upon trust but when the trust determines, the land is to revert to them. Such rights of reverter were not clearly dealt with in the 1925 legislation (the problem is discussed thoroughly in Megarry & Wade, *The Law of Real Property* (5th ed.) at various points in the text). They were dealt with most satisfactorily if the land was treated as settled land and the reverter was clearly overreachable under s.1(4) of the SLA 1925. The new s.2(1A) makes the position clear. If A executes a deed declaring that C and D hold land upon trust for A's son while he is training to be a barrister and conveys it to them upon these trusts then the reversion to A may fall either under the trust or be prior to the trust. Section 2(1A) makes it clear that this is of no consequence. A sale by C and D to a stranger to the trust will convey the land free of the reversion to A, providing the fee simple has been vested in C and D by the conveyance to them.

The second case deals with rights of reverter which fall within s.1 of the Reverter of Sites Act 1987 (c. 15). That Act replaced the statutory right of reverter under various nineteenth century acts (see Sweet & Maxwell's *Conveyancing Practice* 6-153) with a statutory trust for sale. That now becomes a trust of land. To fit in with the overall scheme of the 1996 Act the beneficiaries of this trust are deprived of the right to be consulted before a sale and the right to occupy the trust property (the 1996 Act, Sched. 2, para. 6).

5.7.3 Overreaching—the Ad Hoc Trust of Land

Section 2(2) of the LPA 1925 permits an ad hoc trust for sale. This is a special overreaching trust for sale which overreaches equitable interests prior to the trust for sale. Section 2(2) is amended so that this can now occur in the case of a trust of land. A special overreaching or ad hoc trust for sale exists when the trustees are either appointed by the court or a trust corporation. Thus, Margaret purchases White Towers with her and her friend Peter's money. On ordinary principles she holds White Towers on trust for herself and Peter. Margaret later conveys the land by gift to her sons, W and V. W and V hold the land on trust of land for themselves beneficially but subject to Peter's prior equitable interest. A conveyance on sale by W and V cannot overreach Peter's interest unless there is an ad hoc trust for sale within s.2(2) of the LPA 1925. A purchaser from the trustees is, of course, affected by Peter's interest only according to the ordinary rules of notice even if there is no ad hoc trust of land.

5.8 Powers of Co-Owners

Under pre-1996 law the powers of trustees for sale were the powers of a SLA 1925 tenant for life under Part II of that Act (see s.28 of the LPA 1925). Under the 1996 Act the co-owners are trustees of land with the extensive powers granted by s.6(1) of that Act—that is, "in relation to the land subject to the trust all the powers of an absolute owner". There is accordingly no need in future routinely to include in a conveyance to such co-owners (whether before the new Act there was or not) any extension of their powers. Further, by taking advantage of s.8 of the 1996 Act the powers of the trustees may be further extended or restricted.

6. Purchaser Enquiries

6.1 Into the Terms of the Trust

A purchaser is not affected by notice of the existence of a trust of land providing the overreaching mechanism described above is complied with. So far as this is concerned, it makes no difference whether the terms of the trust are on the face of the legal title or not. A purchaser is, as previously, protected by s.27 of the LPA 1925 which makes it clear that a purchaser who complies with the overreaching machinery of the Act is not concerned with the trusts on which the land is held.

6.2 Into Compliance with the 1996 Act

Section 16 contains detailed provisions to protect the purchaser, and to make enquiry as to whether the Act is complied with unnecessary. The only positive steps a purchaser need take are: (a) to ensure that the legal title is effectively vested in trustees who are able to effect an overreaching convey-ance; and (b) to examine the title to ensure that it contains no statement limiting the trustees' powers to dispose of the land in the way intended. If (under s.8) there is such a limitation then a purchase by a purchaser who has actual notice of the limitation will be invalidated (see s.16(3)(b)). For the position regarding registered land, see para. 6.3 below.

6.3 Enquiries—Registered Land

If there is any restriction on the trustees dealing with the land then this should be entered on the proprietorship register as a restriction. In accord-ance with basic Land Registry rules a purchaser is concerned only with the state of the register. A new s.94(4) requires there to be entered on the Regis-ter prescribed restrictions in respect of titles held on a trust of land.

A purchaser who has actual notice that trustees are acting in breach of a limitation on their powers is not affected by s.16(3) of the 1996 Act as s.16 as a whole does not apply to registered land (s.16(7)). However, a purchaser who intentionally purchases land from trustees acting in breach of trust will be personally bound by basic trust principles (see *Peffer v. Rigg* [1977] 1 W.L.R. 285 and *Lyus v. Prowsa Developments* [1982] 2 All E.R. 953). Such a pur-chaser can deal with the land as a registered proprietor but cannot escape the personal consequences of complicity in a breach of trust. Fraud in equity is a sufficiently wide concept to cover a purchaser who is complicit in a breach of trust, see *Nocton v. Lord Ashburton* [1914] A.C. 932. *Rochefoucauld v. Bous-tead* [1897] 1 Ch. 196 is a particularly helpful authority in allowing the court to prevent a defendant hiding behind the cloak of statutory protection.

6.4 Restriction on Powers

Section 16 must be read in conjunction with s.16(3). The trustees are to take reasonable steps to ensure that any purchaser is made aware of any limitation on their powers made by virtue of s.8. In registered land this will be by means of an appropriate restriction entered on the register. In unregis-tered land the restrictions should be set out in the conveyance to the trustees.

7. Powers of Trustees

Section 6(1) of the 1996 Act confers on trustees of land all the powers of an absolute owner "in relation to the land". For the sake of clarity it might assist to list typical powers which are not affected by this: the power of investment; the powers of maintenance and advancement under ss.31 and 32 of the Trustee Act 1925; and the various powers of delegation of management of trustees.

The new powers of management of land are implied into all trusts of land which exist at the date the Act comes into force.

7.1 Powers to be Exercised qua Trustees

The important limitation on s.6 of the 1996 Act is that the general powers conferred on trustees are given for the purpose of exercising their functions as trustees. That is they are exercisable only by them to do things which the trustees are permitted by the general law to do. This point is further made by s.6(6) which provides that the general powers are not to be exercised in con-travention of any other enactment or any rule of law or equity and s.6(8) which provides that the trustees must comply with any restriction on the exercise of their powers contained in any other enactment. The practical implications of this restriction on the trustees' powers are referred to below (see para. 7.2).

It is important though to note that trustees are constrained by the basic rules of trust. A good example is the rule that a trustee must not profit from the trust. This leads to the principle that "a purchase of trust property by a trustee is voidable at the instance of any beneficiary . . . However honest and fair the sale may be" (Snell's *Equity* 29th ed., citing *Campbell v. Walker* (1800) 5 Ves 678, *Ex p.* James (1803) 8 Ves 337).

The extent to which a purchaser is protected by overreaching is referred to at various points in the text. The basic rule is now contained in s.27 of the LPA 1925. This states "a purchaser of a legal estate for trustees of land shall not be concerned with the trusts affecting the land, the net income of the land or the proceeds of sale of the land whether or not those trusts are declared by the same instrument as that by which the trust of land is created".

It is worth looking at length at the very clear explanation of this principle given in *The Law of Real Property* (Megarry and Wade, 5th ed., p. 404): "The purchaser's immunity from the right of the beneficiaries depends, however, upon the sale being made in accordance with the law and the terms of the trust: a purchaser with notice that the sale is irregular (*e.g.* where the purchase-money is not duly paid to the trustees) will take subject to the trust for sale. In this important respect the beneficiaries have an equitable interest in the land itself, for their benefit; and only a proper sale can overreach this right". This makes it clear in what context overreaching takes place. This point is referred to again as particular powers of the trustees are examined.

In the case of registered land this problem does not arise. If Smith and Jones are joint proprietors then they must be trustees. However, unless there is a restriction on the register then a purchaser is entitled to assume that they have the powers of disposition conferred by the LRA 1925 (see s.18 of that Act).

7.2 Powers of Trustees which are significantly altered by s.6 of the 1996 Act

7.2.1 Sale

It should be noted that ss.12 and 13 of the Trustee Act 1925 (c. 19) remain in force. Section 12 as amended is reproduced in Part IV (p. 47–89). Exercise of the power to sell trust property remains subject to general trust law. This means that: (a) trustees can exercise the power of sale as permitted by s.12 of the TA 1925. This allows a trustee a discretion as to the manner of sale and the conditions of sale; and (b) sales subject to depreciatory conditions are still subject to s.13 of the TA 1925, which limits the possibility of challenging such sales before execution of the conveyance to cases where the purchase money is rendered inadequate. After execution of a sale the transaction may be challenged where the purchaser was acting in collusion with the trustee.

7.2.2 Mortgaging Trust Property

(i) To raise money to make an authorised payment

Section 16 of the TA 1925 is not amended by the 1996 Act. Its effect is that it gives trustees a power to raise money by mortgage which cannot be overridden by the trust instrument. It does not apply to land held for charitable purposes or to trustees under the SLA 1925 unless they are also statutory owners. The power of mortgaging under s.16 is given where trustees require to raise money to make an authorised payment of capital money. Other than mortgages for this purpose the power of mortgaging can be negated by the trust instrument.

(ii) Under s.6 of the 1996 Act

It should be noted that though a wide power of mortgaging is given by s.6 of the 1996 Act it cannot be assumed that the power is unrestricted. The powers conferred by s.6 are conferred "for the purpose of exercising their functions as trustees". It is clear that where trustees are mortgaging trust land for some other purpose then the mortgagee may be aware that there is a breach of trust. The mortgagee will thus be aware that there is a breach of s.6(6) of the 1996 Act. Suppose Smith and Jones are the trustees of a house which they wish to use as a security for Smith's own business debts. This cannot be within the functions of a trustee and must therefore not be within s.6(1) and is also a contravention of a rule of equity within s.6(6). A mortgagee, in order safely to make this loan, must know that Smith and Jones are *sui juris* and are the sole beneficiaries of the trust or that their powers as trustees have been extended beyond s.6(1). On the basic principles of overreaching, a purchaser from trustees of land is intended to be protected by s.27 of the LPA 1925 from circumstances where the trustees do not carry out the terms of the trust. However, a purchaser who knowingly assists in a breach of trust cannot be protected by this (see also p. 47–23). Variation of the implied power conferred by s.6 must (under s.8) be contained in the disposition to the trustees.

7.2.3 Power of Leasing Trust Property

This is now uncircumscribed so far as the length and purpose of leases and their content is concerned. Trustees in leasing trust property remain subject to a duty to obtain the terms which would be obtained by a prudent man of business managing his own affairs (the standard established in *Learoyd v. Whiteley* (1887) 12 App Cas 727).

The previous statutory power of leasing was complex and restrictive (ss.41 to 48 of the SLA 1925). In both trusts for sale and strict settlements it was invariably extended if thought was given to the matter. It was considered widely by practitioners to be unclear as to whether these rules permitted leases containing rent review provisions, although this doubt was unnecessary given the requirement in s.42(1)(ii) of the SLA 1925 that a lease should be at the "best rent reasonably obtainable". Whatever the merit of such a concern, the new power conferred by s.6 disposes of the issue. A purchaser (see the discussion on gifts) will be concerned only if the lease on the face of it, or from facts of which the purchaser is actually aware, is one into which a trustee could not properly enter. Examples would be a lease which is clearly at an undervalue or a lease to any of the trustees (see para. 7.1).

7.2.4 Power to Gift Trust Property

The extended powers given to trustees by s.6 of the 1996 Act do not include the power to gift trust property or dispose of it at an undervalue. Such transactions are not "functions as trustees" to which s.6 applies. Thus, Snell, dealing in general with the position of trustees, says "In discharging his duties he must observe the utmost diligence, or exacta diligentia, in order to escape liability for any loss sustained by the trust estate . . . In carrying out the trusts they must take due care of the trust property by investing it prudently and in the manner directed . . ." (Snell's *Equity*, 29th ed., pp. 213–214).

This means that a title which discloses a gift by trustees is, on the face of it, defective. In most cases the documentation will show that the trustee donors were together absolutely beneficially entitled to the trust property. There will be cases such as a husband and wife gifting their jointly owned property to a child. So far as a subsequent purchaser is concerned the gift cannot have been an overreaching conveyance as no capital money has been paid to trustees. In order to accept the title the purchaser will need to be convinced that all the beneficiaries of the trust had capacity and did consent to the gift.

Trustees remain bound to sell at the best price reasonably obtainable. This principle is most firmly established, see *Buttle v. Saunders* [1950] 2 All E.R. 193: "trustees are not entitled to sell the premises except for the best price reasonably obtainable . . . it is not disputed that that is the duty cast on the trustees". It is thus the case that if it is clear from the conveyance that trustees have sold at an undervalue, for example if this is revealed from the stamp duty being paid at a higher value than the consideration shown, then a purchaser will know there has been a breach of trust. Since all conveyances on sale must now give rise to compulsory registration this state of affairs will rarely be known to a purchaser from the original purchaser from the trustees.

7.2.5 Power to Insure

Trustees of land may insure for any insurable risk up to the full value of the property. The restricted power of insurance in s.19 of the Trustee Act 1925 is accordingly amended to apply to trust property other than land.

8. Exclusion and Restriction of Trustees' Powers

The powers conferred on trustees by ss.6 and 7 of the 1996 Act can be excluded or restricted by the disposition which creates a trust of land. It must be assumed that a declaration of trust is a disposition for this purpose.[2]

The requirement for the variation of trustees' powers to be in the disposition which creates a trust of land may be inadvertently transgressed in some cases. It is usual to describe the trusts in an instrument separate from the disposition. Thus, in a partnership of solicitors, land will be conveyed to a number of the partners on a trust of land. The relationship between the partners will be contained in a separate partnership deed or trust instrument. Where land is conveyed to a number of persons for a particular purpose (*e.g.* as in *Buchanan-Wollaston's Conveyance, Re* [1939] Ch. 378) they might have a separate declaration of trust dealing with issues such as when the property is to be sold. Restrictions contained in the separate declaration of trust or partnership deed do not fetter the trustees' powers under s.6 of the 1996 Act. The position is that as between the beneficiaries and the trustees there may be a breach of trust if the trustees exercise a s.6 power which is restricted by the trust deed. A purchaser may assume that the trustees have unrestricted powers unless the restrictions are contained in the disposition. This argument is somewhat academic in the case of registered land as where the land is registered any restrictions on the trustee-registered proprietors' powers will be entered as restrictions on the proprietorship register.

9. Drafting Express Trusts

Areas in which the drafting of express trusts may be affected by the 1996 Act are as follows.

9.1 Express Trusts For Sale

The purpose of including an express trust for sale in trusts between 1926 and 1996 was to prevent a settlement arising under the SLA 1925. It had the incidental effect that the interests of beneficiaries were (because of the doctrine of conversion) interests in the personalty and not realty. Section 3 of the 1996 Act has, in any event, abolished the doctrine of conversion. This means that the land subject to a trust for sale is to be regarded as land. The interest of a beneficiary under the trust may or may not be an interest in this land depending on how that interest is expressed. A full discussion of this point is found at pp. 47–15, 47–16. The importance of it in practice is that much turns on whether a beneficiary has an interest in possession in land. Such a beneficiary in one to whom there can be delegation under s.9, who may be entitled to be consulted under s.11 and has a right of occupation under s.13.

In drafting a trust many settlors will be anxious to prevent these provisions coming into play and therefore wish to ensure there is no beneficiary who has

---

[2] The reason for this is that s.23(2) of the 1996 Act provides for definitions given in the LPA 1925 to apply. Section 205(1) of the LPA 1925 provides that a "disposition" includes a conveyance and a conveyance includes every assurance of property or an interest therein by any instrument.

an interest in possession in land. Provisions which make it clear that the interest of a beneficiary is only an interest in the income of a fund will have this effect. It does not, in essence, matter whether the trust is expressed as trust for sale or not to achieve this effect, see Precedent 17, p. 47–79.

9.2 Purpose of the Trust

It may be helpful in drafting future trusts to include in them a statement of the purpose of the trust. The reasons for this are that (a) an expression of the purposes of the trust may make it clear whether or not any of the land in the trust may be used for occupation by a beneficiary and (b) such a statement must be taken into account under s.15(1)(b) if there is any dispute brought before the court as to the exercise of the trustees' powers or the nature or extent of any person's interest in property subject to the trust.

9.3 Availability for Occupation

The provision in s.12 of the 1996 Act giving beneficiaries a right of occupation is uncertain in its application. It may or may not apply to beneficiaries who have only an income interest in the trust (see the General Note to s.12, above). Many settlors will wish to ensure that all or particular parts of the land in a trust are not occupied by beneficiaries. The authors' view is that this is achieved where a beneficiary has only an interest in the income of a fund. However, it may well be sensible in addition to include a statement in the trust instrument as to the purposes of the trust and its availability for occupation. In the same way in exercising their powers under s.13 of the 1996 Act (where there are two or more beneficiaries entitled under the Act) the trustees have to give regard to the intentions of the person who created the trust.

9.4 Requirement to Consult Beneficiaries

The requirement of s.11(1) of the 1996 Act (see para. 13.2.1 below) will often be excluded by a simple clause to that effect.

9.5 Appointment of New Trustees

Deeds of trust will commonly contain express provision as to who has the power to appoint new trustees. This will mean that ss.19 and 20 of the 1996 Act will not apply. Either of these provisions giving beneficiaries some say in the appointment of trustees can be excluded by a simple provision in the trust instrument. Professional trustees will routinely wish to exclude s.19 (beneficiaries' power to direct the appointment or retirement of trustees) because they will see it as an obvious potential nuisance. There is less obvious point in excluding s.20 which operates in very limited circumstances (see p. 47–27).

10. Wills and Administration of Estates

10.1 Generally

The 1996 Act has some impact on the drafting of wills but not so much as might at first be hazarded. The general effect is to simplify the administrative parts of wills so that the document as a whole will read more easily to the lay person. Curiously, although the following paragraphs indicate some desirable drafting changes to make in wills, none is imperative. The clauses referred to here cover very similar ground to those suggested for *inter vivos* trusts above.

10.2 The Trust for Sale

It is customary for the residue in a will to be left to the executors and trustees on a trust for sale and then to set out the trusts on which they hold the estate. The reason for this was that if there were successive interests then any land in the estate would be held as settled land under the SLA 1925 unless there was an immediate binding trust for sale (s.205(1)(xxix) of the LPA 1925; s.1(7) of the SLA 1925). No new Settled Land Act settlements can now be created. There is, accordingly, no need to include an administrative trust for sale in the will.

Where successive interests in the residue are created, the estate should be expressed to be held "on trust" by the executors and trustees to give effect to the successive interests.

10.3 Powers of Executors and Trustees

Land is held by the executors or trustees of a will. They will have the extensive powers of management given by s.6 of the 1996 Act. This means there is no need to confer such powers upon the trustees. However, in the management of land held on trust certain powers will still require express provision in the will.

(i) Power of trustee to purchase trust property

This will be required (if there is to be such a power) because of s.6(6) of the 1996 Act (see p. 47–8).

(ii) Power of executors to appropriate without consent

This is required (if there is to be such a power) because both s.7 of the 1996 Act and s.41 of the AEA 1925 require consent of the beneficiaries to a statutory appropriation.

10.4 Exclusion of Provisions of the 1996 Act

In drafting a will, consideration must be given as to whether the testator wishes to exclude the following.
(i) Particular powers of the trustees may be limited or removed (s.8 of the 1996 Act).
(ii) Consulting beneficiaries. The requirement to consult beneficiaries before exercising any function relating to land may be excluded by a simple statement in the will (see s.11 of the 1996 Act and Precedents 11 and 12, pp. 47–77, 47–78).
(iii) Appointment of trustees and retirement of trustees. The provisions of ss.19 and 20 of the 1996 Act which give the beneficiaries a power to direct the appointment or retirement of trustees can be excluded by a simple statement in the will (see Precedents 16a, 16b, p. 47–79).

10.5 Occupation of Trust Land

Where the will anticipates that there may be an ongoing trust then the testator should be directed to the implications of ss.12 and 13 of the 1996 Act.

The will might include: (i) statements as to the purpose of the trust in relation to land to be held under it; (ii) statements as to whether all the land held, or particular land held, is to be available for occupation; and (iii) conditions to be satisfied by a beneficiary occupying all, or particular parts of, trust land.

10.6 Exclusion of Apportionment Rules

The courts in a large number of cases developed a series of rules aimed at holding the balance between income and capital and between interests in possession and reversionary interests. A duty to treat wasting assets as if invested in authorised investments is imposed by *Howe v. Lord Dartmouth* (1802) 7 Ves 137. The mirror image is provided by *Earl of Chesterfield's Trusts, Re* (1883) 24 Ch.D. 643 which, in favour of a tenant for life, requires an assumption that reversionary interests have been converted. So far as realty was concerned these rules and their many branches had no scope for operation (*Woodhouse, Re* [1941] Ch. 332) and were excluded from trusts for sale by s.28(2) of the LPA 1925. That provision is repealed. The rules were excluded from an intestacy because of the conversion worked by the implied trust for sale in s.33 of the AEA 1925. That section is amended to impose a simple trust which, in the case of land, will be a trust of land under the 1996 Act. The discretionary power of sale given to the administration on an intestacy by the amended s.33(1) will exclude the duty to convert (*Pitcairn, Re* [1896] 2 Ch. 199). In a will the property may be left on trust with power to postpone sale and this will have a similar effect. Such a power may not exclude operation of all derivative forms of these rules (see *Allhusen v. Whittell* (1867) L.R. 4 Eq 295 as discussed in *Wills, Re* [1915] 1 Ch. 769 and also *Fisher, Re* [1943] Ch. 377; *Berry, Re* [1962] Ch. 97). It is, in consequence, still safer expressly to exclude the application of all statutory and equitable rules of apportionment. This may still be done by a simple statement that "all statutory and equitable rules of apportionment do not apply to this will".

10.7 Assents of Property on Trust for Sale in Will

Where property is held by the executors on trust before they deal with it as trustees it should be assented to them in that capacity (*King's Will Trusts, Re* [1964] Ch. 542).

Under the pre-1996 Act law the property was vested in the appropriate trustees on trust for sale by an assent. A suitable form of assent is Form No. 9 in the LPA, Sched. 5. Under the post-1996 Act law the trust for sale declared by the will takes effect as a trust of land and the form of assent to be used must accordingly be varied. Instead of the land being expressed to be assented on trust to sell with the express trust for sale set out *in extenso*, the assent is simply to "The Trusts upon the Trusts declared by [The Will]".

11. Partnerships

11.1 Partnership Property

Before the 1996 Act partnership real property was held by up to four partners on a trust for sale. It will now be held on a trust of land. The restriction on the number of trustees which is found in s.34 of the TA 1925 is unaffected by the 1996 Act.

11.2 Abolition of Conversion

Section 22 of the Partnership Act 1890, which provided expressly for the doctrine of conversion to apply to partnership property, is repealed (Sched. 4 of the 1996 Act). The abolition of conversion where there is an express trust for sale is completed by s.3 of the 1996 Act. It must be noted that the repeal of s.22 of the Partnership Act 1890 does not apply to any circumstances involving the personal representative of a partner who died before the 1996 Act's commencement day.

11.3 Partnership Documentation

Partnership property will continue to be conveyed to up to four named partners upon trust. The trusts may, as previously, be contained in a separate trust deed or partnership agreement. If it is desired that there should be a restriction on disposal of partnership property (*e.g.* using land as a security) then restrictions which affect each partner personally will be contained in the partnership agreement; restrictions upon the trustee partner's power of management will be contained in the disposition to them.

12. Delegation

12.1 The Power to Delegate

Section 9 allows the trustees to delegate all, or any part, of their functions to a beneficiary. The trustees can choose whether or not to exercise this power where the following conditions are satisfied: (i) only functions relating to the land are being delegated. Functions unconnected with the land, such as investment of the proceeds of sale, can only be delegated where there is an appropriate express power of delegation; and (ii) delegation must be made to a beneficiary, or beneficiaries, of full age, beneficially entitled to an interest in the land. Section 9 does not allow delegation to a potential beneficiary under a discretionary trust, or to a beneficiary with a contingent interest, or to one whose interest is simply in the income from the trust. This means that the most common situation for delegation will be to an adult beneficiary with a life interest in the property.

Points for the trustees to consider are: (i) whether to delegate all or some of their functions. If the trustees have sufficient confidence in the beneficiary, they can delegate all the functions. On the other hand, they could give the attorney limited powers of management, retaining control over raising money by mortgage or selling. The drafting must clearly reflect the powers being delegated, as powers of attorney are strictly construed (*Bryant Powis & Bryant v. Banque du Peuple* [1893] A.C. 170); (ii) where there is more than one beneficiary eligible to be an attorney, whether to split the functions between the beneficiaries, give a joint power, or simply delegate to one; (iii) whether to make the delegation for a limited period or indefinitely. A limited period might be useful as a trial period; and (iv) the experience and ability of the beneficiary or attorney. Failure to take reasonable care in making the appointment will make the trustees' liable for the attorney's defaults (s.9(8)). Delegation can be to a sole co-trustee who is a beneficiary.

12.2 The Form of the Power

Delegation must be made by all the trustees jointly, using a power of attorney. The Act does not specify any particular format, the requirements as to form are those governing powers of attorney generally. A deed must be used.

Section 9(6) rules out the possibility of this being an enduring power. It will therefore be revoked by the mental incapacity of a trustee. An individual trustee, or each trustee, could make a delegation of their functions, which will survive mental incapacity, by relying on s.3(3) of the Enduring Powers of Attorney Act 1985 (c. 29).

12.3 The Purchaser

Unless the attorney is the registered proprietor, the purchaser must ensure that the power is valid. Proof of the power is the same as for ordinary powers of attorney: the production of the original, or more usually a certified photocopy (s.3 of the Powers of Attorney Act 1971 (c. 27)), is required. This will enable the purchaser to satisfy the Land Registry requirements (the Land Registry may choose to retain the document sent). In inspecting the power, a purchaser will be checking to ensure that there has indeed been a delegation to the person exercising the function, and that this delegation is valid at the time of the transaction.

(i) Dealing with the attorney

Steps need not be taken to ascertain the beneficiary's eligibility or suitability for appointment. Under s.9(2) *any person dealing in good faith* with the attorney can presume that the attorney is a person to whom the delegation could be made. This presumption covers both a purchaser or any other person dealing immediately with the attorney. Of course, it will be rebutted by proof that the person dealing with the attorney knew that the attorney did not fulfil the requirements for appointment, but in the absence of any such actual knowledge, the requirement of good faith will be satisfied by carrying out the normal conveyancing step of inspecting a copy of the power.

Nor is it necessary to check that the power has not been revoked. The title of the purchaser, or any person dealing with the attorney, will be valid even if there has been a revocation provided he did not know of the revocation (s.5(2) of the PAA 1971). Again, the only action the purchaser need take is to inspect the copy power.

(ii) Subsequent purchasers

The task of subsequent purchasers is eased by two forms of statutory declaration.

   (a) Under s.9(2) a declaration made *before or within three months of the purchase* gives a conclusive presumption in favour of the purchaser that the person dealing with the attorney did not have knowledge of any invalidity in the appointment.

   (b) Section 5(4) of the PAA 1971 gives a purchaser the benefit of a conclusive presumption that the person dealing with the attorney did not have knowledge of any revocation. It applies where the transaction between the attorney and the other person took place within 12 months of the creation of the power, or if the person dealing with the attorney before or within three months of the completion of the purchase makes a statutory declaration to the effect that he had no knowledge of any revocation.

   Despite the longer time limits available in the statutes, both declarations (see Precedent 8, p. 47–75) should be made at the time of the first dealing with the attorney and kept with the title. This will prevent later problems with unavailable or deceased parties.

(iii) Registered land

Where the trustees are registered as proprietors and the land is dealt with by the attorney, the purchaser must inspect the power of attorney, as described above. The Land Registry will require no further evidence, beyond a copy of the power, of validity provided the disposition by the attorney is completed within 12 months of the date the power came into operation. After that date, the Land Registry will require evidence that it had not been revoked at the time of the transaction. This will normally be by statutory declaration. Where this is not possible, a certificate by the solicitor to the same effect will be required.

There is no need to inspect copies of the power or require a statutory declaration where the dealing with the attorney was by a person currently registered as the proprietor. In this case, the purchaser can rely upon the state of the register and the registration of the vendor.

12.4 Liability of the Trustees

Trustees must take reasonable care in appointing the attorney. Beyond that, they are not liable for the attorney's mismanagement of the property (s.9(8)). To protect themselves, in making the appointment they must consider the type of management skills required, and the experience and knowledge of the beneficiary. Trustees cannot be called upon to disclose their reasons for making a particular appointment (*Londonderry's Settlement, Re*; *Peat v. Walsh* [1965] Ch. 918) unless the beneficiaries go to the lengths of commencing an action for maladministration.

Any trustee dissatisfied with an attorney's performance can revoke the appointment instantly (s.9(3)). Although the Act provides no format for the revocation, the clearest course is to send a written notice to the attorney, with a copy to the other trustees if they are not joining in the revocation.

12.5 Liability of the Attorney

As a matter of good practice, it should be brought to the attorney's attention that he has the same duties and liabilities as a trustee (s.9(7)) and insurance cover considered. Examples of potential difficulties include the rule that he cannot profit from the trust, and therefore (without express provision in the trust instrument) cannot charge for professional services to the trust. Similarly, the equitable duty to maintain a balance between the beneficiaries will apply. Decisions relating to the property could not favour the life interest at the expense of the remainderman.

An attorney who acts without notice of any revocation of the power will not be liable (either to the donor or any other person) simply by reason of the revocation. This is part of the general rule in s.5(1) of the PAA 1971, and there is no provision in the Act affecting its applicability.

12.6 Revocation of the Power

The important practical point to note is the varied circumstances in which the power will be revoked (s.9(3)). As noted in para. 12.4 above, the power can be revoked at any time by any or all of the trustees. The clearest method will be to send a written notice to the attorney, with a copy to any other trustees not giving notice. But revocation will be equally effective if communicated orally. It may even be implied by, for example, tearing up the power of attorney. As the appointment of a new trustee will also have this effect, a fresh power will have to be executed by the new and continuing trustees if the attorney is to continue acting.

The death of a trustee, or if a trustee ceases for any other reason to be a trustee, is expressly exempted by subs. (3) from revoking the appointment. Mental incapacity or bankruptcy of the trustee would revoke the power, and in those circumstances a new appointment would be necessary.

As noted in s.12(4) a person dealing with the attorney will get good title provided he did not know of any revocation (s.5(2) of the PAA 1971). If revocation occurred after exchange then, provided the attorney had power to bind the trust estate at the time of the contract, specific performance can be had against the trustees as his principals. This will be true even if such purchaser had knowledge of the revocation after exchange but before completion.

13. Consents and the Duty to Consult the Beneficiaries

13.1 Consents

13.1.1 The trustees' duties

There is little of novelty to concern trustees in s.10. The trustees must obtain all the specified consents (including the person with parental responsibility of any infant or the legal representative of a mentally incapable person). If they fail to do so they will be liable for breach of trust. An action could only be brought by a beneficiary who would have to establish loss in order to succeed in a claim for damages. In instances where a proper price has been received in respect of a transaction, what could the damages be? The loss is the property, but the purchaser will probably have good title, and if the full value has been paid, there can be no further claim to damages.

If the trustees' endeavours to obtain a requisite consent fail, they will have to make an application under s.14 to dispense with that consent. The court can make the order whether the consent is unobtainable because the person cannot be traced, or because he refuses to agree to the transaction. In exercising its jurisdiction, the court will have regard to the matters specified in s.15 (discussed at para. 14.1 below).

It should be noted that the provisions of s.10 do not apply to personal representatives (s.18(1)).

13.1.2 Protection of the Purchaser

As far as the purchaser is concerned, if more than two consents are required, he can safely rely on seeing just two (s.10(1)). The purchaser can ignore the consent of a person who is an infant (subs. (3)), but not the consent of the appropriate representative (attorney or receiver) of a person who is mentally incapable. All consents required by the disposition must be produced to the purchaser in respect of land held on charitable, ecclesiastical and public trusts (subs. (2)).

Where the title to the land is registered, the purchaser will only be affected by the need for consent where there is an appropriate restriction on the register. This will have been entered by the Land Registry when the trustees were first registered as proprietors.

13.1.3 Drafting considerations

For settlors the Act extends the possibility of making consent to a transaction a requirement in the case of any trust of land, including one involving successive interests. This was formerly prohibited by s.106 of the SLA 1925 in relation to strict settlements. The trust instrument can make provision for consent, including that of the beneficiaries, to be obtained to any one, all or some dealings. There is no limit, other than the practical considerations, to the number of consents that can be required. Apart from the problems of obtaining an unwieldy number of consents, there could be difficulties with lack of unanimity.

A statement in the trust instrument of the settlor's reasons for requiring a particular consent will help ensure that that person's decision is upheld in the event of an application under s.15 to dispense with that person's consent.

13.2 Consultation

13.2.1 The trustees' position

The Act imposes an automatic duty on trustees to consult the beneficiaries of full age and beneficially entitled to an interest in possession. The duty under s.11 to consult does not arise in respect of beneficiaries with a contingent interest, under a discretionary trust, or whose interest is not in land (*i.e.* where they have a beneficial interest in the income of a trust for sale rather than the land). It will most frequently apply where there is a beneficiary with a life interest in the land, or where there is a beneficiary with an interest under an implied, resulting or constructive trust, *e.g.* of the family home. As the Act limits the duty to consult insofar as it is practical there is no need to obtain a court order where, for example, the relevant beneficiary refuses to reply to correspondence or is unobtainable (subs. (1)(a)).

What is the situation if the beneficiaries do not agree with the trustees' proposals? The duty is *so far as is consistent with the general interest of the trust* to give effect to the beneficiaries' wishes (subs. (1)(b)). This allows the trustees to disregard the disagreement of a beneficiary whose views are not conducive to the welfare of the trust. If the beneficiaries could establish that their consent has been withheld in the interests of the trust, then the trustees must give effect to them in accordance with subs. (1)(b), or make application under s.15 to override their wishes. At the same time, beneficiaries could obtain an injunction under s.15 if the trustees proceed with a transaction and ignore their rights under this section.

Trustees who carry out a function without complying with this duty of consultation could find themselves open to an action for breach of trust. Here, as with s.10 (see para. 13.1.1 above) the difficult practical issue is the measure of damages. Where the trustees can substantiate their actions in the interests of good administration of the trust, and have received full value in respect of any transaction, there is no loss from the breach (*Target Holdings v. Redfern* [1995] 3 W.L.R. 352).

Section 11, like s.10, does not extend to personal representatives (s.18): they therefore do not have this duty to consult.

13.2.2 The Purchaser's position

It is clear that the purchaser is not concerned with whether the requirements of s.11 have been complied with (s.16(1)). This includes both immediate purchasers from the trustees and subsequent purchasers of the land. Thus no inquiries should be made on this matter.

14. Applications to Court

14.1 When to Make Applications

The wording of s.14 is wide enough to give the court jurisdiction to decide the following matters:

(1) Disputes about the exercise of the trustees' functions between (a) the trustees; (b) the trustees and the beneficiaries; (c) the trustees and others with an interest in the property (*e.g.* mortgagees of a beneficial interest, creditors under a charging order, assignees of beneficiaries' interests); and (d) the trustees and those whose consent to a transaction is required by the trust instrument.

The application can be made by any person with an interest in the property. This excludes those simply entitled to consent to a transaction unless they are also beneficiaries. Application can be made by a mortgagee of a beneficiary's interest or a creditor under a charging order. Situations where applications will be made under this section include applications by trustees to dispense with specified consents, applications by a beneficiary for appointment as an attorney under s.9 and applications by a co-owner where another trustee is unwilling to sell. It is important to remember both in advising upon and drafting such an application that the court will have regard to the matters specified in s.15. A successful application will require the circumstances of the case to relate to those criteria. Any express statements in the trust instrument on these matters are likely to carry considerable weight. Section 14 does not apply to property held by personal representatives (s.18(1)).

(2) Authority to enter into transactions which would otherwise be a breach of trust.

(3) The nature and extent of a person's interest in the property. This power, which was not formerly exercisable under s.30 of the LPA 1925, does not alter the rules deciding beneficial interests. Applications can be made to decide whether a person has a beneficial interest, the nature of the co-ownership (joint tenancy or tenancy in common) or the size of the parties' shares.

14.2 Applications by Trustees in Bankruptcy

The practical point here is that an application by a trustee in bankruptcy under s.14 is governed by the criteria now set out in the new s.335A of the Insolvency Act 1986 (c. 45). These will apply equally whether the application for sale is by a trustee in bankruptcy of a cohabitee or of a spouse.

The trustee's application is made in the court with jurisdiction over the bankruptcy. Where the bankrupt is not or has not been married, the main consideration will often be the interests of the bankrupt's creditors (s.335A(2)(a)). The court has the general power in para. (c) to have regard to all the circumstances of the case. This would include the needs of a cohabitee or children. Here the position of cohabitees is, however, weaker as they are merely part of the "circumstances of the case". Spouses are given especial consideration in subs. (2).

In the long run the property will be available for the creditors. The trustee simply has to delay until a year after appointment. After that the court must assume that the interest of the bankrupt's creditors outweigh all other considerations (subs. (3)). This will not be the case where there are exceptional circumstances, though these are notoriously difficult to establish. In *Citro, Re* [1990] 3 All E.R. 952 loss of home and change of school were not sufficient. (For a decision where a sale on a creditor's application was considered unequitable, see *Abbey National v. Moss* (1993) 26 H.L.R. 249).

If the application involves a dwelling house which is or has been the home of the bankrupt, his spouse, or former spouse there are additional factors for the court to consider. These are unchanged from s.336 of the Insolvency Act 1986. The previous position is maintained so that in that case too all applications made a year after the bankrupt's property vests in the trustee in bankruptcy will probably be successful. The position here too is governed by subs. (3), discussed above.

14.3 Drafting Considerations

In drafting trust instruments explicit statements relating to the criteria in s.15 should be made in appropriate situations. The parties' intentions and the purposes for which the property is held should be made clear. They will help prevent expensive argument over these issues.

This elaboration of the purpose of the trust may not be required in every trust of land. It seems unnecessary in many cases of co-ownership of the matrimonial home but it will be useful for the parties to declare their "terms" (intentions and the purpose for the property) in more unusual situations. For example, where property is bought for a mixed use, as a family home and for business purposes, difficulties will be avoided by declaring what is to happen if one of the partners/cohabitees wishes to sell but the other wants to continue the business on the premises.

Where there are successive interests in the property, statements should be included of the settlor's intentions with regard to the trustees' duty to consult the beneficiaries (under s.11) or the power to appoint an attorney (s.9).

15. Appointment and Retirement of Trustees

15.1 Control by Beneficiaries

The Act empowers beneficiaries by s.19 to direct the appointment of substitutional and additional trustees or the retirement of trustees. This applies to all trusts, whenever created. The majority of trusts, however, will be unaffected by these provisions as s.19 will not apply where: (i) there is a living person nominated by the trust instrument to appoint new trustees (s.19(1)); (ii) the beneficiaries are not all of full age and capacity and between them absolutely entitled to the trust property (s.19(1)). The possibility of unborn beneficiaries will make s.19 inapplicable, as will the presence of a contingent interest even if that beneficiary is of full age; (iii) the power is excluded; (iv) the appointment of additional trustees will increase the number of trustees to realty or personalty beyond four in breach of s.36(8) of the TA 1925; and (v) the beneficiaries are not aware of the power. There is no duty under the Act for the trustees to notify them before making an appointment or to inform them of this power. One drafting consideration is that this will be applicable to partnership property, unless excluded. The instrument may provide for the appointment of new trustees.

The Act does not interfere with the right of trustees to make substitutional appointments in the circumstances set out in s.36(1) of the TA 1925 and additional appointments under s.36(8). The practical effect is that on the death of a trustee, for example, the existing trustees can make a new appointment without consulting the beneficiaries. If, however, they receive or have already received a direction from the beneficiaries to make a particular appointment, this must be followed.

15.2 The Beneficiaries' Direction

Beneficiaries must make a written direction, whether for appointment or retirement (s.19(2)). In both these cases, they may give one direction or a series either singularly, or jointly with other beneficiaries (subs. (2)(b)). All the directions must specify for the appointment or retirement of the same person(s).

A direction to appoint should be given by the beneficiaries as soon as they have a unanimous view. This will prevent the trustees making an appointment, as stated above, in ignorance of their views.

The direction to appoint or retire must be given to the existing trustees. In the case of appointment if there are no trustees it is given to the personal representative of the last person who was a trustee (s.19(2)(b)). The Act does not define when a direction is deemed to have been "given". There is nothing in s.19 or in s.23 to make s.196 of the LPA 1925 applicable. It seems inconceivable that the court would not consider a written notice sent to the trustees' last known place of abode or place of business "given". For evidential reasons this should be by registered post or recorded delivery.

Any one beneficiary later becoming dissatisfied with a direction can withdraw it in writing. This must be done before it is complied with (s.21(1)). This may cause difficulty in the other beneficiaries as there is no duty to notify them of the withdrawal. Again, the Act makes no specific provision for serving this notice on the trustees. The best course is to send it to all trustees.

15.3 The Form of Appointment

The Act does not affect the method of appointment. An appointment at the beneficiaries' direction is still made by the continuing trustees, in writing, and usually by deed (ss.36 and 40 of the TA 1925). Such an appointment enjoys the benefits of s.36(7) of the TA 1925, with the new trustee having all the trustees' powers.

15.4 Retirement

Before a trustee retires as a result of a beneficiaries' direction it should be checked that: (1) there will be two trustees or a trust corporation left; (2) either a substitutional appointment is being made or the existing trustees consent to the retirement; and (3) reasonable arrangements have been made to protect the trustees' rights (subs. 3)).

The rights referred to are indemnities for liabilities. The scope of the right to indemnity (other than reimbursement for expenses (s.30 of the TA 1925)) depends upon the express provision made in the trust instrument. Beyond this, there is no general right to indemnity from the trust fund, even by way of insurance (for exceptions to this rule, see a standard text on trusts).

Retirement is by deed (s.19(3)). This will give the benefit of the implied vesting declaration in s.40 of the TA 1925, vesting the property in the continuing trustees (unless a contrary intention is stated). Some property will not vest in this way: shares, and certain leases. In this case, the retiring trustee must take all steps to vest the property in the continuing trustees (s.19(4)). The deed of retirement could also contain a substitutional appointment.

15.5 Drafting Points under ss.19 and 20

Many settlors will want to exclude these provisions. For new trusts, a simple statement in the trust instrument excluding ss.19 and 20 will suffice (s.20(5)).

For pre-commencement trusts an irrevocable deed excluding s.19 must be executed by any living settlors (s.20(6)(7)). This deed will not invalidate an appointment or retirement in compliance with a direction already given. It will invalidate a direction already given but not complied with (subs. (8)). Instructions should be taken on executing such a deed. Delay will not be fatal as clearly the section allows the deed to be executed even after a direction has been given.

15.6 Mentally Incapable Trustees

Section 20 permits the beneficiaries to give directions for the appointment of substantial trustees in place of a mentally incapable trustee. Replacement need not be on a one-for-one basis: the beneficiary can direct the appointment of additional trustees (subs. (2)).

The power applies where the trustee is mentally incapable. This will be a cleary recognisable state of affairs as the direction is given to someone with power to act on the patient's behalf, *i.e.* a receiver, registered attorney under the Enduring Powers of Attorney Act 1985 (c. 29) or a person authorised under Pt. VII of the Mental Health Act 1983 (c. 20).

If the mentally incapable trustee is also a beneficiary, the consent of the person with authority under Pt. VII of the Mental Health Act 1983 must be obtained (the TA 1925, s.36(9)).

It will be particularly useful where there is a sole mentally incapable trustee. In that case, the condition will be satisfied that there is no person entitled and willing and able to act. Where any co-trustee or person nominated under the trust instrument to make appointments is willing to act, then the power is excluded (subs. (1)). As with s.19 the beneficiaries must be of full age and capacity and between them absolutely entitled to the trust property to be able to exercise the power.

15.7 Title Required by Purchaser under ss.19 and 20

Where a trustee is appointed as a result of a beneficiary's direction this should be recited in the trustees' appointment. In favour of a purchaser an appointment depending on that statement and any consequent vesting declaration is valid (s.38(2) of the TA 1925).

15.8 Registered Land

Whenever a new trustee is appointed, a change must be made in the proprietorship register. One of three methods can be used.

(1) A simple transfer by the registered proprietors—retiring and continuing trustees—to the new trustee. No further deed of appointment is required.

The advantage of this is that the Registrar will not investigate the title of the appointees and satisfy himself that they are entitled to make the appointment. This method is not suitable where property other than the registered land is included in the trust.

(2) A deed of appointment can be used, with a supplemental transfer. Again, the Registrar will not investigate the validity of the right to make the appointment.

(3) The deed of appointment (with a copy for filing) is produced to the Registrar who will give effect to an express or implied vesting declaration (s.47 of the LRA 1925), and record the change of trustee. This is a cumbersome method as evidence will have to be produced of the appointor's title to make the appointment.

Any restriction on the Register requiring the consent of a third party to the transaction must be complied with.

PART III: PRECEDENTS

A: CONVEYANCING

1. Conveyance by Solely Entitled Surviving Tenant in Common Incorporating a Deed under s.16(4) of the 1996 Act

THIS CONVEYANCE is made on the   day of
BETWEEN AB of   ("the Trustee") of the first part and
the said AB "the Vendor" of the second part and CD of
"the Purchaser" of the third part.

WHEREAS

1.   [recite purchase by AB and other tenant in common of "the property"].
2.   [recite death of other Trustee(s)].
3.   In the events which have happened the Vendor is absolutely entitled to the land under the trust and is of full age and capacity.

NOW THIS DEED WITNESSETH that

1.   The Trustee conveys ["the property"] to the Vendor beneficially and pursuant to s.16(4) of the Trusts of Land and Appointment of Trustees Act 1996 declares that he is discharged from the trust in relation to that land.
2.   The Vendor with full title Guarantee and in Consideration of the Sum of [   ] receipt of which the Vendor acknowledges conveys the property to the purchaser.
3.   [description of the property].
4.   [certificate of value].

IN WITNESS etc.

Notes:
1.   The Purchaser may rely on the statement under s.16(4) unless he has actual knowledge that AB was mistaken in his belief that he was absolutely entitled.
2.   The death certificate of the deceased Trustees should be produced but no evidence of AB's beneficial entitlement is required or should be requested.

2. Words To Convey To Beneficial Joint Tenants

To AB and CD on trust for themselves as joint tenants in law and equity.

(or in registered land)

The transferees declare themselves to be joint tenants in equity.

Note:

The only change is the absence of an express trust for sale and the absence of an extension of the powers of management (see note at Part II, para. 7)—a greater power of charging the trust property may be desirable for some owners (see Part II, para. 7.2 and Precedent 21 below).

3. Words To Convey To Beneficial Tenants in Common

To AB and CD on trust for themselves as tenants in common (in equal shares or as the case may be or on the trusts of a Deed of Trust made between [AB and CD] of even date herewith).

(or in registered land).

The transferees declare that they are tenants in common equity (in equal shares or as the case may be or on the trusts of Deed of Trust made between [themselves] of even date herewith).

Note:

The parties in the deed of trust may wish to deal expressly with:
any rights of occupation (s.12)
any greater power of charging the trust property (see Part II, para. 7.2).

4. Assent by Personal Representatives in Favour of Trustees of Land

THIS ASSENT is made the   day of   by [names of Personal Representatives] "the Personal Representatives" of [the deceased].

1. The Personal Representatives assent to the vesting in [themselves or the trustees as the case may be] of the property described in the Schedule hereto Upon Trust.

2. [Details of any express power to appoint new trustees given in the Will].

3. [Acknowledgement for production of Probate or Letters of Administration].

Schedule

AS WITNESS ETC

Note:

This is based on Form 9 in Sched. 5 to the LPA 1925 but replacing the trust for sale by a trust of land.

5. Deed of Discharge under s.16(4) of the 1996 Act

This deed of discharge is executed by [name of Trustees] "the Trustees" this   day of   199

WHEREAS

1. THE TRUSTEES are the Trustees of a Trust of Land [recite the Trusts].

2. BY A CONVEYANCE OF EVEN DATE HEREWITH the Trustees conveyed the land subject to the Trust and described in the schedule to [names of Beneficiaries] "the Beneficiaries".

3. The Beneficiaries are absolutely entitled to the said land so conveyed and are of full age and capacity.

NOW THIS DEED WITNESSETH
That the Trustees are discharged from the Trust relating to the land.

EXECUTED AS A DEED.

The Schedule
(description of Property)

Note:

See Part II, para. 5.5 for discussion.

6. Power of Attorney under s.9 of the 1996 Act

1.   This Power of Attorney is made the   day of   199 by [names of Trustees] "The Trustees" who are the Trustees of [the Trust] "the Trust".

2.   The Trustees in exercise of the power contained in s.9 of the Trusts of Land and Appointment of Trustees Act 1996 delegate to [the named beneficiar(y)(ies)] "the Attorney" all their powers as Trustees of the Trust which relate to land.

3.   The period for which the Trustees delegate such functions to the Attorney is indefinite.

EXECUTED AS A DEED BY THE TRUSTEES

Note:

Before acting under this power it should be checked that:
   (a) the Attorney is still entitled to an interest under the Trust;
   (b) all Trustees giving the power are still Trustees;
   (c) no additional Trustee has been appointed.

7. Power of Attorney under s.9 of the 1996 Act

1.   This Power of Attorney is made the   day of   199 by [names of Trustees] "The Trustees" who are the Trustees of [the Trust] "the Trust".

2.   The Trustees in exercise of the power contained in s.9 of the Trusts of Land and Appointment of Trustees Act 1996 delegate to [the named beneficiar(y)(ies)] "the Attorney" the Powers specified in paragraph 3 for the period specified in paragraph 4.

3.   The Powers so delegated to the Attorney are [all their functions as Trustees] [specified functions].

4.   The period for which the Trustees delegate such functions to the Attorney is [indefinite] [specify a period].

EXECUTED AS A DEED BY THE TRUSTEES

Note:

Before acting under this power it should be checked that:
   (a) the Attorney is still entitled to an interest under the Trust;
   (b) all Trustees giving the power are still Trustees;
   (c) no additional Trustee has been appointed.

8. Statutory Declaration under s.9 of the 1996 Act and s.5 of the PAA 1971

I [X, Y of   ] do solemnly and sincerely declare

1.   I [purchased (or otherwise as the case may be)] the property by a [conveyance dated the   day of 199   (or otherwise as the case may be)] which is now produced to me and marked "X, Y" from AB and CD ("the Trustees") acting by EF ("the Attorney").

2.   I believed throughout the transaction that the Attorney was the Attorney of the trustees under a Power of Attorney made the day of 199   under s.9(1) of the Trusts of Land and Appointment of Trustees Act 1996 and I had no knowledge on that date that the Attorney was not a person to whom delegation under s.9 of that Act could not be made and nor did I know of any revocation of that Power of Attorney.

AND I MAKE this solemn declaration conscientiously believing it to be true and by virtue of the provisions of the Statutory Declarations Act 1835.

Declared at

Before me etc.

Note:

This declaration should be sworn within three months of completion of the purchase. It could be made at the time of the initial dealing with the Attorney (see Part II, para. 12).

9. Execution by Attorney

SIGNED as a deed and delivered by [name] as Attorney for [Trustees' names] by Power of Attorney dated   day of 199 .

In the presence of

Note:

An Attorney may execute in the Attorney's name or the donor's—since there will almost always be more than one Trustee, the Attorney will sensibly execute the deed once in his own name. The Trustees will join in to give a receipt where there is any capital money arising on the transaction.

10. Statements by Co-owners for Inclusion in a Transfer

1.   The Buyers declare their intention in purchasing the property is to provide [premises for use as a guest house or a home for themselves and their children or as the case may be].

2.   The Buyers agree the property is not to be sold without the agreement of both Buyers unless one of the following conditions is satisfied:

      (a) both Buyers cease to reside in the property

      (b) [there is no child in full time education under the age of 18 living with either Buyer in the property].

Note:

In the event of a dispute about sale or other disposition such statements will be considered by the court but will not be decisive (see Part II, para. 14).

B: WILL AND TRUST INSTRUMENTS, CLAUSESAND DOCUMENTS

11. Settlement of Land: General Form

THIS SETTLEMENT IS made this   day of   199
BETWEEN AB of ("the Settlor") and CD of etc and EF of etc
("the Trustees").

WHEREAS

(recite Conveyance of Land to the Trustees upon a Trust of Land
to hold upon a settlement of even date being this settlement).

THIS DEED WITNESSETH

1.   The expressions following have the following meanings unless
the context requires otherwise:
    1.1   "the Trustees" means the Trustees for the time being;
    1.2   "the Trust Fund" means any land or proceeds of sale
             of land or other property investments or money held
             by the Trustees under this settlement however arising.
2.   The Trustees hold the Trust Fund upon the following trusts:
    (i)   During the life of GH of etc to pay GH the net income
            and profits from the Trust Fund
    (ii)   [. . . further gifts.]
3.   [Other Administrative Provisions].

Notes:
1.   Being in possession of an interest under a Trust is not the same as
being in possession of the property which is held in that Trust.
This is discussed further at pp. 47–15, 47–16.
2.   Unlike pre-Act Trusts there will be no express trust for sale and a
strict settlement cannot arise whatever the beneficial interests.

12. Statement under s.1(3) of the 1996 Act

Notes:
1.   An existing settlement under the Settled Land Act 1925 may be
altered by creating a new settlement. This will usually occur when
a power of appointment under the settlement is exercised. If the
derivative settlement is not intended to be a SLA 1925 settlement
then it should contain the following statement:
"This Trust is not a Settlement Under the Settled Land Act
1925".
2.   In consequence the provisions of the SLA 1925 (particularly ss.31
and 32 dealing with compound and referential settlements) have
no relevance.
3.   Land held under the new settlement is held on a Trust of Land
and is accordingly vested in the Trustees, who have the powers
contained in the Trusts of Land and Appointment of Trustees
Act 1996 unless these are restricted.

13. Exclusion of s.11: New Trust

Note:

It may be envisaged that settlors will routinely exclude s.11(1) from new Trusts so that the Trustees are not required to consult the beneficiaries in exercise of their powers under ss.6 and 7. The relevant provision need say only:
"Section 11(1) of the Trusts of Land and Appointment of Trustees Act 1996 does not apply to the Trust".

14. Deed of Application under s.11 of the 1996 Act — Made by Settlor of Existing Trust

This deed is made the   day of   199 by [the Settlor[s]] "the Settlor[s]"

WHEREAS

1.   BY A TRUST INSTRUMENT MADE THE   day of 199   the Settlor[s] created the Trusts therein contained "the Trust".

2.   THE SETTLOR[s] [is/are] desirous of applying s.11(1) of the Trusts of Land and Appointment of Trustees Act 1996 "the subsection" to the Trust.

NOW THIS DEED WITNESSETH

That the subsection does apply to the Trust.

EXECUTED AS A DEED

[The Settlor[s]]

Note:

If s.11(1) is not applied to a trust existing when the Act comes into force the Trustees acting in relation to land have no duty to consult the Beneficiaries of full age entitled to an interest in possession in land (see Part II, para. 13.2.1) and generally give effect to those wishes.

15. Provision in Trust Instrument to "Exclude" s.12 of the 1996 Act

Land [or specified land] held under this Trust is not held by the Trustees so as to be available for occupation by [the Beneficiaries/or specified Beneficiaries] and the purposes of the Trust do not include making the land available for such occupation.

16a. Clause Excluding ss.19 and 20 of the 1996 Act

"Sections 19 and 20 of the Trusts of Land and Appointment of Trustees Act 1996 do not apply to this Trust".

Note:

This will exclude the Beneficiaries' right to give the Trustees directions for the appointment or retirement of Trustees (see Part II, para. 15).

16b. Deed to Displace ss.19 and 20 of the 1996 Act — Existing Trust

1.   This Deed is made by [name(s) of Settlor(s)] "the Settlor(s)" in relation to a Trust "the Trust" particulars of which are set out in the Schedule hereto.
2.   Pursuant to s.21(6) of the Trusts of Land and Appointment of Trustees Act 1996 the Settlor(s) declare(s) that ss.19 and 20 of that Act do not apply to the Trust.

AS WITNESS ETC

Schedule

[set out brief details of the Trust]

Note:

In the case of an existing Trust, ss.19 and 20 can be excluded by any living Settlors who are *sui juris* (s.21(6)) (see Part II, para. 15.5).

17. Form of General Gift or Trust: Beneficiaries for Life Interested Only in Income

I give all my real and personal property of any kind whatsoever **including entailed property** to my Trustees upon Trust to sell the property and after payment of all my debts testamentary expenses and legacies to hold the same on the following Trusts:

— to pay the income to my widow [for her life] [until she remarries].

Note:

The purpose of this form of gift is to avoid giving a beneficiary an interest in possession in land (see Part II, para. 9.1).

18. Will — Form of General Gift or Trust to Beneficiaries for Life Interested in Possession

I give all my real and personal property of any kind whatsoever **including entailed property** to my Trustees upon Trust

— for my widow [for her life] [until she remarries]

etc.

Note:

This form of gift ensures that a beneficiary does have an interest in possession in land (see Part II, para. 9.1).

19. Excluding Statutory and Equitable Apportionments

Both in regard to capital and income of any kind whatsoever whenever arising the Trustees may disregard any statutory or equitable rules of apportionment and in particular treat all income as arising on its receipt regardless of any period for which it is payable.

Note:

For the effect of the abolition of the doctrine of conversion on the statutory and equitable apportionments, see Part II, para. 10.6. In practice they should (if intended not to apply) be excluded expressly.

20. Deed Imposing Conditions in Relation to Right of Occupation (under s.13)

This Deed is made the   day of   199 by [names of Trustees] "the Trustees".
1.   The Trustees are the Trustees of [details of the Trust] "the Trust".
2.   Pursuant to the Powers given to the Trustees by s.13 of the Trusts of Land and Appointment of Trustees Act 1996 the Trustees have made the provisions for the occupation of certain land held under the Trust which are set out in the Schedule Hereto.

EXECUTED AS A DEED etc by the Trustees.

Schedule
1.   [right of occupation of (description of land) given to AB] for [description of term] on the following conditions
[(i) Conditions]
2.   The following beneficiary's(ies'), right to occupy trust land is [excluded] [restricted as follows ...]
[(i) ... names and details of beneficiar(y)(ies)].

Notes:
1.   The purpose of this simple deed is for the Trustees in giving possession to a Beneficiary to impose conditions as to their occupation under s.13(3).
2.   There are no formal requirements for the exclusion of the right of occupation under s.13 or the imposition of conditions. It may well be desirable to do this by deed for sake of clarity in dealing with the Beneficiaries.

21. Exclusion, Restriction and Enlargement of Powers under s.8

The extensive powers conferred on Trustees of land may be restricted in any way the Settlor chooses. Section 8 provides for that restriction to be made **in the disposition to be the Trustees.**

No disposition without Consent

(i)   The Trustees shall not [sell] [lease] [charge] [or otherwise dispose of] [the Trust property] without the consent of [AB].

Particular Dispositions Prohibited

(ii)   The Trustees shall not [sell] [lease] [charge] [or otherwise dispose of] [the Trust property] [during the minority of [AB]] [before [a stated date]].

Wider Power of Charging to Secure Personal or any Debts

(iii)   The Trustees may charge the Trust property to raise money for any purpose whatsoever including as security for any debt of their own or any other person.
[This is helpful because of the restrictive wording of s.6 in cases where the Trustees wish to be free to use the property for a hazardous business security in a way which could be seen as obviously not acting prudently as a Trustee].

To Give a Wider Power of Gifting Trust Property

(iv)   "The trustees may dispose of all or any part of the trust property by gift or any other disposition at an undervalue".
[This is helpful if such transactions are a possibility because the wide powers conferred by s.6 are to be exercised only *qua* trustee and do not include a power of gift].

22. Power to Gift Trust Property

The Trustees may

(a)   dispose by gift or by any other disposition at an undervalue of all or any part of the Trust property.

[PROVIDED at least one Trustee has no personal interest except as a Trustee in any such [of the above] transaction(s)].

23. Power to Purchase Trust Property

Add clause (b) to Precedent 22 above.

(b)   sell all or any part of the Trust property to one or more Trustees.

C: APPLICATION TO THE COURT, ss.14 AND 15

24. Originating Application

IN THE COUNTY COURT

IN THE MATTER [ADDRESS OF PROPERTY AND REGISTERED TITLE NO.]

AND IN THE MATTER OF THE TRUSTS OF LAND AND APPOINTMENT OF TRUSTEES ACT 1996, s.14

Applicant

Respondent

I [applicant of address] apply to the Court for an Order in the following terms:

(1)   That the [description of property] "the property" is the property of the Applicant and the Respondent jointly.

(2)   That the property be sold and the proceeds of sale be divided between the Applicant and the Respondent equally or otherwise as may be just.

(3)   That the costs of the Applicant be paid by the Respondent.

THIS APPLICATION is made under s.14 of the TRUSTS OF LAND AND APPOINTMENT OF TRUSTEES ACT 1996.

THE GROUNDS on which I claim to be entitled to the order are

(1)   [state if relevant the relationship between the parties]

(2)   [state how the property comes to be held on a Trust of Land]

(3)   [if relevant specify the financial contribution of the parties].

(4)   [deal with the matters under s.15(1) to which the Applicant wishes the court to have regard
— the intention of the person(s) who created the trust
— the purposes for which the property is held
— the welfare of any minor who occupies or might reasonably be expected to occupy the property
— the interest of any secured credits of any beneficiary
[— the position of any other beneficiary under the Trust].

(5)   [explain reason sale is required: *e.g.* In March 1996 I left the Respondent because of her boring and uncommunicative behaviour and because of her refusal to agree to the sale of the house the proceeds of sale of which I now need to purchase a home to live in. Accordingly I commenced these proceedings.

The name and address of the person on whom it is intended to serve this application is [the respondent].

[conclude with address for service and date and signature of or on behalf of applicant].

25. Example Affidavit in Support of an Application under s.14 of the Trusts of Land and Appointment of Trustees Act 1996

Heading as Action

I Mary Alexander of 3 St Anthony Square Oldcastle make oath and say as follows:

1. I am the Plaintiff in this Application.
2. By a Transfer dated 19 October 1980 I purchased a house for £50,000 at 3 St Anthony Square Oldcastle together with Richard Sugden.
3. At that time we had been living together for approximately four years.
4. Although the house was purchased in our joint names, I provided all the deposit of £3,000 and made the mortgage payments.
5. My income at the time of purchase was £40,000 as a design consultant. Richard was unemployed staying at home to look after the children. In 1984 he became a student and in 1989 started work as a golf professional. From 1990 he contributed £5,000 per annum to the household expenses.
6. We had at the time of the purchase two children.
   Heather May Alexander born 7 May 1978.
   John Richard Sugden born 18 May 1979.
7. We lived in the house with our two children until June of this year when Richard Sugden left me to live in Scotland where he took up employment as a golf club professional in Aberdeen.
8. In view of the above facts, I claim a 75% share in the property.

SWORN at 3 Bank Chambers
Oldcastle by Mary
Alexander the 10th day
of July 1996 before

A Solicitor

D: APPOINTMENT AND RETIREMENT OF TRUSTEES

26. Direction to Trustees to Retire

To [name(s) and address(es) of Trustee(s)].

I (we) (names and addresses of Beneficiaries)

Beneficiar(y)(ies) in [Description of Trust]

DIRECT the above named Trustee(s) to retire from the Trust.

Signed

[each Beneficiary giving the notice].

DATED THIS   DAY OF   199 .

Note:

See Part II, para. 15.2 for discussion.

27. Direction to Trustees to Appoint New Trustee, s.19(2)

DIRECTION UNDER s.19(2) OF THE TRUSTS OF LAND AND APPOINTMENT OF TRUSTEES ACT 1996.

To [names and addresses of each present Trustee] (names and addresses of Beneficiary(ies))

Beneficiar(y)(ies) in [description of trust]

DIRECT that the Trustees appoint [name(s) and address(es) of new Trustee(s)] to be (a) Trustee(s) of the Trust.

Signed

[each Beneficiary giving the notice]

DATED THIS   DAY OF   199 .

Note:

See Part II, para. 15.2 for discussion.

28. This Deed of Retirement and Discharge made by [AB of   ] ("the Retiring Trustee") and [WV and XY] "The Continuing Trustee(s)"

WHEREAS

1.   The Retiring Trustee and the Continuing Trustee(s) are Trustees of (description of Trust).
2.   The Retiring Trustee has been given a direction under s.19(2)(a) of the Trusts of Land and Appointment of Trustees Act 1996 to retire from the Trust.
3.   The Continuing Trustees consent to such retirement.
4.   The Trust property described in Schedule One is to be vested in the continuing Trustees.

NOW BY THIS DEED

1.   The Retiring Trustee retires from and is discharged from the Trust pursuant to s.19(3) of that Act.
2.   The Retiring and Continuing Trustees declare that the property subject to the trust vests in the continuing Trustees on the terms of the Trust.

IN WITNESS ETC

SCHEDULE ONE

Notes:
1.   Recital 3 is not necessary as they execute the deed but it adds clarity.
2.   A vesting declaration (cl.4) is not strictly necessary (s.40(1)(b)) but again adds clarity to the deed.

29. Direction under s.20 of the Trusts of Land and Appointment of Trustees Act 1996

1.   THIS DIRECTION is given by [names and addresses of Beneficiaries] "the Beneficiaries" who are the Beneficiaries of [description of Trust] to [the receiver of the Trustee, his Attorney or authorised person under Part VII of the Mental Health Act 1983] who is [the receiver or as the case may be)] "the appointor" of [name and address of incapable Trustee] under s.20 of the Trusts of Land and Appointment of Trustees Act 1996.
2.   BY THE DIRECTION THE BENEFICIARIES DIRECT THAT THE APPOINTOR APPOINTS [name and address] AS A TRUSTEE IN PLACE OF [name of incapable Trustee].

AS WITNESS OUR HANDS etc.

30. Deed of Appointment of New Trustee in Place of Retiring Trustee at Beneficiaries' Direction

THIS DEED OF APPOINTMENT is made the   day of
BETWEEN [AB of (and CD) of   ] (the continuing Trustees)
[X of] the Retiring Trustee and [Y of   ] the New Trustee.

WHEREAS

1.   The Retiring Trustee and the Continuing Trustees are Trustees of [describe the Trust] the Trust.

2.   The property described in Schedule One is vested in the Retiring Trustee.

3.   The Retiring Trustee has been given a direction to retire under s.19(2)(a) of the Trusts of Land and Appointment of Trustees Act 1996.

4.   The Retiring and Continuing Trustees have been given a direction to appoint the New Trustee under s.19(2)(b) of that Act.

5.   The property described in Schedule One is to be vested in the New and Continuing Trustees.

NOW BY THIS DEED

1.   The Continuing and Retiring Trustee appoint the New Trustee to be a Trustee of [the Trust] in place of the Retiring Trustee.

2.   The Retiring Trustee retires and is discharged from the Trust pursuant to s.19(3) of that Act.

3.   The Retiring and Continuing Trustees declare that the property subject to the Trust vests in the new and continuing Trustee on the terms of the Trust.

IN WITNESS

        etc

FIRST SCHEDULE

Notes:

1.   The vesting declarations if not expressly made will be implied (s.40 of the Trustee Act 1925) but their inclusion provides a quick reference for a purchaser.

2.   Three types of property listed in s.40 of the TA 1925 will not be included under a vesting declaration: (a) certain mortgage securities; (b) leases with a covenant not to assign (unless consent has previously been obtained); and (c) stocks and shares.

3.   Deeds of Appointment under ss.19 and 20
        (i)   Under s.19 the appointment is made in standard form and is made under s.36 of the TA 1925. It should recite the written direction by the beneficiaries to gain the benefit of s.38 of the TA 1925.
        (ii) Under s.20 the appointment is also made under s.36 in standard form. Where it is made by an Attorney, the Enduring Power of Attorney forms part of the title as does evidence of the registration under the Enduring Powers of Attorney Act 1985. If the appointment is by a receiver or authorised person under Part VII of the Mental Health Act 1983 then the order of the Court of Protection authorising the appointment should be recited and the order forms part of the title.

4.   For registration of title purposes, where a transfer is not used for the appointment of new trustees a supplemental transfer should be used (Precedents 31 and 32).

31. Transfer Appointing New Trustees

Form 19 Heading

1.   For the purpose of giving effect to the appointment of a new Trustee I/We [name(s) and address(es) of] Continuing and Retiring Trustee(s) transfer to (Continuing Trustees) and (New Trustees) all the property comprised in Title No. . . .
2.   (Certificate of Value—Category A)

Execution as a deed by parties.

Notes:
1.   If the Retiring Trustee is dead, his name should be omitted and the Death Certificate produced to the Land Registry.
2.   A Retiring Trustee who is abroad for over 12 months or unable or unfit to act will not execute the deed, but a statutory declaration will be required by the Registry to prove the facts.
3.   Scale 2 fees are payable.
4.   This supplemental transfer is used where there has been a prior deed of appointment. The Registrar will not investigate the validity of the right to make the appointment.
5.   Alternatively the deed of appointment (with a copy for filing) can be produced to the Registry. The Registrar will give effect to an express or implied vesting declaration (s.47 of the LRA 1925), and record the change of Trustee. This is a cumbersome method as evidence will have to be produced of the Appointor's title to make the appointment.
6.   Any restriction on the register requiring the consent of a third party to the transaction must be complied with.

32. Transfer Supplemental to a Deed of Appointment

1.   To give effect to the appointment of New Trustees in the Deed of Appointment dated and made between (Continuing Trustees) (name and address) (Retiring Trustee) (name and address) New Trustee, I/We the Continuing and Retiring Trustee transfer to the New Trustee the land comprised in Title No. . . .
2.   (Certificate of value—category 'A').

Note:

This is used where a separate deed of appointment is used, see Part II, para. 15.8.

33. Notice by (a) Beneficiar(y)(ies) withdrawing a Direction to (a) Trustee(s)

To: [name(s) and address(es) of Trustee(s)]

I/We the undersigned (name(s) and address(es)) as Beneficiar(y)(ies) of (describe the trust) withdraw the Direction to [(name of Trustee) to retire from] [(the Trustee(s) to appoint (name) as a Trustee] of the above Trust.

signed

[each Beneficiary giving the notice]

Notes:
1.   Withdrawal must be in writing (s.21(1)(b)).
2.   A notice of withdrawal by any one Beneficiary will be sufficient to withdraw the direction.

PART IV: PRINCIPAL SECTIONS OF THE 1925 LEGISLATION AS AMENDED

This legislation is amended up to November 12, 1996.

Settled Land Act 1925 (c. 18)

Duration of settlements

3. Land which has been subject to a settlement which is a settlement for the purposes of this Act shall be deemed for the purposes of this Act to remain and be settled land, and the settlement shall be deemed to be a subsisting settlement for the purposes of this Act so long as—

  (a) any limitation, charge, or power of charging under the settlement subsists, or is capable of being exercised; or

  (b) the person who, if of full age, would be entitled as beneficial owner to have that land vested in him for a legal estate is an infant.

Trustee Act 1925 (c. 19)

Power of trustees for sale to sell by auction, etc.

12.—(1) Where a trustee has a duty or power to sell property, he may sell or concur with any other person in selling all or any part of the property, either subject to prior charges or not, and either together or in lots, by public auction or by private contract, subject to any such conditions respecting title or evidence of title or other matter as the trustee thinks fit, with power to vary any contract for sale, and to buy in at any auction, or to rescind any contract for sale and to re-sell, without being answerable for any loss.

(2) A duty or power to sell or dispose of land includes a trust or power to sell or dispose of part thereof, whether the division is horizontal, vertical, or made in any other way.

(3) This section does not enable an express power to sell settled land to be exercised where the power is not vested in the tenant for life or statutory owner.

Power to insure

19.—(1) A trustee may insure any personal property against loss or damage to any amount, including the amount of any insurance already on foot, not exceeding three fourth parts of the full value of the building or property, and pay the premiums for such insurance out of the income thereof or out of the income of any other property subject to the same trusts without obtaining the consent of any person who may be entitled wholly or partly to such income.

(2) This section does not apply to any personal property, which a trustee is bound forthwith to convey absolutely to any beneficiary upon being requested to do so.

Application of insurance money where policy kept up under any trust, power or obligation

20.—(1) Money receivable by trustees or any beneficiary under a policy of insurance against the loss or damage of any property subject to a trust or to a settlement within the meaning of the Settled Land Act 1925, whether by fire or otherwise, shall, where the policy has been kept up under any trust in that behalf or under any power statutory or otherwise, or in performance of any covenant or of any obligation statutory or otherwise, or by a tenant for life impeachable for waste, be capital money for the purposes of the trust or settlement, as the case may be.

(2) If any such money is receivable by any person, other than the trustees of the trust or settlement, that person shall use his best endeavours to recover and receive the money, and shall pay the net residue thereof, after discharging any costs of recovering and receiving it, to the trustees of the trust or settlement, or, if there are no trustees capable of giving a discharge therefor, into court.

(3) Any such money—

(a) if it was receivable in respect of settled land within the meaning of the Settled Land Act 1925, or any building or works thereon, shall be deemed to be capital money arising under that Act from the settled land, and shall be invested or applied by the trustees, or, if in court, under the direction of the court, accordingly;

(b) if it was receivable in respect of personal chattels settled as heirlooms within the meaning of the Settled Land Act 1925, shall be deemed to be capital money arising under that Act, and shall be applicable by the trustees, or, if in court, under the direction of the court, in like manner as provided by that Act with respect to money arising by a sale of chattels settled as heirlooms as aforesaid;

(c) if it was receivable in respect of land subject to a trust of land or personal property held on trust for sale, shall be held upon the trusts and subject to the powers and provisions applicable to money arising by a sale under such trust;

(d) in any other case, shall be held upon trusts corresponding as nearly as may be with the trusts affecting the property in respect of which it was payable.

(4) Such money, or any part thereof, may also be applied by the trustees, or, if in court, under the direction of the court, in rebuilding, reinstating, replacing, or repairing the property lost or damaged, but any such application by the trustees shall be subject to the consent of any person whose consent is required by the instrument, if any, creating the trust to the investment of money subject to the trust, and, in the case of money which is deemed to be capital money arising under the Settled Land Act 1925, be subject to the provisions of that Act with respect to the application of capital money by the trustees of the settlement.

(5) Nothing contained in this section prejudices or affects the right of any person to require any such money or any part thereof to be applied in rebuilding, reinstating, or repairing the property lost or damaged, or the rights of any mortgagee, lessor, or lessee, whether under any statute or otherwise.

(6) This section applies to policies effected either before or after the commencement of this Act, but only to money received after such commencement.

Limitation of the number of trustees

34.—(1) Where, at the commencement of this Act, there are more than four trustees of a settlement of land, or more than four trustees holding land on trust for sale, no new trustees shall (except where as a result of the appointment the number is reduced to four or less) be capable of being appointed until the number is reduced to less than four, and thereafter the number shall not be increased beyond four.

(2) In the case of settlements and dispositions creating trusts of land made or coming into operation after the commencement of this Act—

(a) the number of trustees thereof shall not in any case exceed four, and where more than four persons are named as such trustees, the four first named (who are able and willing to act) shall alone be the trustees, and the other persons named shall not be trustees unless appointed on the occurrence of a vacancy;

(b) the number of the trustees shall not be increased beyond four.

(3) This section only applies to settlements and dispositions of land, and the restrictions imposed on the number of trustees do not apply—

(a) in the case of land vested in trustees for charitable, ecclesiastical, or public purposes; or

(b) where the net proceeds of the sale of the land are held for like purposes; or

(c) to the trustees of a term of years absolute limited by a settlement on trusts for raising money, or of a like term created under the statutory remedies relating to annual sums charged on land.

Appointments of trustees of settlements and trustees of land

35.—(1) Appointments of new trustees of land and of new trustees of any trust of the proceeds of sale of the land shall, subject to any order of the court, be effected by separate instruments, but in such manner as to secure that the same persons become trustees of land and trustees of the trust of the proceeds of sale.

(2) Where new trustees of a settlement are appointed, a memorandum of the names and addresses of the persons who are for the time being the trustees thereof for the purposes of the Settled Land Act 1925, shall be endorsed on or annexed to the last or only principal vesting instrument by or on behalf of the trustees of the settlement, and such vesting instrument shall, for that purpose, be produced by the person having the possession thereof of the trustees of the settlement when so required.

(3) Where new trustees of land are appointed, a memorandum of the persons who are for the time being the trustees of the land shall be endorsed on or annexed to the conveyance by which the land was vested in trustees of land; and that conveyance shall be produced to the persons who are for the time being the trustees of the land by the person in possession of it in order for that to be done when the trustees require its production.

Law of Property Act 1925 (c. 20)

PART I
GENERAL PRINCIPLES AS TO LEGAL ESTATES, EQUITABLE INTERESTS AND POWERS

Legal estates and equitable interests

1.—(1) The only estates in land which are capable of subsisting or of being conveyed or created at law are—

(a) An estate in fee simple absolute in possession;
(b) A term of years absolute.

(2) The only interests or charges in or over land which are capable of subsisting or of being conveyed or created at law are—

(a) An easement, right, or privilege in or over land for an interest equivalent to an estate in fee simple absolute in possession or a term of years absolute;

(b) A rentcharge in possession issuing out of or charged on land being either perpetual or for a term of years absolute;

(c) A charge by way of legal mortgage;

(d) and any other similar charge on land which is not created by an instrument;

(e) Rights of entry exercisable over or in respect of a legal term of years absolute, or annexed, for any purpose, to a legal rentcharge.

(3) All other estates, interests, and charges in or over land take effect as equitable interests.

(4) The estates, interests, and charges which under this section are authorised to subsist or to be conveyed or created at law are (when subsisting or conveyed or created at law) in this Act referred to as "legal estates", and have the same incidents as legal estates subsisting at the commencement of this Act; and the owner of a legal estate is referred to as "an estate owner" and his legal estate is referred to as his estate.

(5) A legal estate may subsist concurrently with or subject to any other legal estate in the same land in like manner as it could have done before the commencement of this Act.

(6) A legal estate is not capable of subsisting or of being created in an undivided share in land or of being held by an infant.

(7) Every power of appointment over, or power to convey or charge land or any interest therein, whether created by a statute or other instrument or implied by law, and whether created before or after the commencement of this Act (not being a power vested in a legal mortgagee or an estate owner in right of his estate and exercisable by him or by another person in his name and on his behalf), operates only in equity.

(8) Estates, interests, and charges in or over land which are not legal estates are in this Act referred to as "equitable interests", and powers which by this Act are to operate in equity only are in this Act referred to as "equitable powers".

(9) The provisions in any statute or other instrument requiring land to be conveyed to uses shall take effect as directions that the land shall (subject to creating or reserving thereout any legal estate authorised by this Act which may be required) be conveyed to a person of full age upon the requisite trusts.

(10) The repeal of the Statute of Uses (as amended) does not affect the operation thereof in regard to dealings taking effect before the commencement of this Act.

Conveyances overreaching certain equitable interests and powers

2.—(1) A conveyance to a purchaser of a legal estate in land shall overreach any equitable interest or power affecting that estate, whether or not he has notice thereof, if—

   (i) the conveyance is made under the powers conferred by the Settled Land Act 1925 or any additional powers conferred by a settlement, and the equitable interest or power is capable of being overreached thereby, and the statutory requirements respecting the payment of capital money arising under the settlement are complied with;

   (ii) the conveyance is made by trustees of land and the equitable interest or power is at the date of the conveyance capable of being overreached by such trustees under the provisions of subsection (2) of this section or independently of that subsection, and the requirements of section 27 of this Act respecting the payment of capital money arising on such a conveyance are complied with;

   (iii) the conveyance is made by a mortgagee or personal representative in the exercise of his paramount powers, and the equitable interest or power is capable of being overreached by such conveyance, and any capital money arising from the transaction is paid to the mortgagee or personal representative;

   (iv) the conveyance is made under an order of the court and the equitable interest or power is bound by such order, and any capital money arising from the transaction is paid into, or in accordance with the order of, the court.

(1A) An equitable interest in land subject to a trust of land which remains in, or is to revert to, the settlor shall (subject to any contrary intention) be overreached by the conveyance if it would be so overreached were it an interest under the trust.

(2) Where the legal estate affected is subject to a trust of land, then if at the date of a conveyance made after the commencement of this Act by the trustees, the trustees (whether original or substituted) are either—

(a) two or more individuals approved or appointed by the court or the successors in office of the individuals so approved or appointed; or

(b) a trust corporation,

any equitable interest or power having priority to the trust shall, notwithstanding any stipulation to the contrary, be overreached by the conveyance, and shall, according to its priority, take effect as if created or arising by means of a primary trust affecting the proceeds of sale and the income of the land until sale.

(3) The following equitable interests and powers are excepted from the operation of subsection (2) of this section, namely—

(i) Any equitable interest protected by a deposit of documents relating to the legal estate affected;

(ii) The benefit of any covenant or agreement restrictive of the user of land;

(iii) Any easement, liberty, or privilege over or affecting land and being merely an equitable interest (in this Act referred to as an "equitable easement");

(iv) The benefit of any contract (in this Act referred to as an "estate contract") to convey or create a legal estate, including a contract conferring either expressly or by statutory implication a valid option to purchase, a right of pre-emption, or any other like right;

(v) Any equitable interest protected by registration under the Land Charges Act 1925 other than—

(a) an annuity within the meaning of Part II of that Act;

(b) a limited owner's charge or a general equitable charge within the meaning of that Act.

(4) Subject to the protection afforded by this section to the purchaser of a legal estate, nothing contained in this section shall deprive a person entitled to an equitable charge of any of his rights or remedies for enforcing the same.

(5) So far as regards the following interests, created before the commencement of this Act (which accordingly are not within the provisions of the Land Charges Act 1925), namely—

(a) the benefit of any covenant or agreement restrictive of the user of the land;

(b) any equitable easement;

(c) the interest under a puisne mortgage within the meaning of the Land Charges Act 1925 unless and until acquired under a transfer made after the commencement of this Act;

(d) the benefit of an estate contract, unless and until the same is acquired under a conveyance made after the commencement of this Act;

a purchaser of a legal estate shall only take subject thereto if he has notice thereof, and the same are not overreached under the provisions contained or in the manner referred to in this section.

Manner of giving effect to equitable interests and powers

3.—(1) All equitable interests and powers in or over land shall be enforceable against the estate owner of the legal estate affected in manner following (that is to say):

(a) Where the legal estate affected is settled land, the tenant for life or statutory owner shall be bound to give effect to the equitable interests and powers in manner provided by the Settled Land Act 1925.

(b) ...

(c) In any other case, the estate owner shall be bound to give effect to the equitable interests and powers affecting his estate of which he has notice according to their respective priorities. This provision does not affect the priority or powers of a legal mortgagee, or the powers of personal representatives for purposes of administration.

(2) ...

(3) Where, by reason of a statutory or other right of reverter, or of an equitable right of entry taking effect, or for any other reason, a person becomes entitled to require a legal estate to be vested in him, then and in any such case the estate owner whose estate is affected shall be bound to convey or create such legal estate as the case may require.

(4) If any question arises whether any and what legal estate ought to be transferred or created as aforesaid, any person interested may apply to the court for directions in the manner provided by this Act.

(5) If the estate owners refuse or neglect for one month after demand to transfer or create any such legal estate, or if by reason of their being out of the United Kingdom or being unable to be found, or by reason of the dissolution of a corporation, or for any other reason, the court is satisfied that the transaction cannot otherwise be effected, or cannot be effected without undue delay or expense, the court may, on the application of any person interested, make a vesting order transferring or creating a legal estate in the manner provided by this Act.

(6) This section does not affect a purchaser of a legal estate taking free from an equitable interest or power.

(7) The County Court has jurisdiction under this section where the land which is to be dealt with in the court does not exceed £30,000 capital value.

Creation and disposition of equitable interests

4.—(1) Interests in land validly created or arising after the commencement of this Act, which are not capable of subsisting as legal estates, shall take effect as equitable interests, and, save as otherwise expressly provided by statute, interests in land which under the Statute of Uses or otherwise could before the commencement of this Act have been created as legal interests, shall be capable of being created as equitable interests:

Provided that, after the commencement of this Act (and save as hereinafter expressly enacted), an equitable interest in land shall only be capable of being validly created in any case in which an equivalent equitable interest in property real or personal could have been validly created before such commencement.

(2) All rights and interests in land may be disposed of, including—

(a) a contingent, executory or future equitable interest in any land, or a possibility coupled with an interest in any land, whether or not the object of the gift or limitation of such interest or possibility be ascertained;

(b) a right of entry, into or upon land whether immediate or future, and whether vested or contingent.

(3) All rights of entry affecting a legal estate which are exercisable on condition broken or for any other reason may after the commencement of this Act, be made exercisable by any person and the persons deriving title under him, but, in regard to an estate in fee simple (not being a rentcharge held for a legal estate) only within the period authorised by the rule relating to perpetuities.

Satisfied terms, whether created out of freehold or leasehold land to cease

5.—(1) Where the purposes of a term of years created or limited at any time out of freehold land, become satisfied either before or after the commencement of this Act (whether or not that term either by express declaration or by construction of law becomes attendant upon the freehold reversion) it shall merge in the reversion expectant thereon and shall cease accordingly.

(2) Where the purposes of a term of years created or limited, at any time, out of leasehold land, become satisfied after the commencement of this Act, that term shall merge in the reversion expectant thereon and shall cease accordingly.

(3) Where the purposes are satisfied only as respects part of the land comprised in a term, this section shall have effect as if a separate term had been created in regard to that part of the land.

Saving of lessors' and lessees' covenants

6.—(1) Nothing in this Part of this Act affects prejudicially the right to enforce any lessor's or lessee's covenants, agreements or conditions (including a valid option to purchase or right of pre-emption over the reversion), contained in any such instrument as is in this section mentioned, the benefit or burden of which runs with the reversion or the term.

(2) This section applies where the covenant, agreement or condition is contained in any instrument—

(a) creating a term of years absolute, or

(b) varying the rights of the lessor or lessee under the instrument creating the term.

Saving of certain legal estates and statutory powers

7.—(1) A fee simple which, by virtue of the Lands Clauses Acts, the School Sites Acts, or any similar statute, is liable to be divested, is for the purposes of this Act a fee simple absolute, and remains liable to be divested as if this Act had not been passed and a fee simple subject to a legal or equitable right of entry or re-entry is for the purposes of this Act a fee simple absolute.

(2) A fee simple vested in a corporation which is liable to determine by reason of the dissolution of the corporation is, for the purposes of this Act, a fee simple absolute.

(3) The provisions of—

(a) . . .

(b) the Friendly Societies Act 1896 in regard to land to which that Act applies;

(c) any other statutes conferring special facilities or prescribing special modes (whether by way of registered memorial or otherwise) for disposing of or acquiring land, or providing for the vesting (by conveyance or otherwise) of the land in trustees or any person, or the holder for the time being of an office or any corporation sole or aggregate (including the Crown);

shall remain in full force.

(4) Where any such power for disposing of or creating a legal estate is exercisable by a person who is not the estate owner, the power shall, when practicable, be exercised in the name and on behalf of the estate owner.

Saving of certain legal powers to lease

8.—(1) All leases or tenancies at a rent for a term of years absolute authorised to be granted by a mortgagor or mortgagee or by the Settled Land Act 1925 or any other statute (whether or not extended by any instrument) may be granted in the name and on behalf of the estate owner by the person empowered to grant the same, whether being an estate owner or not, with the same effect and priority as if this Part of this Act had not been passed; but this section does not (except as respects the usual qualified covenant for quiet enjoyment) authorise any person granting a lease in the name of an estate owner to impose any personal liability on him.

(2) Where a rentcharge is held for a legal estate, the owner thereof may under the statutory power or under any corresponding power, create a legal term of years absolute for securing or compelling payment of the same; but in other cases terms created under any such power shall, unless and until the estate owner of the land charged gives legal effect to the transaction, take effect only as equitable interests.

Vesting orders and dispositions of legal estates operating as conveyances by an estate owner

9.—(1) Every such order, declaration, or conveyance as is hereinafter mentioned, namely—
  (a) every vesting order made by any court or other competent authority;
  (b) every vesting declaration (express or implied) under any statutory power;
  (c) every vesting instrument made by the trustees of a settlement or other persons under the provisions of the Settled Land Act 1925;
  (d) every conveyance by a person appointed for the purpose under an order of the court or authorised under any statutory power to convey in the name or on behalf of an estate owner;
  (e) every conveyance made under any power reserved or conferred by this Act,
which is made or executed for the purpose of vesting, conveying, or creating a legal estate, shall operate to convey or create the legal estate disposed of in like manner as if the same had been a conveyance executed by the estate owner of the legal estate to which the order, declaration, vesting instrument, or conveyance relates.

(2) Where the order, declaration, or conveyance is made in favour of a purchaser, the provisions of this Act relating to a conveyance of a legal estate to a purchaser shall apply thereto.

(3) The provisions of the Trustee Act 1925 relating to vesting orders and orders appointing a person to convey shall apply to all vesting orders authorised to be made by this Part of this Act.

Title to be shown to legal estates

10.—(1) Where title is shown to a legal estate in land, it shall be deemed not necessary or proper to include in the abstract of title an instrument relating only to interests or powers which will be overreached by the conveyance of the estate to which title is being shown; but nothing in this Part of this Act affects the liability of any person to disclose an equitable interest or power which will not be so overreached, or to furnish an abstract of any instrument creating or affecting the same.

(2) A solicitor delivering an abstract framed in accordance with this Part of this Act shall not incur any liability on account of an omission to include therein an instrument which, under this section, is to be deemed not necessary or proper to be included, nor shall any liability be implied by reason of the inclusion of any such instrument.

Registration in Middlesex and Yorkshire as respects legal estates

11.—(1) It shall not be necessary to register a memorial of any instrument made after the commencement of this Act in any local deeds registry unless the instrument operates to transfer or create a legal estate, or to create a charge thereon by way of legal mortgage; nor shall the registration of a memorial of any instrument not required to be registered affect any priority.

(2) Probates and letters of administration shall be treated as instruments capable of transferring a legal estate to personal representatives.

(3) Memorials of all instruments capable of transferring or creating a legal estate or charge by way of legal mortgage, may, when so operating, be registered.

Limitation and Prescription Acts

12. Nothing in this Part of this Act affects the operation of any statute, or of the general law for the limitation of actions or proceedings relating to land or with reference to the acquisition of easements or rights over or in respect of land.

Effect of possession of documents

13. This Act shall not prejudicially affect the right or interest of any person arising out of or consequent on the possession by him of any documents relating to a legal estate in land, nor affect any question arising out of or consequent upon any omission to obtain or any other absence of possession by any person of any documents relating to a legal estate in land.

Interests of persons in possession

14. This part of this Act shall not prejudicially affect the interest of any person in possession or in actual occupation of land to which he may be entitled in right of such possession or occupation.

Presumption that parties are of full age

15. The persons expressed to be parties to any conveyance shall, until the contrary is proved, be presumed to be of full age at the date thereof.

16–18.—[*Repealed but N.B. the repealed s.18 is amended by Sched. 4 to the 1996 Act and s.16 is amended by Sched. 3.*]

Infants and Lunatics

s.19. [*Repealed*]

Infants not to be appointed trustees

20. The appointment of an infant to be a trustee in relation to any settlement or trust shall be void, but without prejudice to the power to appoint a new trustee to fill the vacancy.

Receipts by married infants

21. A married infant shall have power to give valid receipts for all income (including statutory accumulations of income made during the minority) to which the infant may be entitled in like manner as if the infant were of full age.

Conveyances on behalf of persons suffering from mental disorder and as to land held by them in trust

22.—(1) Where a legal estate in land (whether settled or not) is vested in a person suffering from mental disorder, either solely or jointly with any other person or persons, his receiver or (if no receiver is acting for him) any person authorised in that behalf shall, under an order of the authority having jurisdiction under Part VII of the Mental Health Act 1983, or of the court, or under any statutory power, make or concur in making all requisite dispositions for conveying or creating a legal estate in his name and on his behalf.

(2) If land subject to a trust for land is vested, either solely or jointly with any other person or persons, in a person who is incapable, by reason of mental disorder, of exercising his functions as trustee, a new trustee shall be

appointed in the place of that person, or he shall be otherwise discharged from the trust, before the legal estate is dealt with by the trustees.

s.23. [*Repealed*]

Trusts of land

24.—(1) The persons having power to appoint new trustees of land shall be bound to appoint the same persons (if any) who are for the time being trustees of any trust of the proceeds of sale of the land.

(2) A purchaser shall not be concerned to see that subsection (1) of this section has been complied with.

(3) This section applies whether the trust of land and the trust of proceeds of sale are created, or arise, before or after the commencement of this Act.

s.25. [*Repealed*]
s.26. [*Repealed*]

Purchaser not to be concerned with the trusts of the proceeds of sale which are to be paid to two or more trustees or to a trust corporation

27.—(1) A purchaser of a legal estate from trustees of land shall not be concerned with the trusts affecting the land, the net income of the land or the proceeds of sale of the land whether or not those trusts are declared by the same instrument as that by which the trust of land is created.

(2) Notwithstanding anything to the contrary in the instrument (if any) creating a trust of land or in any trust affecting the net proceeds of sale of the land if it is sold, the proceeds of sale or other capital money shall not be paid to or applied by the direction of fewer than two persons as trustees, except where the trustee is a trust corporation, but this subsection does not affect the right of a sole personal representative as such to give valid receipts for, or direct the application of, proceeds of sale or other capital money, nor, except where capital money arises on the transaction, render it necessary to have more than one trustee.

s.28. [*Repealed*]
s.29. [*Repealed*]
s.30. [*Repealed*]

Trust of mortgaged property where right of redemption is barred

31.—(1) Where any property, vested in trustees by way of security, becomes, by virtue of the statutes of limitation, or of an order for foreclosure or otherwise, discharged from the right of redemption, it shall be held by them in trust—

(a) to apply the income from the property in the same manner as interest paid on the mortgage debt would have been applicable; and

(b) if the property is sold, to apply the net proceeds of sale, after payment of costs and expenses, in the same manner as repayment of the mortgage debt would have been applicable.

(2) Subsection (1) of this section operates without prejudice to any rule of law relating to the apportionment of capital and income between tenant for life and remainderman.

(3) ...

(4) Where—

(a) the mortgage money is capital money for the purposes of the Settled Land Act 1925;

(b) land other than any forming the whole or part of the property mentioned in subsection (1) of this section is, or is deemed to be, subject to the settlement; and

(c) the tenant for life or statutory owner requires the trustees to execute with respect to land forming the whole or part of that property a vest-

ing deed such as would have been required in relation to the land if it
had been acquired on a purchase with capital money,
the trustees shall execute such a vesting deed.

(5) This section applies whether the right of redemption was discharged
before or after the first day of January, nineteen hundred and twelve, but has
effect without prejudice to any dealings or arrangements made before that
date.

s.32. [*Repealed*]

Dispositions on Trust for Sale

Application of Part I to personal representatives

33. The provisions of this Part of this Act relating to trustees of land apply
to personal representatives holding land in trust, but without prejudice to
their rights and powers for purposes of administration.

Undivided Shares and Joint Ownership

Effect of future dispositions to tenants in common

34.—(1) An undivided share in land shall not be capable of being created
except as provided by the Settled Land Act 1925 or as hereinafter mentioned.

(2) Where, after the commencement of this Act, land is expressed to be
conveyed to any persons in undivided shares and those persons are of full
age, the conveyance shall (notwithstanding anything to the contrary in this
Act) operate as if the land had been expressed to be conveyed to the grantees, or, if there are more than four grantees, to the four first named in the
conveyance, as joint tenants in trust for the persons interested in the land:

Provided that, where the conveyance is made by way of mortgage the land
shall vest in the grantees or such four of them as aforesaid for a term of years
absolute (as provided by this Act) as joint tenants subject to cesser on
redemption in like manner as if the mortgage money had belonged to them
on a joint account, but without prejudice to the beneficial interests in the
mortgage money and interest.

(3) A devise bequest or testamentary appointment, coming into operation
after the commencement of this Act, of land to two or more persons in undivided shares shall operate as a devise bequest or appointment of the land to
the personal representatives of the testator, and (but without prejudice to the
rights and powers of the personal representatives for purposes of administration) in trust for the persons interested in the land.

(3A) In subsections (2) and (3) of this section references to the persons
interested in the land include persons interested as trustees or personal representatives (as well as persons beneficially interested).

s.35. [*Repealed*]

Joint tenancies

36.—(1) Where a legal estate (not being settled land) is beneficially limited
to or held in trust for any persons as joint tenants, the same shall be held in
trust, in like manner as if the persons beneficially entitled were tenants in
common, but not so as to sever their joint tenancy in equity.

(2) No severance of a joint tenancy of a legal estate, so as to create a tenancy in common in land, shall be permissible, whether by operation of law or
otherwise, but this subsection does not affect the right of a joint tenant to
release his interest to the other joint tenants, or the right to sever a joint
tenancy in an equitable interest whether or not the legal estate is vested in the
joint tenants:

Provided that, where a legal estate (not being settled land) is vested in joint
tenants beneficially, and any tenant desires to sever the joint tenancy in

equity, he shall give to the other joint tenants a notice in writing of such desire or do such other acts or things as would, in the case of personal estate, have been effectual to sever the tenancy in equity, and thereupon the land shall be held in trust on terms which would have been requisite for giving effect to the beneficial interests if there had been an actual severance.

Nothing in this Act affects the right of a survivor of joint tenants, who is solely and beneficially interested, to deal with his legal estate as if it were not held in trust.

(3) Without prejudice to the right of a joint tenant to release his interest to the other joint tenants no severance of a mortgage term or trust estate, so as to create a tenancy in common, shall be permissible.

Rights of husband and wife

37. A husband and wife shall, for all purposes of acquisition of any interest in property, under a disposition made or coming into operation after the commencement of this Act, be treated as two persons.

Land Registration Act 1925 (c. 21)

Land held on trust for sale

94.—(1) Where registered land is subject to a trust of land, the land shall be registered in the names of the trustees.

(2) Where an order, obtained under section seven of the Settled Land Act 1884, is in force at the commencement of this Act, the person authorised by the order to exercise any of the powers conferred by the Settled Land Act 1925 may, in the names and on behalf of the proprietors, do all such acts and things under this Act as may be requisite for giving effect on the register to the powers authorised to be exercised in like manner as if such person were registered as proprietor of the land, and a copy of the order shall be filed at the registry.

(3) Where, by virtue of any statute, registered land is made subject to a trust of land, the trustees (unless already registered) shall be registered as proprietors thereof, and shall in the prescribed manner apply for registration accordingly, and no fee shall be charged in respect of such registration or consequential alteration of the register, but this subsection has effect subject to the provisions of this Act relating to the registration of the Public Trustee and the removal of an undivided share from the register before the title to the entirety of the land is registered.

(4) There shall also be entered on the register such restrictions as may be prescribed, or may be expedient, for the protection of the rights of the persons beneficially interested in the land.

(5) Where a deed has been executed under section 16(4) of the Trusts of Land and Appointment of Trustees Act 1996 by trustees of land the registrar is entitled to assume that, as from the date of the deed, the land to which the deed relates is not subject to the trust unless he has actual notice that the trustees were mistaken in their belief that the land was conveyed to beneficiaries absolutely entitled to the land under the trust and of full age and capacity, and

(6) Where a proprietor ceases in his lifetime to be a tenant for life, he shall transfer the land to his successor in title, or, if such successor is an infant, to the statutory owner, and on the registration of such successor in title or statutory owner it shall be the duty of the trustees of the settlement, if the same be still subsisting, to apply for such alteration, if any, in the restrictions as may be required for the protection of the minor interests under the settlement.

Restriction on number of trustees

95. The statutory restrictions affecting the number of persons entitled to hold land subject to a trust of land and the number of trustees of a settlement apply to registered land.

Administration of Estates Act 1925 (c. 23)

Trust for sale

33.—(1) On the death of a person intestate as to any real or personal estate, that estate shall be held in trust by his personal representatives with the power to sell it.

(2) The personal representatives shall pay out of—

(a) the ready money of the deceased (so far as not disposed of by his will, if any); and

(b) any net money arising from disposing of any other part of his estate (after payment of costs),

all such funeral, testamentary and administration expenses, debts and other liabilities as are properly payable thereout having regard to the rules of administration contained in this Part of this Act, and out of the residue of the said money the personal representative shall set aside a fund sufficient to provide for any pecuniary legacies bequeathed by the will (if any) of the deceased.

(3) During the minority of any beneficiary or the subsistence of any life interest and pending the distribution of the whole or any part of the estate of the deceased, the personal representatives may invest the residue of the said money, or so much thereof as may not have been distributed, in any investments for the time being authorised by statute for the investment of trust money, with power, at the discretion of the personal representatives, to change such investments for others of a like nature.

(4) The residue of the said money and any investments for the time being representing the same, and any part of the estate of the deceased which remains unsold and is not required for the administration purposes aforesaid, is in this Act referred to as "the residuary estate of the intestate."

(5) The income (including net rents and profits of real estate and chattels real after payment of rates, taxes, rent, costs of insurance, repairs and other outgoings properly attributable to income) of so much of the real and personal estate of the deceased as may not be disposed of by his will, if any, or may not be required for the administration purposes aforesaid, may, however such estate is invested, as from the death of the deceased, be treated and applied as income, and for that purpose any necessary apportionment may be made between tenant for life and remainderman.

(6) Nothing in this section affects the rights of any creditor of the deceased or the rights of the Crown in respect of death duties.

(7) Where the deceased leaves a will, this section has effect subject to the provisions contained in the will.

Powers of management

39.—(1) In dealing with the real and personal estate of the deceased his personal representatives shall, for purposes of administration, or during a minority of any beneficiary or the subsistence of any life interest, or until the period of distribution arrives, have—

(i) as respects the personal estate the same powers and discretions, including power to raise money by mortgage or charge (whether or not by deposit of documents), as a personal representative had before the commencement of this Act, with respect to personal estate vested in him, and such power of raising money by mortgage may in the case of land be exercised by way of legal mortgage; and

47–101

(ii) as respects the real estate, all the functions conferred on them by Part I of the Trusts of Land and Appointment of Trustees Act 1996; and

(iii) all the powers necessary so that every contract entered into by a personal representative shall be binding on and be enforceable against and by the personal representative for the time being of the deceased, and may be carried into effect, or be varied or rescinded by him, and, in the case of a contract entered into by a predecessor, as if it had been entered into by himself.

(2) Nothing in this section shall affect the right of any person to require an assent or conveyance to be made.

(3) This section applies whether the testator or intestate died before or after the commencement of this Act.

Savings

51.—(1) Nothing in this Part of this Act affects the right of any person to take beneficially, by purchase, as heir either general or special.

(2) The foregoing provisions of this Part of this Act do not apply to any beneficial interest in real estate (not including chattels real) to which a person of unsound mind or defective living and of full age at the commencement of this Act, and unable, by reason of his incapacity, to make a will, who thereafter dies intestate in respect of such interest without having recovered his testamentary capacity, was entitled at his death, and any such beneficial interest (not being an interest ceasing on his death) shall, without prejudice to any will of the deceased, devolve in accordance with the general law in force before the commencement of this Act applicable to freehold land, and that law shall, notwithstanding any repeal, apply to the case.

For the purposes of this subsection, a person of unsound mind or defective who dies intestate as respects any beneficial interest in real estate shall not be deemed to have recovered his testamentary capacity unless his receiver has been discharged.

(3) Where an infant dies after the commencement of this Act without having been married and without issue, and independently of this subsection he would, at his death, have been equitably entitled under a trust or settlement (including a will) to a vested estate in fee simple or absolute interest in freehold land, or in any property settled to devolve therewith or as freehold land, such infant shall be deemed to have had an entailed interest, and the trust or settlement shall be construed accordingly.

(4) This Part of this Act does not affect the devolution of an entailed interest as an equitable interest.

PART V: TRANSFER OF LAND. TRUSTS OF LAND. LAW COMMISSION REPORT (LAW COM. No. 181)

TRUSTS OF LAND

CONTENTS

---

* Appendices B and C are not reproduced in this Handbook.

TRUSTS OF LAND

Summary

In this report the Law Commission, as part of its programme for the simplification of conveyancing, makes recommendations as to the reform of the law relating to trusts of land.

We consider that the present dual system of trusts for sale and strict settlements is unnecessarily complex, ill-suited to the conditions of modern property ownership, and liable to give rise to unforeseen conveyancing complications. We propose that it should be replaced by an entirely new system, applicable to all trusts of land except existing Settled Land Act settlements, set out in broader and simpler provisions designed to resolve existing difficulties whilst continuing to provide security for beneficiaries and purchasers alike.

The report contains a draft Bill to give effect to the recommendations.

THE LAW COMMISSION

Item IX of the First Programme

TRANSFER OF LAND

TRUSTS OF LAND

To the Right Honourable the Lord Mackay of Clashfern, Lord High Chancellor of Great Britain.

PART I

INTRODUCTION

1.1 This report sets out our recommendations for reform of the law relating to trusts of land. Our review of strict settlements and trusts for sale began in October 1984 as part of our property law programme.[1] In October 1985 we published a working paper containing a range of proposals for reform of the law relating to trusts of land.[2] We invited the submission of observations and suggestions from interested individuals and organisations. We received many valuable comments, for which we are most grateful. A list of the commentators is set out in Appendix B [*not reproduced in this Handbook*].

The present law

1.2 As we observed at the outset of the working paper, the law on settled land and on trusts for sale is more than adequately dealt with in existing legal writings. For that reason, the working paper contained only a brief introductory summary of the present law, confining detailed explanation to particular points under discussion and referring the reader to the standard textbooks[3] for a more general account of the law. The same approach has been adopted in this report. For ease of reference, the introductory summary given in the working paper is reproduced[4] below:

"*The present system*

[2.1] At present there are two possible ways of creating successive interest in land, and one of creating concurrent interests. Where success-

---

[1] Item IX of the First Programme.
[2] Working Paper No. 94, *Trusts of Land*.
[3] Megarry and Wade, *The Law of Real Property*, 5th ed., (1984), pp. 311–464; Cheshire and Burn's *Modern Law of Real Property*, 14th ed., (1988), pp. 169–337.
[4] With original footnotes, renumbered for the purpose of this Report.

ive interests are concerned, whichever system is used, the beneficial interest of the life tenant and the remainderman are equitable only.[5] The difference between the two systems lies principally in how the legal estate is held and who has the powers of management. Where successive interests are created under the Settled Land Act 1925, the tenant for life has a beneficial life interest. However, for the purposes of dealing with the land he also holds the legal estate.[6] He has wide powers of management. A purchaser will be able to acquire a legal fee simple absolute from the tenant for life free from the equitable interest created by the settlement provided that the purchaser pays the purchase money to at least two trustees or to a trust corporation. Where successive interests are created behind a trust for sale, the legal estate is held by the trustees, and generally it is they who have the powers of management. A purchaser will be able to acquire the legal estate free from the equitable interest from the trustees by paying the purchaser money to the trustees.

[2.2]   Concurrent interests in land usually exist behind a trust for sale.[7] The only permitted concurrent interest in the legal estate is a joint tenancy. Legal tenancies in common were abolished by s.34 of the Law of Property Act 1925. Therefore the effect of a conveyance to two or more people as beneficial joint tenants is that they hold the legal estate as joint tenants on trust for sale, for themselves as beneficial joint tenants, and the effect of a conveyance to two or more people as tenants in common is that they too hold the legal estate as joint tenants on trust for sale, but for themselves as tenants in common."

The problems

1.3 Those aspects of the present law which have given rise to most difficulty are fully discussed in the following pages of this report. They may for convenience be summarised as follows: firstly, the current dual system is unnecessarily complicated, the settled land provisions being particularly so; secondly, the trust for sale mechanism is not appropriate to the conditions of modern home ownership; thirdly, it is possible for testators or grantors to trigger the (complex) mechanisms of the strict settlement quite unintentionally. The problems were outlined in the Working Paper as follows:[8]

"A. *Dual system*

[3.2]   The following problems are those that arise because, at present, successive interests in land can be created either as settled land under the Settled Land Act 1925 or as interest behind a trust for sale. It has often been suggested that a dual system is unnecessary and that one system for successive interests would be sufficient. Originally the two systems performed different functions.[9] The strict settlement, using combinations of life interests and entailed interests (which before 1926 could exist as legal estates), was intended to keep land within the ownership of a particular family. In many cases the tenant for life would occupy the land. The trust for sale was used either where a sale was actually intended, or where the land concerned was intended to be an investment, to be bought and sold as market conditions demanded, the tenant for life being paid the income from it. By the mid-19th century it was apparent that strict settlements caused difficulty in that, if the settle-

---

[5] Law of Property Act 1925, s.1.
[6] This is not so if he is an infant, or in some other way incapacitated, when there are complex provisions as to who should exercise the powers of the tenant for life.
[7] Law of Property Act 1925, ss.34–36. Where land is settled under the Settled Land Act 1925 and there are joint tenants for life, there will be no trust for sale.
[8] With original footnotes, renumbered for the purpose of this Report.
[9] For a full historical account see Simpson, *An Introduction to the History of Land Law*, (1961), pp. 188–194, 218–224.

ment was not well drafted, the powers of the tenant for life were too limited to enable the land to be managed properly, and however the settlement was drafted, sale of the land was extremely difficult as no person had the power to convey the fee simple. A series of reforming statutes culminating in the Settled Land Act 1925 increased the powers of the tenant for life and ensured that there was also some person able to convey the fee simple in the land. At the same time the Law of Property Act 1925, s.1 prevented life interests from existing as legal estates, so that all settlements had to take effect behind a trust. The effect of these reforms has been to remove many of the differences between the two systems of settlement. In either system the land can be sold and the strict settlement is no longer an effective method of keeping land in the family. The remaining differences centre on who makes the decisions with respect to the land. It is arguable that the differences are not sufficient to justify the continuing existence of two systems.

[3.3] *Priority given to settled land.* The legislation is so phrased that when successive interests are created, a trust for sale must be expressly adopted (except where imposed by statute); otherwise the Settled Land Act will apply. This means that where trusts of land are created without proper advice it is almost certain that the land will be settled. This is most likely to occur where wills are, as often happens, drawn up without advice. In some cases this will be what the testator would have wanted, but in many cases it will not be and additional expense for the beneficiaries may result because additional documents and a different form of probate are required. If an inadvertent settlement is created by will and the executors do not realise this, problems may be caused for purchasers (see below).

[3.4] *Definition of trust for sale.* Inadvertent settlements may arise not through failure to decide which is required but through failure to create a valid trust for sale. The definition of a trust for sale as an immediate binding trust for sale has been criticised.[10] As a definition it is poor because it defines a thing as a particular kind of that thing. The word "binding" has caused particular problems because a trust should be binding anyway and the courts have considered that it must mean something other than the trustees being under a duty to sell.[11]

[3.5] *Rights of residence.* In other cases, settled land has been created inadvertently because a right of residence has been conferred on a person for his or her lifetime. It is not entirely clear that the conferment of such a right was intended to be sufficient to bring the land within the Settled Land Act. The technical question to be decided was whether land "stands for the time being limited in trust for any persons by way of succession".[12] However the courts have made it clear that they will treat such land as settled land especially if there is no other way to protect the rights of the life resident.[13] Giving such a person all the powers of disposition and management of a tenant for life has been much criticised. There should be some provision for giving rights of residence during a

---

[10] Law of Property Act 1925, s.205(1)(xxix), and see Megarry and Wade, *The Law of Real Property*, 5th ed., (1984), pp. 386–388.
[11] *Re Parker's Settled Estates* [1928] Ch. 247; *Re Ryder and Steadman's Contract* [1927] 2 Ch. 62; *Re Norton* [1929] 1 Ch. 84; *Re Beaumont Settled Estates* [1937] 2 All E.R. 353; *Re Sharpe's Deed of Release* [1939] Ch. 51.
[12] Settled Land Act 1925, s.1(1).
[13] *Re Duce and Boots Cash Chemists (Southern) Ltd* [1937] Ch. 642; *Bannister v. Bannister* [1948] 2 All E.R. 133; *Binions v. Evans* [1972] Ch. 359.

person's lifetime which do not cause technical complications. This problem is discussed further below.[14]

B. *Making good title*

[3.6]   If a purchaser of land subject to a trust for sale fails to comply with the provisions of s.27 of the Law of Property Act 1925, which states that the purchase price must be paid to at least two trustees (or a trust corporation) the conveyance will not be void, although interests under the trust for sale will not be overreached. If a purchaser of settled land fails to comply with the provisions of s.18 of the Settled Land Act 1925, the conveyance will be void except in so far as it binds the beneficial interest of the tenant for life. In some circumstances a purchaser may be protected by s.110 of the Settled Land Act, which is discussed in the following paragraph. It is questionable whether it is necessary for the position of a purchaser to vary in this way.

[3.7]   The drafting of s.110 of the Settled Land Act 1925 has led to the suggestion that it fails to give purchasers enough protection and that they may have to examine the trust instrument themselves, contrary to the general principles of the Settled Land Act 1925. This is probably a theoretical problem rather than a practical one. A real problem that has arisen is the relationship between s.110 and s.18 of the Act. Section 110 is meant to give some protection to a purchaser if he buys in good faith, but under s.18, if land is settled land, then any unauthorised disposition is void. It is not certain which prevails, nor is it clear whether s.110 offers any protection where the purchaser does not know that he is dealing with the tenant for life.[15]

[3.8]   Where settled land is created by will (particularly a home-made one) it is easy for the executors not to realise this and they may, for example, vest the land in trustees rather than in the tenant for life. It may then be difficult for either the tenant for life or the trustees or their successors to make a good title to a later purchaser.[16]

[3.9]   There is no formal provision for the termination of a trust for sale. This means that purchasers of land which has been subject to a trust for sale may be put in the position of having to investigate the trusts in order to ascertain that the trust for sale has ended.[17]

C. *Control by beneficiaries*

[3.10]   In general the beneficiaries of a trust of land are treated no differently from the beneficiaries of a trust of any other kind of property.

---

[14] Para. 16.16 of the Working Paper, as follows (footnotes omitted):

"*Inadvertent settlements*. Inadvertent settlements fall into two categories. The first are those where the intention is to create some sort of trust or settlement, and the settlor, by failing expressly to subject the land to a trust for sale, brings it within the Settled Land Act 1925. If, as is likely, this is a trust in a will, the executors may not realise the true effect of the provisions and the wrong procedure may be followed, causing problems for subsequent purchasers.... The second type of inadvertent settlement occurs when a person is given the right to reside in a property during his lifetime, and subject to that right the property is conveyed or passes on death to another. At present the result of such an arrangement may be that the land is settled land under the Settled Land Act 1925, and the person with the right of residence is the tenant for life with full powers of disposition and management. This result may be thought to be unsatisfactory, as there was no intention to confer such an extensive interest on the tenant for life. However, these cases should not necessarily be seen as wrongly decided. As Megarry and Wade put it, "it has to be remembered that the deliberate policy of the Act is that the statutory powers must always be available, so that the land is not sterilised, and that these powers cannot be restricted or fettered, whatever the settlor's intentions. This policy may naturally produce unintended results, but that is not necessarily a good reason for excluding a case from the purview of the Act."

[15] Compare *Weston v. Henshaw* [1950] Ch. 510 with *Re Morgan's Lease* [1972] Ch. 1.

[16] As, for example, in *Re Duce and Boots Cash Chemists (Southern) Ltd* [1937] Ch. 642.

[17] Except where joint tenants were holding on trust for themselves and there is only one survivor: Law of Property (Joint Tenants) Act 1964.

This may, itself, be the cause of some problems. Land is not like most other kinds of property: each piece is, in principle, unique, and, more importantly, it may be the place where the beneficiaries live, or want to live in the future. Questions of control over the land are therefore particularly important.

[3.11] *Those entitled to settled land in remainder.* It is impossible for a reminderman to prevent the sale of the land, unless there is lack of good faith on the part of the tenant for life. This leaves the remainderman in a very weak position because the land may have already been sold before he becomes aware of the tenant for life's intention to sell.[18]

[3.12] *Duty to consult.* The trustees of land held on a statutory trust for sale[19] have a duty to consult the beneficiaries.[20] There is no such duty where express trusts for sale are concerned. Even as regards statutory trusts the provision is weak. It only applies "so far as is practicable". The trustees only have to give effect to the wishes of the beneficiaries "so far as consistent with the general interest of the trust" and a purchaser is not affected by the trustees' failure to carry out or comply with the result of any consultation.

[3.13] *Delegation.* It has been suggested that the power to delegate the management of land to a tenant for life of land held on trust for sale is inadequate. If the power to delegate is not exercised, the tenant for life is left with no control, which may be unsatisfactory if the trust for sale is being used as a substitute for settled land. If the power is exercised, ownership and management are separated, which may be undesirable. The trustees retain the legal interest. If the tenant for life is not in possession, he may not be able to bring an action in his own name to protect the reversion of any property leased. As he is not the covenantee, he cannot sue on the covenants in the lease. It may be that these difficulties do not cause problems in practice as the trustees always take appropriate action, but, in theory at least, they do exist.... In addition it has been said,[21] "Psychologically in the management of a country estate this duty to act in the name of another seems unsound". Whether this is true today seems less likely. Ownership and management are commonly separated, for example in limited companies, and we doubt that there is any general issue of principle at stake. Making trustees delegate certain powers in certain situations would minimise the difference between the two systems.

[3.14] *Sale subject to consent.* In settled land it is not possible to make the sale of the land or the exercise of other powers subject to the consent of some other person,[22] for example, a remainderman. Making the consent of a beneficiary necessary for the sale of land held on trust for sale does not seem to have caused any problems and a similar provision could be made for settled land.

D. *Specific Settled Land Act problems*

[3.15] *Complexity.* Perhaps the greatest difficulty of the Settled Land Act 1925 is its sheer complexity. Three different aspects will serve to illustrate this.
  (i) The Act always requires the use of at least two documents, the vesting deed which vests the legal estate in the tenant for life (or whoever is entitled to exercise his powers) and the trust instru-

---

[18] See, for example, *England v. Public Trustee* (1968) 112 S.J. 70.
[19] See para. 2.2 of the Working Paper (set out in para. 1.2 of this Report).
[20] Law of Property Act 1925, s.26(3) substituted by the Law of Property (Amendment) Act 1926, Sched.
[21] Potter, "Strict Settlement and Trust for Sale", (1944) 8 Conv. (N.S.) 147, 157.
[22] Settled Land Act 1925, s.106.

ment which declares the trusts.[23] If land is acquired after the settlement has been created, a subsidiary vesting deed must be executed vesting the land in the tenant for life (or whoever is entitled to exercise his powers).[24] Hence where there are frequent purchases of land for a settlement, there may be a considerable number of vesting deeds. There are no equivalent provisions for trusts for sale. The deed which vests the land in trustees for sale may also declare the trusts, or there may be two separate documents where that is convenient.[25]

(ii) The Settled Land Act 1925 does not only provide for the straightforward settlement of a life interest followed by interests in remainder. It also covers a wide range of conditional interests and determinable fees, and land conveyed to infants. Here there is no tenant for life in the proper sense and the Act has to make elaborate provisions giving certain people all the powers of the tenant for life.[26]

(iii) Because the Act applies in certain circumstances without this being appreciated by the settlor, it can happen that no trustees are appointed by him. Thus a simple gift of land to X for life remainder to Y creates a settlement and it is necessary for trustees to be appointed. Again this necessitates complex provisions as to who are to be the trustees where none are appointed.[27]

[3.16] *Conflict of interest.* It has been suggested that there is an inherent conflict involved in the position of the tenant for life. The legal estate and all the powers of dealing with it are vested in him and under s.16 of the Settled Land Act 1925 he is a trustee. Yet he is, at the same time, the principal beneficiary. While it is quite usual for a trustee to be a beneficiary, given the lack of any other restraints on the tenant's powers, the conflict may become real. It seems that where there is a conflict of interests, the tenant for life is not treated like an ordinary trustee. It has been held that the court will not intervene if the tenant for life allows the estate to become derelict, but only if there is evidence that he has refused to exercise his powers.[28] Thus the remaindermen may inherit an estate much diminished in value and have no remedy. Similarly the interests of the remaindermen may be adversely affected by a sale of the settled land at a low price. Again, they may have no effective remedy[29] as they may not discover the sale until years after it took place and, even if they could establish a breach of trust, the tenant for life may be dead and his estate not worth suing. While it is clear that the courts, recognising the risks arising from conflicts of interest, usually make the purchase of trust property by a trustee virtually impossible,[30] in one case where the tenant for life purchased the settled land without the proper procedure being adopted, the sale was simply allowed to stand.[31]

E. *Trust for sale—specific problems*

[3.17] *Co-ownership.* The Law of Property Act 1925 imposes a statutory trust for sale wherever land is conveyed to co-owners—whether in equity they are joint tenants or tenants in common.[32] Thus, wherever a

---

[23] Settled Land Act 1925, ss.4, 5.
[24] Settled Land Act 1925, s.10.
[25] Law of Property Act 1925, s.27(1): the purchaser is not concerned with the trusts.
[26] Settled Land Act 1925, ss.20–24.
[27] Settled Land Act 1925, ss.30–34.
[28] *Re Thornhill's Settlement* [1941] Ch. 24.
[29] *England v. Public Trustee* (1968) 112 S.J. 70.
[30] Pettit, *Equity and the Law of Trusts*, 5th ed., (1984), pp. 374–376.
[31] *Re Pennant's Will Trusts* [1970] Ch. 75.
[32] Law of Property Act 1925, ss.34, 36.

couple buy a house, they become trustees for sale of it although a sale is probably not what they intend. In 1925, owner-occupation of dwellings was far less usual than nowadays and, where it did exist, it was less likely that a house would be purchased in joint names.[33] The co-ownership envisaged by the Law of Property Act would have arisen in a different context, where, for example, property was left to children in equal shares. In such a case, a sale at some stage was likely. As far as co-ownership is concerned, a system devised for one set of social circumstances is being used for very different circumstances.

[3.18]   *The doctrine of conversion.* The doctrine of conversion states that where land is held on trust for sale, the interests of the beneficiaries are deemed to be interests in the proceeds of sale, even before the land has been sold. The doctrine developed during the 18th century.[34] In the early cases, the nature of the beneficial interests was in question because the law of inheritance differed depending on whether property was real or personal. The doctrine of conversion meant that land held on trust for sale devolved as personalty. When reform of land law was being considered, it was the doctrine of conversion that made the trust for sale a useful tool in the simplification of conveyancing: since the interests were not in the land anyway, it was easy to provide that a purchaser should take free of them.[35] Now, however, the doctrine of conversion causes problems. To say that a person with an equitable joint tenancy or an equitable tenancy in common has no interest in the house but only an interest in the proceeds of sale, when no sale is contemplated, is wholly artificial. The courts have refused to allow the doctrine of conversion to operate fully in some cases.[36] The position therefore now is that the doctrine of conversion applies for some purposes but not for others, depending on the particular circumstances. This is clearly unsatisfactory.

[3.19]   *Powers conferred by s.30 of the Law of Property Act 1925.* Problems have arisen with s.30 of the Law of Property Act 1925 as to who can apply under the section, the extent of the powers of the court and the factors to be taken into account in exercising the court's discretion. On the face of it, the section only enables an application to be made if the trustee is refusing to sell. However the courts have found ways of protecting beneficiaries who wish to prevent a sale.[37] It also appears that a trustee who has no beneficial interest in the land may be unable to apply, so that the section does not provide a remedy where the trustees cannot agree to a sale.[38]

[3.20]   While the court is given power to make such order as it thinks fit, it is not certain whether this extends to ordering one co-owner who has sole occupation to pay an occupation rent to the other who is not in

---

[33] Co-ownership arises when two or more people rent property, as would have been more usual in 1925, but most of the problems seem to occur when the co-owners own the fee simple or a long lease.
[34] Lightwood, "Trusts for Sale", (1927) 3 C.L.J. 59.
[35] See Fourth Report of the Acquisition and Valuation of Land Committee, Cmd. 424, 1919, especially Appendix IV Part I, the Memorandum by B. L. Cherry.
[36] e.g. *Williams & Glyn's Bank v. Boland* [1981] A.C. 487.
[37] See, e.g. *Bull v. Bull* [1955] 1 Q.B. 234.
[38] See Law Reform Committee, 23rd Report, para. 3.63.

occupation.[39] It is probably desirable that they should have power to do so, as this provides a possible solution to the problem that where a sale is refused because of the wishes of one co-owner, the other is deprived of a valuable financial asset.

[3.21] A considerable amount of case law exists as to how the discretion should be exercised. Generally the court will look at the purpose for which the trust was created, and see whether the purpose still exists.[40] Particular difficulties have arisen as to the weight to be given to the children's interests,[41] and where one co-owner is bankrupt.[42]

[3.22] *Occupation right.* It is not clear whether a tenancy in common confers on beneficiaries as against trustees a right to occupy the land.[43]

[3.23] *Creation of tenancy in common.* It has been suggested that a tenancy in common cannot be created informally by *e.g.* financial contributions, because s.34(1) of the Law of Property Act states that undivided shares can only be created "as provided by the Settled Land Act 1925 or as hereinafter mentioned". The Settled Land Act 1925, s.36(4) states that undivided shares can only be created under a trust instrument or under the Law of Property Act 1925. This means that only expressly created or statutorily imposed undivided shares can exist. However the courts seem to have accepted the existence of informally created tenancies in common behind a trust for sale.[44] The position could be clarified by statute.

[Paragraphs [3.24] (severance) and [3.25] (ascertaining the equitable interests) are not reproduced: the problems mentioned in the working paper are not peculiar to trusts of land and thus fall outside the scope of

---

[39] See further para. 8.10 of the Working Paper, as follows (footnotes omitted):

"*Occupation rents.* If each beneficiary has a right to occupy, should the courts have the power to order, for example, one co-owner to pay money to the other in respect of that occupation? The present law is discussed at some length at first instance in *Dennis v. McDonald* [[1982] Fam. 63, at pp. 70–71], where Purchas J. accepted that "the true position under the old authorities was that the Court of Chancery and Chancery Division would always be ready to inquire into the position as between co-owners being tenants in common either at law or in equity to see whether a tenant in common in occupation of the premises was doing so to the exclusion of one or more of the tenants in common for whatever purpose or by whatever means. If this was found to be the case, then if in order to do equity between the parties an occupation rent should be paid, this would be declared and the appropriate inquiry ordered. Only in cases where the tenants in common not in occupation were in a position to enjoy their right to occupy but chose not to do so voluntarily, and were not excluded by any relevant factor, would the tenant in common in occupation be entitled to do so free of liability to pay an occupation rent". However, it appears that such a power to require payment of a rent only exists if the situation is one where the court would have power to order a sale. The question that arises is whether this power should be placed on a statutory footing, or whether it is best to leave the court with the widest powers possible under a re-drafted s.30. The advantage of legislating is, as always, that it would bring greater certainty, and so make settlements out of court more likely. The disadvantage in this particular case is that to bring greater certainty, one would have to define, with some precision, the situations in which an occupation rent could be paid, and to do so would restrict what is at present a broad jurisdiction. In addition, one might have to lay down principles on which the rent is to be calculated, a matter on which there is relatively little law. Should it be related to the market rent, or to the fair rent as if a tenancy of the dwelling were regulated under the Rent Act 1977 or to the "reasonable rent" as if it were a restricted contract? An alternative measure might be the income lost to the non-occupier through not being able to invest the money he would have received had the property been sold. The circumstances in which the rent might be ordered to be paid seem to be so varied that any attempt at precise definition is likely to lead to unjust results. Accordingly, we suggest that, at most, there should be a provision along the lines that the occupation rent should, so far as equitable and practicable, compensate a beneficiary for his loss of occupation rights."

[40] *Re Buchanan-Wollaston's Conveyance* [1939] Ch. 738; *Bull v. Bull* [1955] 1 Q.B. 234; *Barclay v. Barclay* [1970] 2 Q.B. 677.

[41] Compare *Rawlings v. Rawlings* [1964] P. 398, 419 and *Burke v. Burke* [1974] 1 W.L.R. 1063, 1067.

[42] *Re Holliday* [1981] Ch. 405; *Re Lowrie* [1981] 3 All E.R. 353.

[43] It was accepted in *Bull v. Bull* [1955] 1 Q.B. 234 that they did have a right of occupation but this has been criticised. See Crane (1955) 19 Conv. (N.S.) 146. In *Williams & Glyn's Bank v. Boland* [1981] A.C. 487 Lord Wilberforce noted Denning L.J.'s view in *Bull v. Bull* with approval.

[44] See further para. 6.5 of the Working Paper [reproduced in this Report at footnote 51].

the present report. Work in this area was felt best left over to become the subject of a separate project in the future].

F. *Powers of trustees*

[3.26]   The Law Reform Committee has already discussed some problems relating to the powers of trustees of land and of the tenant for life.[45] These are discussed below in the context of our fifth proposal. Two further problems which should be mentioned are:

(i) *Power to mortgage.* Where land is held by co-owners, there is generally a trust for sale. Trustees for sale have the powers of a tenant for life under the Settled Land Act. As such, they cannot raise the initial purchase price by mortgage.[46] This probably does not matter often, because the co-owners as beneficiaries are unlikely to object, and mortgagees do not in practice do so. However, it is one more illustration of the difficulties caused by using an inappropriate structure for co-ownership.

(ii) *Power to appoint attorney.* Since co-owners are trustees for sale, if there are only two co-owners (as is usually the case) one cannot appoint the other as his or her attorney.[47] This causes inconvenience and expense, as a third party must be involved. In addition trustees should use a special trustee form of attorney rather than the general one, and failure to use the right form may delay or invalidate a transaction.[48]

G. *Bare trusts*

[3.27]   Generally, where two or more people hold interests in land, then either the Settled Land Act will apply or there will be a trust for sale. However, a bare trust is within neither system, and so is to some extent an anomaly. A bare trust exists when the entire beneficial interest is vested in one person and the legal estate in another. The trustee in such a case has no duties other than to obey the beneficial owner, who is, to all intent, the real owner. Such a trust may arise, for example, because land held on trust for several beneficiaries has become vested in one adult beneficiary, or because land is being held by a nominee. A more frequent situation which may involve a bare trust arises where the property of any unincorporated association is held on trust for its members by trustees.[49] Generally bare trusts do not cause problems for purchasers, because either the purchaser is aware of the equitable interest and investigates to ensure the sale is with the consent of the beneficial owners, or he is unaware and takes free of them as a bona fide purchaser of the legal estate for value without notice. However, the overreaching machinery provided by s.2 of the Law of Property Act 1925 does not apply to bare trusts,[50] and there may be situations where a purchaser fails to obtain a good title.

Summary

[3.28]   It will be seen from the preceding paragraphs that many of the problems spring from the existence of two systems which can each be

[45] Law Reform Committee, 23rd Report, Powers and Duties of Trustees, Cmnd. 8733.
[46] See *Emmet on Title*, 19th ed., para. 10.140.
[47] Trustee Act 1925, s.25(2), as substituted by Powers of Attorney Act 1971, s.9(2).
[48] *Walia v. Michael Naughton Ltd, The Times*, 1 December 1984. [Since reported at [1985] 1 W.L.R. 1115 and [1985] 3 All E.R. 673. See now also s.3(3) of the Enduring Powers of Attorney Act 1985 and Law Society's Gazette, 18 May 1988, p. 4. Preliminary work has been carried out in this area, which falls beyond the scope of the present report and may become the subject of a separate project in due course].
[49] *Worthing Rugby Football Club Trustees v. Inland Revenue Commissioners* [1985] 1 W.L.R. 409.
[50] Except where the bare trust has arisen because a trust for sale has ended and the purchaser buying from trustees for sale can assume the trust continues: Law of Property Act 1925, s.27.

used for much the same purpose and yet have major differences in the way they operate. Added to this is the preference that the legislation shows for the creation of settled land, so that land may inadvertently come within the Settled Land Act 1925, even though this is inappropriate. However although it appears at first sight that the legislation governing the two systems covers all possible situations, it has become apparent that this is not so. Bare trusts are not catered for, and lifetime rights of residence have only been made to fit within settled land with difficulty.[51]"

The proposals

1.4 The proposals made in the working paper were grouped under five headings. Proposal I was that the present dual system of trusts for sale and strict settlements should be replaced by an entirely new system, under which all land held on trust would be held by trustees with a power to sell and a power to retain the land. Proposal II suggested that there should be no new settled land, and that all successive interests should fall under a trust for sale. Proposal III was that, where successive interests are created, there should no longer be a presumption in favour of the strict settlement. Proposal IV sketched out a new system of co-ownership. Finally, Proposal V contained a few specific suggestions, which could be combined with any of the preceding proposals.

1.5 In the working paper, we expressed a preference for the scheme set out in Proposal I. It was our view that the introduction of a completely new system would be the most satisfactory means of resolving the current problems. We consider that the principal difficulty with the present law is its obvious complexity. In comparison with trusts of personalty, the law relating to trusts of land appears extremely complex and convoluted. Despite this, it does not cover all those situations in which land is held on trust. In recommending that the law relating to trusts of land should be set out in the form of broader and simpler provisions, our aim is to place trusts of land on a similar footing to that of trusts of personalty. We consider that this simplification will resolve many of the particular difficulties while providing security for purchasers of land.

1.6 On consultation, we found there to be considerable support for Proposal I. Several of those who responded strongly approved of our proposed new system. However some consultees did favour the retention of the exist-

---

[51] See also as the co-ownership and trusts for sale, paras. 6.4 and 6.5 of the Working Paper, as follows:

"[6.4] *Co-owners.* The automatic imposition of a trust for sale on co-owners who may have purchased the property for their own occupation is highly artificial and difficult to explain to a lay client. As has been said, the structure of co-ownership laid down in 1925 is no longer suitable for modern conditions. Under this proposal, land held by co-owners would be held on trust, but there would be no duty to sell. Since there is no duty to sell, the doctrine of conversion would not be applicable, as this doctrine depends on there being a duty to sell, with equity assuming that the sale has taken place, even when it has not.

[6.5] At present, although it is clear that the 1925 legislation was intended to impose a trust for sale in all cases of beneficial co-ownership, there are some circumstances which it did not expressly cover. These are identified by Megarry and Wade [*The Law of Real Property*, 5th ed. (1984), p. 438] as follows:

(i) a conveyance to A (an infant) and B (an adult) as tenants in common;
(ii) a conveyance to A and B as joint tenants, where equity requires them to take as beneficial tenants in common, e.g. because they are partners, or contribute purchase-money in unequal shares;
(iii) a conveyance to X purchasing as trustees for A and B who are equitable owners in common of the purchase-money; and
(iv) a declaration by A as sole owner, that he holds on trust for himself and B in equal shares.

In addition the courts have assumed that where land is purchased in the name of one person alone, and another person contributes to the purchase price, the land is held by the sole legal owner on trust for sale for himself and the other person who contributed [*Bull v. Bull* [1955] 1 Q.B. 234, *Williams & Glyn's Bank v. Boland* [1981] A.C. 487]. We would suggest that clear provision should be made so that wherever concurrent interests in land are created, that land should be held under the new trust."

See now para. 3.5 of this Report and clause 1 of the draft Bill, implementing the above proposal by means of a comprehensive definition of "trust of land".

ing dual system. The majority of these were, in effect, suggesting that there is a need for Settled Land Act settlements or their functional equivalent—a need for which neither Proposal I nor Proposal II would provide. Opposition to Proposal I was largely in these terms. Nevertheless, the information which we received in response to the working paper confirmed that although some strict settlements are currently in existence, very few new settlements are being created. In addition, we consider that, if the powers of delegation held by trustees of land are broadened, settlors will be able to create what is, in effect, an "enhanced" strict settlement. This being the case, we consider that the merits of a unitary system far outweigh the possible disadvantages of "phasing out" the Settled Land Act.

1.7 We confirm our initial preference for a single trust of land to apply to both concurrent and successive interests in land. The interests themselves will be unchanged: the difference lies in the trust machinery. Under the new system, trustees will hold the legal estate on trust with a power to sell and a power to retain the land, and, as at present, it will always be possible to convey the legal estate free of equitable interests.

The structure of the report

1.8 This report is arranged in three parts. Part I being this introductory section. Part II is further divided into three sections. The first of these discusses how the trust of land will affect the holding of different kinds of interest. The next section sets out the structure of the trust. Finally there is a discussion of miscellaneous matters. Part III summarises the recommendations made in the main body of the report. A draft bill to give effect to those recommendations is annexed (Appendix A), as is a schedule setting out the main statutory provisions affected, in both original and amended form (Appendix C) [*not reproduced in this Handbook*].

PART II

THE TRUST OF LAND

A. INTERESTS

2.1 In the working paper,[52] we set out the main interests for which any system, whether it be unitary or dual, should provide, these being: concurrent interests, successive interests, the interests of minors, the interests of purchasers, and interests under bare trusts.

Concurrent Interests

3.1 At present, most concurrent interests fall under a trust for sale, either expressly or by implication.[53] The defining feature of the trust for sale, at least as it was originally designed, is that the trustees are under a duty to sell the trust land. Implicit in this is the notion that this land should be held primarily as an investment asset rather than as a "use" asset.

3.2 This formulation may well have been suitable or convenient for the purposes which it was designed to serve. However, since the passing of the 1925 property legislation, social conditions have altered to such an extent that the invariable imposition of a duty to sell now seems wholly artificial.

---

[52] Working Paper No. 94, paras. 4.1–4.6.

[53] Sections 34 and 36 of the Law of Property Act 1925 impose an implied trust for sale wherever there is equitable co-ownership of land. Although these statutory provisions are, to say the least, unclear as to whether or not a trust for sale arises where there is equitable co-ownership behind a sole legal title, the decision in *Bull v. Bull* [1955] 1 Q.B. 234 establishes that it will do so. This interpretation was approved by the House of Lords in *Williams and Glyn's Bank Ltd v. Boland* [1981] A.C. 487. Similarly, it would seem that an implied trust for sale will arise where there is co-ownership at law but not in equity (*Wilson v. Wilson* [1969] 3 All E.R. 945). The obvious instance in which equitable co-ownership will not trigger a trust for sale is that of joint life tenancies under a strict settlement.

This is largely because the incidence of owner-occupation has, over the last sixty-three years, risen to such a level that most dwellings are now owner-occupied.[54] Most of these are occupied by joint owners. One consequence of this is that the imposition of a duty to sell seems clearly inconsistent with the interests and intentions of the majority of those who acquire land as co-owners. In such cases the intention will rarely be that the land should be held pending a sale; it is much more probable that it will be retained primarily for occupation. In other words, the property will not be held simply as an investment asset, but rather as a "use" asset.

3.3 The courts have sought to neutralise this artificiality by developing the principle that, where the "collateral purpose" of the trust is, for example, to provide a family or matrimonial home,[55] and where that purpose still subsists, the court may, in the exercise of its discretion under section 30 of the Law of Property Act 1925, refuse to order a sale.[56] In that a single trustee is no longer able to force a sale (as against occupiers' interests), the "use" value of the property is given recognition.[57] It is, however, somewhat illogical that the courts should be required to develop and maintain a doctrine which takes as its foundation the artificiality of the trust for sale.

3.4 As a corollary of the duty to sell, and in accordance with the doctrine of conversion,[58] any interest held under a trust for sale is an interest in the proceeds of the sale of the land. Consequently, the beneficiaries are deemed not to have an interest in land as such.[59] Once again, the courts have intervened to mitigate the artificiality of the position.[60] This intervention has, however, resulted in an unsatisfactory division between those circumstances in which an interest under a trust for sale will be held to be an interest in land and certain others in which it will not, or might not.[61]

3.5 Our proposals in relation to concurrent interests are focused upon two features of the trust for sale. Our principal recommendations are, firstly, that all land which previously would have been held under an implied trust for

---

[54] Although there are no available figures for 1925, some indication of the rate of owner-occupation may be gleaned from the fact that in 1914 7% of houses were owner-occupied, the figure in 1938 being 43%. (Source: Housing Policy Technical Volume, Pt. 1, (1977). Figures are for England and Wales only.) By 1984 the percentage had risen to 61%. (Source: Social Trends, (1986). Figures are for Great Britain as a whole.) See also Working Paper No. 94, para. 3.17.

[55] Although recent case-law has centred largely on what is termed a "family-based" approach, the collateral purpose may take some other form. (The term "primary purpose" is often used as an alternative to "collateral purpose", use of the former term reflecting a trend towards the exclusion of the duty to sell.)

[56] This discretion has been exercised very broadly indeed. In *Williams v. Williams* [1976] Ch. 278, at 285, Lord Denning M.R. suggested that "... [judges] nowadays have great regard to the fact that the house is bought as a home in which the family is to be brought up. It is not treated as property to be sold nor as an investment to be realised for cash". Similarly, Ormrod L.J. observed in *Re Evers' Trust* [1980] 1 W.L.R. 1327, at 1332, that "... [t]his approach to the exercise of discretion ... enables the court to deal with substance, that is reality, rather than form, that is, convenience of conveyancing...".

[57] Contrast the approach taken in *Re Mayo* [1943] Ch. 302. See para. 12.3.

[58] This doctrine is based on the rule that "equity looks on that as done which ought to be done". Given that land held under a trust for sale is held under a duty to sell, equity "anticipates" this sale and "converts" the interests of the beneficiaries into interests in personalty. The "old" view of the doctrine was well expressed by Cross L.J. in *Irani Finance Ltd v. Singh* [1971] Ch. 59, at 80: "The whole purpose of the trust for sale is to make sure, by shifting the equitable interests away from the land and into the proceeds of sale, that a purchaser of the land takes free from the equitable interests. To hold these to be equitable interests in the land itself would be to frustrate this purpose."

[59] See Anderson, "The Proper, Narrow Scope of Equitable Conversion in Land Law", (1984) 100 L.Q.R. 86, for the argument, based on a review of the case law from the early eighteenth century onwards, that this "absolutist" interpretation of the doctrine of conversion has only recently crept into judicial doctrine.

[60] The clearest example of this is the decision in *Williams and Glyn's Bank Ltd v. Boland* [1981] A.C. 487, particularly Lord Wilberforce's observation that "... to describe the interests of spouses in a house jointly bought to be lived in as a matrimonial home as merely an interest in proceeds of sale, or rents and profits until sale, is just a little unreal ...".

[61] There may, for example, be a distinction between "family" purposes and commercial ones. Where land is held uniquely for investment the courts might be less ready to characterise the doctrine as "unreal". Indeed, even where "family" trusts are concerned there are indications that the *Boland* approach will not be uniformly followed. For example, Lord Oliver's judgement in *City of London Building Society v. Flegg* [1987] 2 W.L.R. 1266 echoes the dictum of Cross L.J. in *Irani Finance Ltd v. Singh* [1971] Ch. 59 (see footnote 58).

sale[62] should now be held under the new system by trustees with a power to retain and a power to sell,[63] and, secondly, that the doctrine of conversion should cease to apply. Thus, the main purpose of the trust will no longer be the realisation of the capital value of the land. Although this purpose is often seen as a merely notional one, judicial interpretation has not been so consistent as to exclude the occasional reappearance of the "old" approach.[64] The new system will be more readily intelligible to non-lawyers than the trust for sale. The point here is not simply that it should be easier for practitioners to explain the law to their clients, but also that co-ownership should take a form which non-lawyers can make sense of for themselves.

3.6 A scheme giving trustees of land a power to sell and a power to retain the land would correspond much more closely to the perceptions of most co-owners. Although many of these owners might be surprised to learn that they are trustees of any kind, the new system, given its simplicity and the fact that it bases the powers of trustees on those of an absolute owner, should be a considerably more accessible concept than that of the trust for sale. This scheme will, in addition, put the exercise of judicial discretion under section 30 on a rather better footing than at present. Although the courts have exercised this discretion quite broadly, the starting point has always been that there is a duty to sell. This has confined the development of judicial doctrine to the formulation of reasons why sale should not take place. If the trustees have, as we recommend, a power either to sell or to retain rather than a power merely to postpone sale, the terms of the discretionary jurisdiction will be more in accord with the circumstances which they are required to accommodate. The jurisdiction will be framed with sufficient breadth to permit a genuinely flexible approach.[65] Furthermore, the doctrine of conversion being founded upon the duty to sell, the removal of that duty will carry with it the foundation of the doctrine. Therefore, we recommend that the doctrine of conversion should be abolished in relation to all trusts, whenever created. The equitable interests of the beneficiaries will continue to be overreached if payment is made to two trustees, the interests becoming interests in the proceeds of sale if or when the land is sold.[66] In this way, the practical utility (in conveyancing terms) of the doctrine will remain undiminished.

3.7 We consider that where a trust of land is expressly created, the settlor should still be able to impose a duty to sell upon the trustees. However, where a duty to sell is so imposed, a power to retain will be statutorily implied, whether or not there is a contrary intention. Furthermore, the express imposition of a duty to sell will not carry with it the implication that the interests of the beneficiaries are "converted" to personalty. These interests will, as outlined above, remain interests in land until sale actually occurs.

Successive Interests

4.1 Successive interests may at present be accommodated under either a trust for sale or a strict settlement. One of the more obvious difficulties with the present system is that the strict settlement is accorded priority over the trust for sale. Wherever successive interests in land are created they take effect under a strict settlement unless there is an express provision to the effect that they are to be held on trust for sale. Consequently, it is all too easy for a testator inadvertently to bring into operation the Settled Land Act mechanism with all its attendant complexities.[67] Although the testator's

---

[62] Including cases of equitable co-ownership behind a sole legal title: see footnote 53. This is achieved in the draft Bill by the comprehensive definition of "trust of land" in clause 1.
[63] This will be one consequence of giving trustees of land the powers of an absolute owner. See para. 10.6.
[64] See, for example, footnote 61.
[65] We consider that the courts should have a broad power to deal with any dispute involving a trust of land.
[66] We are at present reviewing the operation of the overreaching mechanism: see Working Paper No. 106.
[67] Typically, this might occur where a testator devises property to his wife for the duration of her life, and thereafter to his children absolutely.

"intention" may in such circumstances be a rather elusive factor,[68] there cannot be many cases in which it would not be desirable to avoid the potential complications. The difficulty is in part that the complexity of strict settlements may expose the beneficiaries to added trouble and expense (in, for example, obtaining probate or appointing trustees), neither of which may seem justifiable where the property concerned is a small family home. Perhaps more significantly, Settled Land Act conveyancing is so rare that many practitioners may not be sufficiently familiar with the provisions of the Act to recognise the implications of such a will. Where the correct formalities have not been complied with, and the conveyance has been obtained from the wrong person, purchasers will be faced with the additional expense of remedial action.[69]

4.2 Similarly, a strict settlement may be created inadvertently wherever a person is granted a right to occupy property during their lifetime. In the case of *Bannister* v. *Bannister*[70] the Court of Appeal held that a life interest which arose under a constructive trust "... ha[d] the effect of making the beneficiary a tenant for life within the meaning of the Settled Land Act, 1925."[71] This interpretation of the Settled Land Act gives such beneficiaries the full powers of a life tenant in circumstances which suggest that the grant may not have been intended to carry with it these powers of sale and management. Although the courts might in the future regard the residential licence as a more apt construction in these situations, there may nevertheless be situations in which the strict settlement offers the only means of protecting the life interest.

4.3 Our recommendation is that it should no longer be possible to create Settled Land Act settlements and that, consequently, all successive interests should fall under the new system. Existing settlements will not be affected. In so recommending, we are conscious that there are some who consider that the Settled Land Act mechanism should continue to be available. In considering these responses, our view was that there were, in opposition to these, compelling reasons for adopting the course which we recommend. The information made available to us on consultation strongly suggests that, in recent years, the incidence of new express settlements has steadily declined, to the extent that there are today almost no new settlements.[72] Presumably, one explanation for this is that the strict settlement was designed to give effect to a form of "family" ownership which is not as prevalent, nor as much favoured, as it then was.[73] Indeed, the Settled Land Act mechanism is not a particularly effective means of keeping land "in the family".[74]

4.4 The essential distinction between the strict settlement and the trust for sale, as ways of providing for successive interests in land, is that each offers a quite different scheme for management of the trust land. Whereas in the trust for sale control of the land lies with the trustees, under a strict settlement the life tenant has most of the powers of management. Therefore, the question is whether, given that there may be some circumstances in which one might wish to give full powers of management to the current occupier of the land,

---

[68] To maintain that a particular testator "intended" or did not "intend" the consequences which a strict settlement might entail is to make a rather contrived judgement as to what that testator *would* have agreed to had the legal technicalities been in his mind.

[69] See, for example, *Re Duce and Boots Cash Chemists (Southern) Ltd* [1937] Ch. 642, and, generally, Prof. E. C. Ryder, "Settled Land: Mistakes and Their Consequences", (1962) C.L.P. 194.

[70] [1948] 2 All E.R. 133; see also *Binions v. Evans* [1972] Ch. 359.

[71] [1948] 2 All E.R. 133, at p. 137.

[72] Those practitioners who responded to our request for information indicated that there are very few strict settlements currently "on file", most of these having been established decades ago. Only one firm expressly proposed to create new settlements in the future.

[73] For examples of the traditional role of the strict settlement, see English and Saville, *Strict Settlement: A Guide For Historians.*

[74] There is, of course, nothing to prevent the life tenant selling the land so as to realise its capital value. In addition, liability to taxation is such as to render the "dynastic" strict settlement quite unattractive. (See Mellows, *The Law of Succession*, 4th ed., chapter 24.)

this objective can only be effectively achieved within the framework of the Settled Land Act. An important consideration here is that, although this feature of the Settled Land Act may have its advantages, it is one which has, in practice, produced some undesirable consequences. Of these, the most obvious is the conflict of interests inherent in the position of the tenant for life, who, on the one hand, has a duty to act as trustee[75] but, on the other, is the principal beneficiary.[76] This may be of particular importance where the life tenant exercises the power to sell the estate. The terms or timing of the sale, or, indeed, the question of whether there ought to be a sale at all, are matters which will be of legitimate concern to the remaindermen, yet the latter have little or no legal right to intervene.[77] Furthermore, although the life tenant may be a trustee, there are indications that the duties which attach to this role will not be as rigorously enforced as they are in other trust situations.[78]

4.5 Besides the "family" settlement, there are other examples of situations in which the strict settlement might be preferred to the trust for sale or trust under the new system. In the context of matrimonial arrangements, it may, for example, be desired that the survivor should have the powers of a life tenant but that the capital should ultimately pass to the children of a previous marriage. In many of these instances, it may be simpler to do this by way of the Settled Land Act machinery. More generally, it might be considered appropriate that the current occupier of the land, being uniquely placed to do so, should have responsibility for the overall maintenance of the property, or for the collection of rents. We consider that these facilities should, in substance, continue to be available; settlors should be allowed to place control of the trust in the hands of those beneficiaries who are most directly interested in the trust land. Thus, our recommendations include a proposal that the new system should include such powers of delegation as are necessary to permit this.[79]

4.6 The principal advantage of the new system is its simplicity. It will eliminate many of the difficulties which are liable to follow from the constitution of an implied strict settlement, particularly where the existence of that settlement has gone unrecognised.[80]

4.7 Under the new system, successive interests will be held under the same provisions as those governing trusts of concurrent interests. Where at present successive interests would be *expressly* subjected to a trust for sale, the new system will replace the old machinery in the same way as it will in the case of concurrent interests. The reforms will thus include not only the improvements set out above, but also the increased flexibility which should result from the implementation of our recommendations as to, for example, the powers of trustees and the delegation of those powers. The most extensive reforms, however, will be those which follow where the new system replaces the implied or express strict settlement.

4.8 Where at present strict settlements would arise by implication—where, that is, there is a grant of a life interest in land, or where successive interests are created by will—the recommended reforms will be particularly beneficial. The problem of the "unintended" strict settlement is perhaps the most immediate and substantial difficulty in the present system. Furthermore, where a trust arises by implication, there is an added premium on the qualities of simplicity and flexibility. Under our proposals, such life interests

---

[75] Settled Land Act 1925, s.16.
[76] See further para. 3.16 of the Working Paper (set out in para. 1.3 of this report).
[77] As Prof. Ernest Scamell, (1957) C.L.P. 152, at p. 162, observes: "... It is true that some protection against a capricious *exercise* of a tenant for life's powers is provided by section 107 of the Act which requires him to act as a trustee in such exercise, but this section does not apply to a capricious non-exercise of his powers, and in any event the cases show that the duties imposed by the section are very slight."
[78] See Working Paper No. 94, para. 3.16 (set out in para. 1.3 of this Report).
[79] See para. 11. Trustees under a trust for sale may already delegate their powers of management to a beneficiary under section 29 of the Law of Property Act 1925.
[80] See para. 4.1.

will take effect under the new system, the trustees' powers of sale and management being limited accordingly. Given that these interests are not generally intended to carry with them the powers of a tenant for life, particularly the power of disposition, it seems advantageous that the overall power of management should be vested in trustees,[81] not least because the freedom of action which is built into the role of the tenant for life[82] may, in this connection, be particularly undesirable.

4.9 The introduction of a unitary trust mechanism should eliminate many of the conveyancing difficulties which can at present arise where the existence of a strict settlement goes unrecognised.[83] Similarly, whereas at present the existence of an implied strict settlement will usually trigger the operation of sections 30 to 34 of the Settled Land Act (which contain some rather complicated provisions as to the nomination of trustees), under the new system the trustees will quite simply be those persons who hold the legal estate in the land.[84] Where there is only one such trustee, the provisions of section 36(6) of the Trustee Act 1925 (as amended[85]) will enable the appointment of an additional trustee or trustees.

4.10 Where the trust is created expressly, the provisions which we recommend should, once again, offer greater simplicity and flexibility. To begin with, there will be some simplification of the formalities of constitution. Whereas the constitution of a strict settlement requires the execution of two separate documents, a vesting instrument and a trust deed, under the new system the only formalities required will be those which are at present essential to the creation of any trust land.[86] For those who wish to avoid disclosure of the apportionment of beneficial interests, the loss of the "curtain principle" may prove inconvenient, but standard trust mechanisms could be used to achieve a similar result.[87] The advantage of the change is that it avoids the complications which can occur where there are a number of vesting deeds.[88]

4.11 One of our foremost concerns was to provide a suitable facility for those settlors who might wish to construct something analogous in substance (if not in form) to the strict settlement. Our recommendation as to the delegation of trust powers will enable settlors to go beyond the delegation provisions of the trust for sale. They will be able to construct what would in effect be an "enhanced" strict settlement. Such a settlement would not be precisely the same as a strict settlement because the trustees will retain the legal title. Delegation will be by way of power of attorney, which means that it will be clear to any potential purchaser or transferee that they are dealing with an attorney.

4.12 Given that such a settlement will be subject to the powers given to the court by the revised section 30,[89] remaindermen will be placed in a much stronger position than they are under a strict settlement. They will be able to apply to the court to challenge any exercise of the trust powers by the trustees or by a life tenant. This means that, although the court may give priority to the wishes of the life tenant,[90] remaindermen will have at their disposal an effective means of protecting their interest.

---

[81] Where no trustees have been appointed by the grantor or settlor, those persons holding the legal estate will act as trustees. (See para. 9.2.)

[82] See para. 4.4, and footnote 74.

[83] See para. 4.1.

[84] See para. 9.2.

[85] See para. 9.1.

[86] Viz., the requirements of the Law of Property Act 1925, s.53(1)(b).

[87] It would, for example, still be possible to execute two documents should this be desired.

[88] Which will be the case where, for example, there have been several acquisitions of land under an existing settlement.

[89] See para. 12.

[90] See para. 12.13.

Minors

5.1 At present, minors cannot hold a legal estate in land, and it is provided that the Settled Land Act machinery should come into operation wherever there is an attempted conveyance of land to a minor.[91] The substitution of the new system in these cases will again simplify matters, without, as the Working Paper makes clear,[92] introducing any substantive changes. Minority will remain a disability and an attempted conveyance to a minor will take effect as a declaration of trust, the land being held by the relevant trustee or trustees under the new system. Where the conveyance is made *inter vivos*, the grantor will hold the land as trustee for the minor. Where the disposition is testamentary, the personal representatives of the settlor will act as trustees. Where land is conveyed to a minor jointly with an adult, the adult will hold the land on trust for himself and the minor, as joint tenants or as tenants in common according to the terms of the conveyance.

5.2 Section 27 of the Settled Land Act is rather ambiguous in that it does not explicitly provide for those situations in which a legal estate is conveyed to minors as tenants in common. Under the new system, an attempted conveyance of land to minors, whether as joint tenants or as tenants in common, will take effect within terms similar to those which will apply to conveyances to a sole minor. Once again, the trustees will be either the personal representatives of the settlor, or the *inter vivos* grantor, and the land will be held for the minors either as joint tenants or tenants in common, whichever is appropriate.

5.3 Subsections (3), (4), (5) and (6) of section 19 of the Law of Property Act 1925 make provision for conveyances on trust or by way of mortgage. It being our recommendation that a conveyance of a legal estate in land to a minor should create a trust in favour of that minor, these provisions will no longer be necessary.

Purchasers

6.1 We are at present reviewing the mechanisms which were provided for the protection of purchasers and beneficiaries by the legislation of 1925.[93] The new system will retain the mechanism by which purchasers may, on the fulfilment of certain conditions, take the legal estate free of the interests of the beneficiaries.[94] It may be that our work on overreaching will result in a recommendation that the balance between the interests of beneficiaries and purchasers be altered. Nevertheless, purchasers will be in no less secure a position than purchasers of land held on trust for sale. In (substantially) duplicating those provisions which currently apply to trusts for sale, and in extending them to circumstances which would at present fall under the provisions of the Settled Land Act, purchasers of what would now be a settled land estate will find the process of conveyance rather simpler.

6.2 Moreover, such purchasers will no longer be faced with the hazards of an ineffective disposition of settled land[95] or an "unrecognised" strict settle-

---

[91] Law of Property Act 1925, s.1(6), Settled Land Act 1925, s.1(1)(ii)(d). Under s.27(1) of the latter Act, such a conveyance takes effect as a contract for valuable consideration to execute a full settlement but in the meantime to hold the land in trust, for the infant. As a minor cannot be a tenant for life, s.26 provides that the trustees of the settlement should have the powers of a tenant for life.

[92] Working Paper No. 94, para. 6.6

[93] See Working Paper No. 106.

[94] Our recommendations will not interfere with those provisions which limit the number of legal estates which may be held and the number of persons who can hold any one estate.

[95] Any assessment of the nature and extent of this hazard will depend upon an interpretation of sections 18(1) and 110 of the Settled Land Act 1925. The particular question to be asked here is, to what extent does section 110 mitigate the effect of section 18? The problem may be illustrated by reference to the divergence between the approach taken by Danckwerts J. in *Weston v. Henshaw* [1950] Ch. 510, and that adopted by Ungoed-Thomas J. in *Re Morgan's Lease* [1972] Ch. 1. For a full discussion, see Gray and Symes, *Real Property and Real People* (1981), pp. 171–176. It may also be that the effect of section 110 is, in certain circumstances, to require purchasers to examine the trust instrument.

ment.[96] The overreaching mechanism will operate much as it currently does in relation to trusts for sale. This means that there can be no question of a disposition being void; the danger, to the extent that there is one, is that purchasers dealing with a single trustee might not appreciate that they are in fact dealing with trust property. Given that the purchaser will often have notice of the equitable interest of the beneficiaries,[97] and that even where he does not most purchasers nowadays will be alert to the hazard of overriding interests,[98] this danger seems rather more foreseeable than a situation such as that disclosed by the facts of *Weston* v. *Henshaw*.[99]

Bare Trusts

7.1 As we said in the Working Paper:[100] "It is useful in some situations for the legal estate and equitable interests to be separated even though the trustee has none of the usual duties of a trustee. It is important that any proposed change should not make such a separation impossible". At present, so-called bare trusts[101] fall outside the statutory dual system of trusts for sale and strict settlements. The lack of relevant statutory provisions as to such matters as trustees' powers, rights of beneficiaries and protection of purchasers is thought inconvenient and can occasion confusion in practice. However, such trusts will fit without difficulty within our proposed new unitary system. Beneficial owners would, of course, when creating the bare trust remain able to limit the powers of the trustees;[102] for example, the powers of disposition may be made exercisable only with the consent, or at the direction, of a named person.

B. THE TRUST

Creation

8.1 It is our view that the new system should cover all trusts of land, including so-called "bare" trusts.[103] Consequently, we consider that the application of the system should not be conditional upon the fulfilment of any special formalities. The only requirement will be that the trust be properly constituted within the terms of general trust law. This will bring trusts of land into line with trusts of personalty, in that there will be a single body of law covering all such trusts.

8.2 The new system will apply whether the trust is expressly created or statutorily implied. It will apply (in place of a trust for sale) wherever there is a conveyance of land to equitable co-owners. In addition, and in line with our view that all trusts of land should be brought within the new system, it will

[96] See para. 4.1.
[97] Where the property is registered land, the beneficial interests will often be protected by means of an entry restricting the registered proprietor's powers of disposition and caution. Where the land is unregistered, the equitable doctrine of notice prevails, except where there is a right of occupation under the Matrimonial Homes Act 1983, in which case that interest may be registered as a Class F land charge within the terms of section 2(7) of the Land Charges Act 1972.
[98] After *Boland*, one of the foremost concerns of purchasers and their advisers will be the avoidance of potential overriding interests. It is worth noting here that one of the recommendations of the Third Report on Land Registration (Law Com. No. 158, para. 3.34(7)) is that any registered proprietor or chargee against whom an overriding interest is asserted should be entitled to seek indemnity.
[99] [1950] Ch. 510. The facts of this case were that a mortgagee lent money on the security of a legal mortgage to a borrower who, although a tenant for life of a strict settlement, had in his possession title deeds showing him to be absolute and beneficial owner of the estate. It was on the basis of these deeds that the mortgagee took the mortgage and paid the mortgage money over to the borrower.
[100] Working Paper No. 94, para. 4.6.
[101] "A simple (or bare) trust is one in which property is vested in one person on trust for another, the nature of the trust not being prescribed by the settlor but being left to the construction of the law, as where property is transferred to T 'on trust for B absolutely'. In such a case, T must permit B to enjoy the trust property, and must obey his instructions as to disposing of it." *Snell's Principles of Equity*, 28th ed. p. 104.
[102] See para. 10.10.
[103] See footnote 101.

also apply wherever equitable interests in land arise by way of resulting, constructive, or implied trusts. Successive interests in land being necessarily equitable, these will in future automatically be subject to the new system. All this is simply achieved by the all-embracing definition of "trust of land" in clause 1 of the Bill.

8.3 One of the major policies underlying our recommendations is that use of the Settled Land Act 1925 should in the future be reduced to a minimum. The reasons for this policy have been discussed in those paragraphs which deal with successive interests.[104] At this point, suffice it to say that we are convinced—after a review of the evidence available to us—that the introduction of a unitary system would be particularly beneficial. Our recommendations are designed to ensure that, after the commencement date, there should be no new strict settlements. If an existing settlement acquires more land, that land will be held under the new system. Similarly, where land which is already settled land would continue to be so only by virtue of a new instrument, that land would also be held under the new system. In addition to a general provision stating that there should be no new settlements, the Bill expressly provides for those circumstances in which a strict settlement will at present arise.[105]

Trustees

9.1 Where a trust arises by way of a conveyance to co-owners, the trustees will, as at present, be the first four named in the conveyance. They will, however, hold the legal estate on trust under the new system rather than on trust for sale. Where new trustees are to be appointed,[106] we recommend that section 36 of the Trustee Act 1925 should apply as at present, subject however to an amendment. We recommend that where the beneficiaries are ascertained, *sui juris*, and unanimous, they should be able to exercise the right of appointment currently exercised by the remaining trustees. The beneficiaries' right would take priority over the trustees' right under section 36(1)(b). However, in order that purchasers might continue to enjoy the protection of section 38 of the Trustee Act,[107] the beneficiaries will exercise their right indirectly. In other words, they will merely *direct* the appointment of a new trustee, the formal deed of appointment being executed by the remaining trustees. Where the mental disorder of an existing trustee necessitates the new appointment, the beneficiaries would be able to give the direction to the trustee's receiver of (if no receiver was acting) to any person authorised for that purpose by the Court of Protection.[108] In order to avoid confusing distinctions, the amendment will apply to trusts of personalty as well as trusts of land.

9.2 Where successive interests are created, the trustees will be either those persons appointed by the settlor or, failing this, whoever has the legal estate currently vested in him. Where necessary, the court will have recourse to the

[104] Paragraphs 4.1–4.12.
[105] See clauses 13, 14, 15, 16 and 17.
[106] e.g. where a trustee is dead, remains out of the U.K. for more than a year, desires to be discharged, refuses or is unfit to act, is incapable of acting or is an infant; has been removed under a power in the trust instrument; or where existing trustee(s), being not more than three (none a trust corporation) wish to appoint an additional trustee.
[107] Section 38 provides that: (1) a statement, contained in any instrument by which a new trustee is appointed for any purpose connected with land, to the effect that a trustee has remained out of the U.K. for more than a year or refuses or is unfit to act, or is incapable of acting, or that he is not entitled to a beneficial interest in the trust property in possession, shall, in favour of a purchaser of a legal estate, be conclusive evidence of the matter stated; and (2) in favour of such purchaser, any appointment of a new trustee depending on that statement and any vesting declaration, express or implied, consequent on the appointment, shall be valid.
[108] The new subsection (1B) of section 36, inserted by clause 18(2) of the draft Bill, adopts the wording of section 22 of the Law of Property Act 1925 (as amended). The position of the mentally incapacitated trustee who has delegated his powers by enduring power of attorney has not been examined as part of the present exercise: this has been left over to be dealt with as part of a separate examination of the use of powers of attorney by trustees.

power which it currently possesses under section 41 of the Trustee Act 1925.[109] Where there is an attempted conveyance of land to a minor, an *inter vivos* "conveyance" will constitute a declaration by the grantor that he holds the land on trust for that minor. In testamentary dispositions to a minor, the personal representatives will become trustees. Where the trust of land arises on intestacy, the administrators of the estate will, as at present, become trustees.

Powers

10.1 In determining the nature and extent of the trust powers there are two related considerations. Firstly, there is the question of *what* powers should be created and, secondly, there is the question *how* those powers should be distributed and located. These two considerations are clearly related, as the scheme of distribution will determine the utility and efficacy of the powers themselves. This point is well illustrated by a comparison of the trust for sale with the strict settlement—in each of these, substantially the same powers[110] are arranged to quite different effect: with the former, they are vested in the trustees for sale, whilst with the latter, they are generally vested in the tenant for life. We consider that a scheme of distribution should provide for optimum flexibility, and that the best way of achieving this is to start from the basis of the trust for sale model—namely that of the trustee-manager—grafting onto this powers of delegation which are broad enough and flexible enough to enable distribution of trust powers to the beneficiaries with current interests.

10.2 Should they wish to do so, settlors will be able to use the provisions of the new system to ensure that the trust powers are vested in the life tenant; it will, in other words, be possible, by expressly directing that there should be a particular delegation, to achieve much the same result as that which at present flows automatically from the constitution of a strict settlement. In addition, the new system will enable settlors to set limits upon the exercise of the trustees' powers. With the strict settlement it is, of course, not possible to limit the freedom of action of the tenant for life to any real effect,[111] which is why settlors can do little to give remaindermen an effective say in the management of the land. Although the trust for sale is quite flexible in this respect, and although remaindermen can be given some foothold—by making the sale of the land subject to the consent of certain named persons[112]— the duty to sell cannot be delegated to the life tenant for more than one year.[113] Consequently, it is impossible to give an occupying beneficiary all the powers of a tenant for life under a strict settlement. Under the new system, trustees will have a power to sell and a power to retain, and they will be able, without limitation as to time, to delegate these powers to any beneficiary with a present, vested, interest in possession. Thus, under the new system, settlors will be able to construct a settlement which, while giving an occupying beneficiary powers analogous to those of a tenant for life under a strict settlement, also inhibits (if they so wish) that beneficiary's powers of disposition. In this way the new system will couple the simplicity of a unitary trust with an enhancement of the flexibility which is provided within the current system.

10.3 Where a trust arises impliedly, the trust powers will, of course, be vested in trustees. It is our view that, given the circumstances in which an

---

[109] Section 41 of the Trustee Act 1925 provides that the court may, whenever it is expedient to appoint a new trustee or trustees and it is found inexpedient, difficult or impracticable to do so without the court's assistance, make an order appointing a new trustee or trustees, either in substitution for, or in addition to, any existing trustee or trustees.

[110] See section 28 of the Law of Property Act 1925.

[111] See para. 4.4.

[112] Law of Property Act 1925, s.28(1).

[113] Section 25 Trustee Act 1925. See also para. 11.1. Under section 29 of the Law of Property Act 1925, the trustees' *powers* (but not sale) may be (revocably) delegated for a longer period.

implied trust of land is most likely to arise, namely where there is concurrent co-ownership, or where a life interest in land is created, this is quite acceptable. Either there will be little change to the present position, as where the trust is one of concurrent interests, or there will be some measure of improvement, as where the trust replaces the implied strict settlement. In this latter case, particularly where there is a non-testamentary grant of a life interest in land, it seems right that the trust powers should remain vested in trustees rather than in the holder of that life interest.[114] Nevertheless, where appropriate, the power of delegation will be available.

10.4 As regards the nature and extent of the trust powers themselves, we consider that trustees of land should be put in much the same position as an absolute owner. The circumstances of most trusts of land will be such that those persons to whom the legal label of "trustee" is attached are quite likely to regard themselves as the "owners" of the trust land. Even where this is not the case, it is desirable that the trustees should have the powers necessary to make efficient use of the land. Our proposals are designed to reflect this state of affairs whilst maintaining the general equitable duties of trustees.[115] Therefore, although the powers will be approximate to those of an absolute owner, they will not be quite as readily exercisable.

10.5 In recommending that trustees of land should have all the powers of an absolute owner, our aim is not simply to tack additional powers on to those which trustees for sale currently possess, so as to arrive at a more "complete" inventory. Rather, it is to make the scheme of powers as broadly based and as flexible as possible. The powers of trustees for sale are expressed as a rather complex and fragmented set, and, in accordance with our policy that trusts of land should be analogous to those of personalty, it is our view that this composite of powers should be dissolved into a simple and widely-framed provision.[116]

10.6 Perhaps the most significant consequence of giving trustees the powers of an absolute owner is that these trustees will now have a power either to sell or to retain the land. This will, of course, be one of the more fundamental elements in the specification of the trust under the new system. For example, the inclusion of these powers provides a foundation for restructuring of the jurisdiction of the court under section 30. Similarly, it facilitates the construction of a unitary trust in that (coupled with extended powers of delegation) it substantially retains the facility which is at present offered by the Settled Land Act.

10.7 Trustees of land will have a power to apply proceeds of sale of trust land, or any part thereof, to the purchase of land, either for occupation by the beneficiaries or for investment. Although trustees for sale do have a power to apply trust money to the purchase of land, the courts have interpreted the scope of this power rather restrictively. Thus, in *Re Power's Will Trusts*[117] it was held that, where the trustees were expressly given all the powers of investment of an absolute owner, this power could not be exercised to purchase land for occupation by beneficiaries. Similarly, it has been held that where all the trust land has been sold the trustees cease to be trustees for sale and hence cease to be within the statutory provisions.[118]

---

[114] It is seen as one of the drawbacks of the present system that such holdings necessarily attract the powers of a tenant for life under a strict settlement. See para. 4.2.

[115] See para. 10.9.

[116] Section 28 of the Law of Property Act provides that trustees for sale shall have all the powers held by the tenant for life and the trustees of a strict settlement. This definition by analogy is rather clumsy, and does not provide trustees for sale with a sufficiently extensive set of powers.

[117] [1947] Ch. 572. See *Emmet on Title*, 19th ed., para. 23.032, for the suggestion that such a purpose might be brought within the power of investment by allowing the life tenant into occupation as a licensee on an undertaking to pay outgoings and to give vacant possession on three months notice. It is further suggested that this decision may not apply at all to statutory powers.

[118] *Re Wakeman* [1945] Ch. 177. Cf. *Re Wellstead's Will Trusts* [1949] Ch. 296.

10.8 Our recommendation is that trustees should have a broad power to apply some or all of any proceeds of sale to the purchase of land, either as an investment or for occupation by the beneficiaries. This power would extend to the purchase of freehold or leasehold legal estates. It would not be restricted to property where the lease has more than sixty years left to run:[119] we felt that such a restriction was neither necessary nor desirable in today's economic climate, in which shorter leases may often be regarded as good and prudent investments, appropriate to the particular circumstances of the trust and the beneficiaries. The fixing of a minimum period, of whatever length, could only be the result of an arbitrary decision and, bearing in mind that there are circumstances in which it is quite conceivable that even a freehold might represent an imprudent or inappropriate investment, it seemed sensible to give trustees maximum flexibility, leaving general equitable rules to govern the use of such flexibility. In addition, the powers of trustees of land to mortgage, lease, or sell the land should be analogous to those held by absolute owners. Any money realised by the exercise of these powers will be held upon the same trusts as the land is or was held.

10.9 Although the powers conferred by clause 4 of the draft Bill are very broad, their exercise will not be unfettered. General equitable rules will continue to ensure that these powers can only be properly exercised in the interests of the beneficiaries.[120] This will, of course, put trusts of land on much the same footing as those of personalty. To the extent that this power includes a power to invest proceeds of sale, its exercise will also be governed by the Trustee Investment Act 1961.

10.10 There may of course be some express limitation of these powers, either by way of provisions subjecting their exercise to the consent of some person or persons, or by way of express restrictions in the trust instrument. In either of these cases, there will be no derogation from the principle that a purchaser should not be required to examine a trust instrument to determine the validity of a conveyance. Therefore, we recommend that purchasers should not be affected by an express limitation of the trustees' powers unless they have notice of that limitation. Clearly, it is in the interest of beneficiaries that there should be some means of ensuring that purchasers do have notice of such a restriction. Accordingly, we further recommend that the trustees should have a duty to take reasonable steps to ensure that any restriction upon their powers is brought to the attention of prospective purchasers. In the case of registered land, trustees should be required to apply for a restriction to be entered on the register of title. Failure on the part of trustees to take such reasonable steps—whether by way of registration (where appropriate) or otherwise—would place them in breach of trust. Beneficiaries with an interest in registered land may protect their position by entering a caution on the register[121] (there is, however, no equivalent measure available to beneficiaries with an interest in unregistered land).

---

[119] Capital money arising under the Settled Land Act 1925 may not be invested in leasehold land with less than 60 years to run: section 73(1)(xi).

[120] The duties of trustees are fully set out in the textbooks. See, for example, *Snell's Principles of Equity*, 28th ed., Pt. II, ch. 7; Pettit, *Equity and the Law of Trusts*, 5th ed., ch. 17.

"The duties of trustees are many. ... In carrying out the trusts [the trustees] must take due care of the trust property by investing it prudently and in the manner directed; they must give information to the beneficiaries when required, and in some cases submit to their directions; they must comply with any directions of the court and when in difficulty seek its aid; and, finally, they must make no profit out of the trust unless authorised." *Snell's Principles of Equity*, 28th ed., pp. 212–213.

In addition, under the principle *delegatus non potest delegare*, trustees are under a duty to act personally unless delegation of their functions is authorised by the trust instrument or by statute: *Ibid.*, at p. 263.

[121] *Elias v. Mitchell* [1972] Ch. 652.

Delegation of Trust Powers

11.1 Our recommendations include a proposal that trustees of land should have a rather broader power of delegation[122] than they have at present. The major purpose of this extended power is, as we have seen, to enable a beneficiary under a trust of land to be given much the same powers as a tenant for life under a strict settlement. The power of delegation of trustees for sale is insufficient for this purpose because, although the trustees may delegate their powers of management to a beneficiary,[123] the duty to sell cannot be effectively delegated.[124] We recommend that this bar should be removed so as to allow the delegation (without limitation as to time) of all the trust powers in relation to land to any beneficiary with a present, vested, interest. These powers might not be delegated to beneficiaries who have a future or contingent interest, or to those who have a purely monetary interest. The effect of this reform would be to allow the delegation of all the trust powers in relation to land to those persons to whom trustees for sale may at present delegate only their powers of management.

11.2 Delegation will be effected by the grant of a power of attorney.[125] This means that, as with the trust for sale,[126] delegation will be on a personal, revocable, basis, with the trustees retaining the legal estate. Thus, even where the trust powers are delegated to a beneficiary, that beneficiary will not be in a position which exactly mirrors that of a tenant for life. The fact that delegation is by way of power of attorney means that, in any dealings with the trust land, it will be clear to those with whom the beneficiary is dealing that he is only acting *qua* attorney. This may be said to have certain disadvantages,[127] but there are important counter-balancing benefits, particularly for purchasers and, to a lesser extent, for the other beneficiaries. It is to be presumed that most settlors would favour such a restraint.

11.3 One effect of delegation under section 29 of the Law of Property Act is that the trustees are no longer liable to the other beneficiaries for the acts or defaults of the person(s) to whom the powers of management have been delegated.[128] It is our view that this makes the trustees' liability too narrow. As it is our recommendation that delegation should take place within the terms of section 25 of the Trustee Act 1925, so it will follow that trustees of land will be liable to the other beneficiaries for the acts or defaults of the donee(s). Therefore, the trustees will have a clear incentive to adopt a supervisory role.

Powers of the Court

12.1 The courts have interpreted section 30 of the Law of Property Act so broadly as to enable them, in settling a dispute relating to a trust for sale, to give effect to what they perceive to be the purpose of the trust or the intention of the parties in acquiring the trust land. It is our view that the courts

---

[122] Although delegation would be one of the *powers* of an absolute owner, its exercise would conflict with a trustee's *duty* to act personally unless authorised by the trust instrument or by statute: *Snell's Principles of Equity*, 28th ed., p. 263.
[123] Section 29, Law of Property Act 1925.
[124] Section 25 of the Trustee Act 1925, as amended by the Powers of Attorney Act 1971, provides that a trustee may delegate the trusts, powers and discretions vested in him as trustee for a maximum of 12 months only. However, section 3(3) of the Enduring Powers of Attorney Act 1985 (which was intended simply to enable beneficial co-owners to give enduring powers despite attendant trusteeship) appears to allow trustees to delegate, by means of an enduring power of attorney, considerably more widely than is permitted by section 25 of the Trustee Act 1925.
[125] It is one of the curious features of the Law of Property Act that there is no provision as to how delegation should be effected.
[126] Law of Property Act 1925, section 29(1).
[127] See, for example, the comments of Potter, "Strict Settlement and Trust for Sale", (1944) 8 Conv. (N.S.) 147, at p. 157.
[128] Section 29(3).

should have a similarly broad power to settle disputes concerning trusts of land under the new system.

12.2 There are, however, two main problems with this interpretation. The first, which might be described as a problem of "form", is that this approach sits uneasily upon the statutory formulation of the trust for sale. Although the "primary purpose" doctrine may mitigate the artificiality of this formulation, nevertheless it begs many questions about the nature of the trust for sale. The second, or "substantive", problem is that the doctrine cannot satisfactorily deal with the implications of the duty to sell. The imposition of this duty continues to restrict adversely the courts' discretion.

12.3 The source of the first problem is that any interpretation of the section 30 discretion should, logically, be rationalised in terms of the trust for sale scheme as a whole. The formal terms of the trust for sale are, as we have seen,[129] quite unsuited to modern conditions of home ownership. Whether or not one remains within the traditional approach, these terms impose some degree of artificiality upon any exercise of the discretion. If, on the one hand, primacy is given to the duty to sell (following the interpretation adopted by Simonds J. in *Re Mayo*),[130] the trust for sale is defined in such a way as to remain within the constraints imposed by a "traditional" approach.[131] If, on the other hand, the doctrine of the "primary purpose" is applied, this artificiality can only be neutralised by formulating reasons for the displacement of the primacy of the duty to sell. There is something odd about a doctrine whose essential purpose is so obviously the circumvention of an inconvenient provision. It is not that there is anything illogical or unrealistic about the substance of the approach, rather it is that this "creative" interpretation hangs upon the practical unsuitability of the statutory definition. It is somewhat unsatisfactory that court practice should be thus adapted to the inadequacies of the trust for sale.

12.4 As regards the second problem, the imposition of a duty to sell means that, although the court may make "such order as it thinks fit", this discretion may be restricted to a power to either order or refuse a sale.[132] This makes the court's discretion rather "one-dimensional". On this view, it is not (for example) possible for the court to refuse to order a sale and yet impose an occupation rent.[133] This obviously limits the effectiveness of the discretion as a means of doing justice to all parties.[134]

12.5 Our recommendations in relation to section 30 should be viewed in the context of the proposed new system as a whole. It is our view that a restructuring of the trust powers, and in particular the elimination of the duty to sell, should clear the way for a genuinely broad and flexible approach. The courts will not be required to give preference to sale, and, in making orders, will not be restricted to making ones which are simply ancillary to sale.

12.6 As regards the circumstances in which applications to the court should be allowed, our general view is that the courts should be able to intervene in

---

[129] See para. 3.
[130] [1943] Ch. 302. at p. 304: "It appears to me that the judicial discretion conferred by s.30 of the Law of Property Act 1925, must be exercised in the same way as the discretion which is exercisable by the court in the case of an instrument containing an express trust for sale. The trust for sale will prevail unless all [the] trustees agree in exercising the power to postpone."
[131] For which see para. 3.
[132] See, for example, the comments of Purchas J. in *Dennis v. McDonald*, [1982] Fam. 63, at p. 73: "I do not think that [section 30] enables the court to make orders where an order for sale is not made. Only orders ancillary to an order for sale which are necessary to implement the sale are envisaged by the words of the section. The words are "*and* the court may make such order as it thinks fit" and not "*or* the court may make such other orders," etc."
[133] Though, as in *Dennis v. McDonald*, an order for payment of an occupation rent may be justified in terms other than those of the Law of Property Act.
[134] Though see *Re Evers' Trust* [1980] 1 W.L.R. 1327 for an instance in which a refusal to order a sale was conditional upon an undertaking by an occupying co-habitant to indemnify her co-trustee. The threat of sale can be an inducement to negotiate terms.

any dispute relating to a trust of land.[135] Looking at the way in which the courts have approached trusts for sale, it seems that they are already disposed to taking this approach.[136] There is at present one important restriction, this being that it is not at present possible to apply to the court to prevent either a sale or the exercise of a power.[137] We recommend that any interested person should be able to apply to the court either to force or prevent a sale, or to force or prevent the exercise of the trustees' powers. This would mean that, in contrast to the trust for sale, any beneficiary or trustee will be able to ask the court to exercise any of the powers described in the next two paragraphs.

12.7 As with the question of trust powers generally, our aim is to express the courts' powers by way of a broad provision rather than by drawing up an inventory. This may not give the courts many more powers than they currently exercise in relation to trusts for sale; our recommendations as to the making of applications and orders may be of greater importance in securing added flexibility.[138] Similarly, if the trustees have more powers, then the courts' overall "capacity" will be increased accordingly.

12.8 Generally, this broad power will include powers to interfere with the trustees' exercise of any of the trust powers, to dispense with any contents, or to regulate beneficiaries' occupation of land.[139]

12.9 As regards the exercise of these powers, it is our view that the court's discretion should be developed along the same lines as the current "primary purpose" doctrine. This approach was moulded to practical requirements,[140] and we consider that it gets the balance more or less right. Nevertheless, we recommend that section 30 should set out some guidelines for the exercise of the court's discretion, the aim being to consolidate and rationalise the current approach. The criteria which the courts have evolved for settling disputes over trusts for sale are ones which will continue to have validity in the context of the new system.[141] One function of the guidelines will be to put these criteria on a statutory footing. For example, although it seems clear that the courts will not be slow to protect the interests of children, much may depend upon whether the trust purpose is deemed to be the provision of a "matrimonial" home or of a "family" home.[142] Our recommendation here is that the welfare of children should be expressly defined as an independent consideration. The aim is to ensure that the interests of children are not linked to the interests of particular beneficial owners.

12.10 Aside from the welfare of children, the court is directed to have regard to five other factors: the intentions of the settlor; the purpose for which the land was acquired; the wishes of any adults entitled to interests in possession; the interests of any creditor who has obtained a charging order under the Charging Orders Act 1979 against any person for whose benefit trust land is held; and any other matters which appear to the court to be relevant. These guidelines are not designed to restrict the exercise of judicial

---

[135] Under the Trustee Act 1925, section 57, or the Settled Land Act 1925, section 64, the courts already have jurisdiction to add to the powers of trustees of land.

[136] For example, in *Bull v. Bull* [1955] 1 Q.B. 234, the court adopted a broad definition of the trust for sale so as to bring the case within the terms of section 30.

[137] This may also be seen as following from the imposition of the duty to sell.

[138] To put it in other words, it seems that any restriction upon the court's powers results more from the fact that the conditions under which applications may be made are quite narrow, than from a restrictive definition of the powers themselves.

[139] As to beneficiaries' rights of occupation, see para. 13.3 *et seq.*

[140] Even though it may have developed "in spite of" the statutory formulation of the trust for sale.

[141] It is envisaged that there will be much of value in the existing body of case law, even though these cases assume that there is a duty to sell.

[142] If the purpose is defined as that of providing a "family" home, then provision for children is implicit in that purpose. If, on the other hand, the purpose is deemed to be that of providing a "matrimonial" home, the interests of children may be linked to those of the beneficial owners. Compare the cases of *Dennis v. McDonald* [1982] 2 W.L.R. 275, and *Re Holliday* [1980] 3 All E.R. 385 with that of *Re Evers' Trust* [1980] 1 W.L.R. 1327. See Webb (1982) 98 L.Q.R. 519.

discretion by either narrowing it in breadth or giving certain interests formal priority over certain others.[143] They are simply designed to indicate some of the more important factors to which the courts should have regard.

12.11 The Insolvency Act 1986 provides for cases in which an application for sale under section 30 is consequential to the insolvency of one of the beneficial owners. Where an application for sale is made by the trustee in bankruptcy of an insolvent, the Insolvency Act provides that this application should be heard in the bankruptcy court, applying the guidelines set out in section 336 of that Act. These guidelines are, however, only applicable to cases of insolvency in which the property concerned is a dwelling house held on trust by the bankrupt jointly with a spouse or former spouse. In other words, the section 336 guidelines do not cover all cases of insolvency. That section does not cover land in which the bankrupt is beneficially interested but which is held on trust for him by his spouse.

12.12 We consider that, if cases of insolvency are to be dealt with in accordance with a separate set of rules, then these rules should apply to all cases of insolvency, regardless of whether or not the property concerned is a dwelling house. We do, however, recognise that applications for the sale of a family home should not be treated on exactly the same basis as other categories. Therefore, we recommend that the provisions of the Insolvency Act 1986 should be extended to cover all applications for sale in which a beneficiary has been adjudged bankrupt, but that paragraphs (b), (c) and (d) of subsection 336(4) of the Insolvency Act 1986 (respectively requiring the court to have regard to: the conduct of the spouse or former spouse, so far as contributing to the bankruptcy; the needs and financial resources of the spouse or former spouse; and the needs of any children) should apply only where the trust land is or has been the home of the bankrupt or the bankrupt's spouse or former spouse.

12.13 The discussion of court powers has thus far proceeded largely on the assumption that we are concerned with concurrent interests. As regards successive interests, the effect of our recommendations will be to replace in this respect the relevant provisions of the Settled Land Act 1925[144] with section 30 of the Law of Property Act 1925 (as amended). This section will be broader and stronger than the existing provisions. One particularly advantageous consequence of this is that remaindermen will be able to make applications under section 30 for a review of the decisions of the trustees, or of any beneficiary to whom the trust powers have been delegated. It may, in this context, be appropriate to consider whether the life tenant's wishes should be given priority over the wishes of other beneficiaries, particularly as we are concerned that the new system should, as much as possible, enable settlors to reproduce the conditions of a strict settlement. It is, however, our view that there should be no restrictions upon the exercise of the court's discretion. The guidelines set out in the revised section 30 reflect our concern that the wishes of the settlor be given some weight.

Position of Beneficiaries

13.1 Clearly, a primary concern of beneficiaries is that the trust land should be managed for their benefit.[145] Given the general requirement that trustees

---

[143] Clearly, the terms of these guidelines may influence the exercise of the discretion in some way. For example, it may be that the courts' approach to creditors' interests will be altered by the framing of the guideline as to the welfare of children. If the welfare of children is seen as a factor to be considered independently of the beneficiaries' holdings, the courts may be less ready to order the sale of the home than they are at present.

[144] Section 64. This section gives the court a power to authorise a tenant for life to conclude any transaction which (although outside his powers) would be for the benefit of the land or of those persons interested in it. In addition to this, recourse may be had to the (more extensive) provisions of the Variation of Trusts Act 1958.

[145] The difficulty here is, of course, that what is in the interest of one beneficiary may not be in the interest of another.

must act within the terms of the trust,[146] there are two factors to be considered in determining how well served beneficiaries are by a given scheme. First, there is the question whether the trustees' powers are such as to enable them to manage the trust land in the interests of all the beneficiaries. Second, there is the question whether the beneficiaries have a sufficient say in the exercise of these powers.

13.2 It being our recommendation that trustees of land should be given powers similar to those of an absolute owner, the trust powers will be wide enough to permit efficient management of the land. In specifying the scope of these powers, it seems necessary to set out expressly the position regarding beneficiaries' rights of occupation. It is not clear whether trustees for sale have a power to let beneficiaries into occupation, and it may also be that, although under the new system the trustees will have the powers of an absolute owner, this would not be considered a proper exercise of those powers.

13.3 We recommend that certain beneficiaries should have a right to occupy the trust land. This right will extend only to beneficiaries with a present, vested, interest in the land.[147] Given that not all land held on trust will be held for occupation,[148] the right will be further restricted to the occupation of land which has been provided or acquired for beneficiaries' occupation, whether from the commencement of the trust or at any time later. In letting any eligible beneficiary into occupation of this land, the trustees will have a power to agree to impose reasonable terms as to occupation rents, repairing obligations, and outgoings.

13.4 Where more than one beneficiary is eligible to occupy trust land, the trustees will have a discretionary power to exclude or restrict the occupation right of any of them. In exercising their discretion, the trustees will be directed to have regard to the purpose of the trust, the circumstances of the eligible beneficiaries, and any other relevant factors. Those beneficiaries whose right of occupation has been so restricted may be granted some form of compensation.[149]

13.5 As regards the question of consultation, where the beneficiaries are also the only trustees of the trust, the effect of our recommendations will be to put them (corporately) in much the same position as an absolute owner. Where, however, there are beneficiaries who are not also trustees, the question of consultation and intervention arises far more acutely.[150] At present, the Law of Property Act provides that trustees should as far as possible consult the beneficiaries and, so far as consistent with the general interest of the trust, give effect to their wishes.[151] In the case of an express trust for sale, this provision applies only if expressly included in the trust instrument. We recommend that the provision be amended so that it applies to all trusts of land (whether for sale or not), unless expressly excluded in the trust instrument.

13.6 Within the new system, beneficiaries will be in a comparatively better position than beneficiaries of current trusts of land.[152] For example, given that the terms governing applications under section 30 will be less restrictive than they are at present,[153] beneficiaries will have greater scope to challenge the decisions of the trustees and generally influence the management of the trust land.

---

[146] If they are not to be in breach of trust.

[147] In other words, those with a purely monetary interest, or with a future or contingent interest, will be excluded. Where the trust is a discretionary one, beneficiaries will only come within the class if and when the trustees have exercised the discretion in their favour.

[148] It may be held for investment, either wholly or in part.

[149] Either by way of payments made by the occupying beneficiary or by way of an increased share in the profits of the land. See clause 7 of the draft Bill.

[150] Of course, it may be that a beneficiary has been delegated all the trust powers.

[151] Section 26(3).

[152] It should be noted that, as regards beneficiaries under a trust of concurrent interests, the very nature of their interest will be changed. They will have an interest in the land rather than merely in the proceeds of sale.

[153] See para. 12.

Termination of the Trust

14.1 Under section 17 of the Settled Land Act 1925, where the estate owner holds the land free from other equitable interests under a trust instrument the trustees are bound to execute a deed declaring that they are discharged from the trust. A purchaser can then assume that the land is no longer settled land. There has never been a comparable provision for trusts for sale. In the working paper we suggested that there should be such a provision for all trusts of land, and this proposal was particularly well received by consultees.

14.2 It is not possible to reproduce the provisions of section 17 exactly because that section assumes that the legal estate is held by someone who is beneficially entitled to the land. Trustees for sale already have a duty, if requested by a beneficiary entitled to have the legal estate vested in him, to transfer the legal estate to the beneficiary. Where the proceeds of sale are held in trust for persons of full age in undivided shares absolutely, those persons can require the trustees to vest the land in them as joint tenants on trust for sale.

14.3 The effect of our reforms will be to give trustees a power to convey the land to those who are absolutely entitled to it. This power will be exercisable whether or not the conveyance is requested by the beneficiary or beneficiaries. In so conveying the land, trustees will be under a duty to execute a deed of discharge so as to protect purchasers.

C. OTHER MATTERS

Family Charges and Rentcharges

15.1 Strict setttlements will at present arise wherever land is charged with the payment of a charge or annuity for the benefit of any person.[154] As it is our policy that there should be no new strict settlements, it is necessary to make alternative provision for this kind of arrangement. We recommend that land which is subjected to a rentcharge or family charge should be held under the new system, the legal owner holding the land on trust for the benefit of himself and the person(s) to whom the charge is payable. This will have little practical effect on dealings with the charged land. At present, if the beneficiary of the strict settlement conveys the legal estate as subject to the charge, then the conveyance need not be in the prescribed form for conveyances of settled land. The purchase money need not be paid to two trustees, and the purchaser or transferee takes the land subject to the charge. Under the new system, conveyances will be of equal simplicity. The trustee may either convey the land as encumbered by the charge, or appoint a second trustee so as to overreach the charge in accordance with the provisions of section 2 of the Law of Property Act.[155]

Entailed Interests

16.1 In the working paper[156] we proposed that the creation of new entailed interests should be prevented. This proposal met with strong approval from several consultees. At present, entailed interests can only be constituted behind a strict settlement. Given that our recommendations are designed to minimise use of the Settled Land Act 1925, it seems logical to suggest that there should be no new entails, particularly as the latter would have little purpose outwith the framework of a strict settlement. We recommend that an attempt to create an entailed interest in land should operate as a grant of a fee simple absolute, unless the grantor has an equitable interest only. In this latter case, the attempt to create an entail will take effect as a declaration of trust on the part of the settlor or the personal representative that the land is

---

[154] Settled Land Act 1925, s.1(1)(v).
[155] We are currently engaged in a review of the law relating to overreaching. See Working Paper No. 106.
[156] See Working Paper No. 94, para. 6.8.

held on trust (under the new system) for the grantee absolutely. It is at present possible to create entailed interests in personalty. Given that we are concerned to approximate the positions of trusts of real and personal property, we further recommend that it should no longer be possible to create entailed interests in personal property.

Conditional and Determinable Fees

17.1 By virtue of section 7 of the Law of Property Act 1925, a fee simple which is subject to a legal or equitable right of entry or re-entry is a fee simple absolute and hence a legal estate. Our recommendations are not designed to affect this provision, and these estates would continue to be legal estates. However, where a person is granted a conditional or determinable fee in land which does not come within section 7 the land would be held on trust under the new system, the trustees being the grantor or personal representatives (as appropriate).

Charities

18.1 At present, land held under charitable trusts is covered by section 29 of the Settled Land Act 1925.[157] As it is our aim that the Settled Land Act should in future be used as little as possible, we consider that charitable trusts of land should come within the scope of our project. Although the Bill contains a general definition which has the effect that all land held on trust should be subject to the provisions of the Law of Property Act 1925 as amended,[158] we take the view that there is a need to provide explicitly for the position with regard to trusts for charitable, ecclesiastical, or public purposes.[159] It is not intended that there should be any alteration of (or any other effect upon) the Charities Act 1960, section 29.[160]

18.2 Certain provisions of the Bill will apply only to charitable, ecclesiastical and public trusts. We recommend that where a purchaser has notice that he is dealing with land held on charitable trusts, he should satisfy himself that the trustees have obtained any required consents or orders. In addition to the general requirement that trustees with limited powers should bring these limitations to the attention of purchasers, there is a further specific provision to the effect that trustees holding registered land under charitable trusts should enter an appropriate restriction on the register of title.

Intestacy

19.1 At present, where a person dies intestate all his property, whether real or personal, which is not already money, is held on trust for sale.[161] Where a person dies leaving a will his property is not subjected to a trust for sale unless a trust for sale is created by that will.[162] In cases where a trust for sale has been imposed either by will or on intestacy, the situation differs from that of "ordinary" trusts for sale in that the eventual beneficiaries do not on the death of the testate or intestate become beneficiaries under the trust for sale.[163]

---

[157] This section provides that land vested in trustees on or for charitable ecclesiastical or public trusts is deemed to be settled land for the purposes of that section only. This provision does not, however, cover all charitable trusts of land. It seems clear that some land is conveyed to trustees on trust for sale to be held for charitable purposes. In such cases the trustees have a duty to sell, but in other respects section 29 applies.

[158] See clause 1.

[159] Hence the inclusion of clause 17.

[160] Which prevents the sale of certain charitable land without the permission of the Charity Commissioners.

[161] Administration of Estates Act 1925, s.33(1). The personal representatives of the deceased have power to postpone sale for such period as they think proper.

[162] In such a case, the Administration of Estates Act 1925 gives the executors the powers of trustees for sale. It should be noted that section 39 also applies to intestate estates, and it is not altogether clear how sections 33 and 39 are meant to relate to each other.

[163] The personal representatives are in a fiduciary position and the rights of the beneficiaries are protected by the court, which ensures that the assets are duly administered. The beneficiaries do not have direct equitable interests in the property which is to be distributed.

19.2 Our proposals are not designed to alter the relationship between personal representatives and beneficiaries under either an intestacy or an express trust for sale. We do, however, recommend that trusts for sale should no longer automatically arise on intestacy, since no practical justification for this could be perceived. Accordingly, we propose that section 33 of the Administration of Estates Act 1925 be amended so as to provide that, in cases of intestacy, the deceased's estate should be held by his personal representatives on trust under the new system. The personal representatives would hold the property, after meeting those costs and expenses which are at present set out in subsection 33(2), on the same terms as those of subsections 33(2)–(7). This amendment is designed to affect both real and personal property.

19.3 As it is our policy that trusts of land which arise on death should be similar in nature to *inter vivos* trusts, we recommend that the Administration of Estates Act 1925 should be amended so as to provide personal representatives with the powers conferred on trustees of land under section 28 of the Law of Property Act 1925 (as amended).[164]

PART III

SUMMARY OF RECOMMENDATIONS

20.1 The present dual system of trusts for sale and strict settlements should be replaced by an entirely new system, applicable to both concurrent and successive interest in land, and placing trusts of land on a footing similar to that of trusts of personalty. Trustees would hold the legal estate on trust with a power to sell and a power to retain the land and, as at present, would be able to convey the legal estate free of equitable interests.

[Paragraphs 1.4–1.7; Clause 1]

20.2 *Interests*

Concurrent interests—Land which previously would have become subject to an implied trust for sale should be held by trustees with a power to retain and a power to sell. The doctrine of conversion should be abolished in relation to all trusts, whatever the property and whenever created. It should still be possible for a duty to sell expressly to be imposed but a power to retain should be statutorily implied, contrary intention notwithstanding.

[Paragraphs 3.5–3.7; Clauses 8–12; 19; 21]

Successive interests—It should no longer be possible to create Settled Land settlements and all successive interests should fall under the new system. (Existing settlements would not be affected.)

[Paragraph 4.3; Clauses 13–14]

Minors—Minority should remain a disability and an attempted conveyance of land to a minor should take effect as a declaration of trust, the land being held by the relevant trustee(s) under the new system.

[Paragraphs 5.1–5.3; Clause 15]

Purchasers—The new system should retain the overreaching mechanism, which would operate much as it currently does in relation to trusts for sale.

[Paragraphs 6.1–6.2]

---

[164] Because the deceased's property is legally and beneficially vested in the personal representatives, the latter will not be trustees of land simply by virtue of holding land.

Bare trusts—These should come within the new system.

[Paragraph 7.1; Clause 1]

20.3 *The Trust*

Creation—There should be no special formalities, the only requirement being that the trust be properly constituted within the terms of general trust law. The new system should apply to all trusts of land (whenever created and whether express, implied or constructive), with the exception of existing Settled Land Act settlements. There should be no new settled land and land newly acquired by an existing settlement, or which would continue to be settled land only by virtue of a new instrument, should be held under the new system.

[Paragraphs 8.1–8.3; Clauses 1; 13–14]

Trustees—Where a trust arises by way of a conveyance to co-owners, the trustees should be, as at present, the first four named in the conveyance. Where new trustees are to be appointed, section 36 of the Trustee Act 1925 should apply, subject to an amendment (applicable to trusts of personalty as well as trusts of land) enabling beneficiaries who are ascertained, *sui juris* and unanimous to exercise, by direction, a priority right of appointment. Where successive interests are created, the trustees should be those appointed by the settlor, failing which, whoever had the legal estate currently vested in him. An attempted conveyance to a minor *inter vivos* would constitute a declaration of trust by the grantor. In testamentary dispositions to a minor, the personal representatives would become trustees. Where a trust arises on intestacy, the administrators of the estate would, as at present, become trustees.

[Paragraphs 9.1–9.2; Clauses 11; 14; 15; 18]

Powers—Trustees should be given all the powers of an absolute owner, subject to general equitable duties as to the exercise of those powers and, in relation to investment, by the Trustee Investment Act 1961. The powers could be expressly limited but, in the absence of actual notice, purchasers should not be affected by any such limitation. Trustees should be under a duty to take reasonable steps to ensure that any such limitation is brought to the attention of prospective purchasers.

[Paragraphs 10.1–10.10; Clause 4]

Delegation—Delegation should be under section 25 of the Trustee Act 1925, by way of power of attorney, and should allow the delegation (without limitation as to time) of all the trust powers in relation to land to any beneficiary with a present, vested interest.

[Paragraphs 11.1–11.3; Clause 5]

Powers of the Court—Section 30 of the Law of Property Act 1925 should be amended (a) so as to enable any trustee or other interested person to apply to the court to intervene in any dispute relating to a trust of land; (b) to include guidelines for the exercise of the court's discretion.

In cases of insolvency, the provision of section 336 of the Insolvency Act 1986 should be extended to cover all applications for sale in which a beneficiary has been adjudged bankrupt, but paragraphs (b), (c), and (d) of subsection (4) should apply only where the trust land is the home of the bankrupt or his spouse or former spouse.

In relation to successive interests, the relevant provisions of the Settled Land Act 1925 should be replaced by Section 30 of the Law of Property Act 1925 (as amended).

[Paragraphs 12.6–12.13; Clause 6]

Position of Beneficiaries—Beneficiaries with a present, vested interest should have a right to occupy trust land which has been provided or acquired for beneficiaries' occupation, trustees having power to agree or impose reasonable terms as to occupation rents, repairing obligations, and outgoings. Where there is more than one eligible beneficiary, trustees should have a discretionary power, having regard to the purpose of the trust, the circumstances of the eligible beneficiaries and any other relevant factors, to exclude or restrict the occupation right of any of them. Beneficiaries whose right of occupation had been so restricted might be granted compensation. There should be an amendment to the consultation provisions of section 26(3) of the Law of Property Act 1925 to make them applicable to all trusts of land unless expressly excluded.

[Paragraphs 13.3–13.5; Clauses 3; 7]

Termination—Trustees should be empowered to convey the land to those absolutely entitled to it. The power should be exercisable whether or not the conveyance had been requested by the beneficiary or beneficiaries. In so conveying the land, trustees should be under a duty to execute a deed of discharge.

[Paragraph 14.3; Clause 2]

20.4 *Other Matters*

Family charges and rentcharges—Land subject to a rentcharge or family charge should be held on trust under the new system, the legal owner holding the land on trust for the benefit of himself and the person(s) to whom the charge is payable. The trustee may convey the land as encumbered or appoint a second trustee so as to overreach the charge in accordance with section 2 of the Law of Property Act 1925.

[Paragraph 15.1; Clause 14]

Entailed interests—An attempt to create an entailed interest in land should operate as a grant of a fee simple absolute (unless the grantor's interest is equitable only, in which case the attempt would take effect as a declaration of trust). It should no longer be possible to create entailed interests in any property.

[Paragraph 16.1; Clause 16]

Conditional and determinable fees—Where a person is granted a conditional or determinable fee in land which does not come within section 7 of the Law of Property Act 1925, the land should be held under the new system, the trustees being the grantor or personal representatives.

[Paragraph 17.1; Clause 14]

Charities—Trusts for charitable, ecclesiastical or public purposes would be subject to the provisions of the Law of Property Act 1925 as amended. (No alteration of, or other effect upon, the Charities Act 1960, section 29 is intended.) Where a purchaser has notice that he is dealing with land held on charitable trusts, he should satisfy himself that the trustees have obtained any required consents or orders. Trustees holding registered land under charitable trusts should enter an appropriate restriction on the register of title.

[Paragraphs 18.1–18.2; Clause 17]

Intestacy—Section 33 of the Administration of Estates Act 1925 should be amended so as to provide that, in cases of intestacy, the deceased's estate (both real and personal property) be held by his personal representatives on trust with a power to sell. The Administration of Estates Act 1925 should be amended so as to provide personal representatives with the powers conferred on trustees of land under section 28 of the Law of Property Act 1925 (as amended).

[Paragraphs 19.2–19.3; Clauses 11; 20]

(Signed) ROY BELDAM, *Chairman*
TREVOR M. ALDRIDGE
BRIAN DAVENPORT
JULIAN FARRAND
BRENDA HOGGETT

MICHAEL COLLON, *Secretary*

30 December 1988*

---

* All substantive work on this Report was completed before 30 December 1988, but submission and publication were delayed by final editorial work and the completion of the consequential provisions in the annexed draft Bill.

Trusts of Land Bill*
ARRANGEMENT OF CLAUSES

An Act to make provision with respect to land held subject to trusts, the functions of trustees holding land and of personal representatives and the appointment of trustees; to prevent the creation of new entailed interests; to abolish the doctrine of conversion as respects property held by trustees or personal representatives; and for connected purposes.

Be it enacted by the Queen's most Excellent Majesty, by and with the advice and consent of the Lords Spiritual and Temporal, and Commons, in

---

*Explanatory notes follow at the end of the Bill.

this present Parliament assembled, and by the authority of the same, as follows:

Preliminary

Meaning of "trust of land" and "trustees' land"

1.—(1) In this Act—

"trust of land" means any trust (whenever created and whether express, implied or constructive) subject to which land is held, other than a trust which is a settlement to which the Settled Land Act 1925 applies; and

"trustees of land" means the persons holding land on such a trust (including personal representatives holding land as trustees).

(2) In section 205(1) of the Law of Property Act 1925 after paragraph (xxix) there shall be inserted—

"(xxia) 'trust of land' and 'trustees of land' have the same meanings as in the Trusts of Land Act 1989;".

Application of provisions relating to trusts for sale to all trusts of land with amendments

Duration and termination of trusts of land

2.—(1) For section 23 of the Law of Property Act (duration of trusts for sale) there shall be substituted—

"Trusts of land

Duration and termination of trusts of land

23.—(1) Subject to subsection (2) of this section, a trust of land shall, so far as the position of any purchaser of the land is concerned, be deemed to continue until the land has been conveyed to or under the direction of a person who is sui juris and for whom the land is held absolutely under the trust (whether or not he is beneficially entitled to it).

(2) Where trustees of land hold the land on trust absolutely for a person who is sui juris (whether or not he is beneficially entitled to it)—

(a) they may convey the land to him absolutely, notwithstanding that they have not been required to do so; and

(b) if they execute such a conveyance (whether or not they have been so required), they shall execute a deed declaring that they are discharged from the trust so far as that land is concerned.

(3) A purchaser of land in respect of which a deed has been executed in pursuance of subsection (2)(b) is entitled to assume that the land has ceased to be subject to the trust.".

(2) This section applies whether the trust is created before or after the commencement of this Act.

Duty of trustees to consult beneficiaries

3.—(1) Section 26 of the Law of Property Act 1925 (which contains provisions as to consents to the exercise of a trust for sale) shall have effect subject to the amendments in subsections (2) to (4) (which apply those provisions to the exercise by any trustees of land of any functions).

(2) In subsection (1)—

(a) for the words "execution of a trust for sale of land" there shall be substituted the words "exercise of any function by any trustees of land"; and

(b) for the words from "execution" to "trustees for sale" there shall be substituted the words "exercise by them of that function".

(3) In subsection (2) for the words "execution of any such trust or power" and "execution of the trust or the exercise of the power" there shall be substituted respectively the words "exercise of any such function" and "exercise of that function".

(4) In subsection (3) for the words "Trustees for sale" and "the rents and profits of the land until sale" there shall be substituted respectively the words "Trustees of land" and "the land".

(5) For the second sentence of subsection (3) (trustees' duty to consult with beneficiaries not to apply in express trusts unless contrary intention in disposition creating trust) there shall be substituted—

"This subsection shall apply except in so far as provision to the contrary is made by the disposition creating the trust.".

(6) In subsection (4) for the words "trust for sale" there shall be substituted the word "trust".

(7) This section applies whether the trust was created before or after the commencement of this Act.

Powers of management of trustees

4.—(1) For section 28 of the Law of Property Act 1925 (powers of management etc. conferred on trustees for sale) there shall be substituted—

"Powers of management etc. of trustees of land

28.—(1) Subject to the provisions of this section and to any restrictions imposed by any enactment on the exercise by trustees of land of any particular power, such trustees shall have all the powers of an absolute owner in relation to the land subject to the trust.

(2) Without prejudice to the powers conferred on them by the Trustee Investments Act 1961 or otherwise, trustees of land may purchase—

(a) an estate in fee simple absolute in possession in any land in England or Wales; or

(b) a term of years absolute in any such land,

for any purpose they think fit.

(3) In exercising their powers under subsection (1) or (2) of this section trustees of land shall have regard to the rights and claims of all the persons interested in the land (whether beneficially or otherwise).

(4) In subsections (2) and (3) "trustees of land" includes the trustees of the proceeds of sale of land which immediately before its sale was subject to a trust of land or was or was deemed to be settled land for the purposes of the Settled Land Act 1925; and the reference in subsection (3) to "land" shall be construed accordingly.

(5) Where under a trust of land the land subject to the trust becomes vested absolutely in persons of full age in undivided shares (whether beneficially or not), the trustees may, subject to the following provisions of this section, partition the land or any part of it and provide by way of mortgage or otherwise for the payment of any equality money.

(6) The trustees shall give effect to any such partition by conveying the land partitioned in severalty (whether or not subject to any legal mortgage created for raising equality money) to persons of full age either absolutely or on trust, according to the rights of the persons interested under the partition.

(7) Before exercising their powers under subsection (5) the trustees shall obtain the consent of the persons, if any, of full age who are interested in possession in the land (other than as mere annuitants) or, in the case of a person suffering from mental disorder, of his receiver or authorised attorney; but a purchaser may assume that all such consents which are necessary have been obtained.

(8) Where a share in the land is affected by an incumbrance, the trustees may either give effect to it or provide for its discharge from the property allotted to that share as they think fit.

(9) If a share in the land is absolutely vested in a minor, subsections (5) to (8) of this section shall apply as if he were of full age, except that the trustees may act on his behalf and retain land or other property representing his share on trust for him.

(10) This section shall not apply if or to the extent that provision to the contrary is made by the disposition creating the trust and, in particular, if that disposition requires any consent to be obtained to the exercise of any power, the power may not (subject to section 26 of this Act) be exercised without that consent.

(11) In subsection (7) "authorised attorney" means an attorney acting under the authority of a power of attorney which is registered under section 6 of the Enduring Powers of Attorney Act 1985."

(2) After that section there shall be inserted—

"Protection of purchasers from trustees with limited powers

28A.—(1) Where the powers of trustees of land are limited by virtue of section 28(10) of this Act—

(a) if the land is registered under the Land Registration Act 1925, the trustees shall apply under section 58 of that Act (power to place restrictions on the register) for an entry to be placed on the register of title to prevent any transaction concerning the land being effected otherwise than in conformity with that limitation; and

(b) if the land is not so registered, the trustees shall take all reasonable steps to bring the limitation to the notice of any purchaser of the land.

(2) Where land subject to a trust is not so registered—

(a) a purchaser of the land is entitled to assume that the powers of the trustees are not limited by virtue of section 28(10) of this Act unless he has actual notice to the contrary; and

(b) in favour of a purchaser without such notice such a limitation shall not invalidate any exercise of those powers.".

(3) This section applies whether the trust was created before or after the commencement of this Act and, where the trust is a trust of the proceeds of sale of land, whether the sale took place before or after its commencement.

Delegation of powers by trustees of land

5.—(1) For section 29 of the Law of Property Act 1925 (delegation of powers of management by trustees for sale) there shall be substituted—

"Delegation of powers by trustees of land

29. The power conferred by section 25(1) of the Trustee Act 1925 (delegation by trustees by power of attorney for period not exceeding 12 months) may be exercised by a trustee of land so as to delegate any functions as respects land subject to the trust for an indefinite period if every donee of the power of attorney is a person of full age with a vested interest in possession in the land (other than a mere annuitant).".

(2) This section applies whether the trust was created before or after the commencement of this Act, but does not affect the operation of section 29 as respects any delegation of powers before that time.

Powers of court in respect of exercise of functions by trustees of land and trust disputes

6.—(1) For section 30 of the Law of the Property Act 1925 (powers of court where trustees for sale refuse to exercise powers) there shall be substituted—

"Powers of court as respects trusts of land

30.—(1) Any person who is a trustee of land or is interested (whether beneficially or otherwise) in the land may apply to the court for an order under this section.

(2) On an application under this section the court may make such order as it thinks fit—

    (a) as to the exercise by the trustees of any of their functions; or

    (b) for the settlement of any dispute which has arisen concerning the trust or the land subject to it.

(3) In considering on such an application whether to order that land subject to a trust be sold, the court shall, subject to subsection (5) of this section, have regard—

    (a) to the intentions of the settlor;

    (b) to the purpose for which the land was acquired;

    (c) if the land includes any dwelling, to the welfare of any minor who occupies or might reasonably be expected to occupy it as his home;

    (d) to the wishes of any persons of full age who are entitled to interests in possession in the land or, in the case of a dispute between them, of the majority (according to the value of their combined interests) of those persons;

    (e) to the interests of any creditor who has obtained a charging order under the Charging Orders Act 1979 against any person for whose benefit any land subject to the trust is or may be held; and

    (f) to any other matters appearing to the court to be relevant.

(4) Where an application under this section relates to the exercise by trustees of their powers under section 7 of the Trusts of Land Act 1989, the court shall have regard also to the matters mentioned in subsection (3)(c) of that section.

(5) Subsection (3) does not apply in the case of an application to which section 335A of the Insolvency Act 1986 applies (applications by the trustee of a bankrupt for the sale of land).

(6) In subsections (1) and (2) of this section "land" includes the proceeds of sale of land which was immediately before its sale subject to the trust in question.

(7) The county court has jurisdiction under this section where the land which is to be dealt with in the court does not exceed the county court limit in capital value or net annual value for rating.".

(2) At the beginning of Chapter V of the Insolvency Act 1986 there shall be inserted—

"Rights under trusts of land

Rights under trusts of land

335A.—(1) Any application by a trustee of a bankrupt's estate under section 30 of the Law of Property Act 1925 (powers of court in respect of powers of trustees of land and trust disputes) for an order under that section for the sale of land shall be made to the court having jurisdiction in relation to the bankrutpcy.

(2) On such an application the court shall make such order under that section as it thinks just and reasonable having regard—

    (a) to the interests of the bankrupt's creditors;

    (b) to all the circumtsances of the case other than the needs of the bankrupt; and

    (c) in a case where section 336(6) applies, to the other matters there mentioned.

(3) Where such an application is made after the end of the period of one year beginning with the first vesting under Chapter IV of this Part of the bankrupt's estate in a trustee, the court shall assume, unless the circumstances of the case are exceptional, that the interests of the bankrupt's creditors outweigh all other considerations.".

(3) In section 336 of the Insolvency Act 1986—

(a) subsection (3) which is superseded by subsection (2) shall be omitted; and

(b) in subsection (4) (factors to be considered by the court on such applications as mentioned in subsections (2) and (3) of that section) the words "or (3)" and "or section 30 of the Act of 1925" shall be omitted; and

(c) after subsection (5) of that section there shall be inserted—

"(6) Where such an application as is mentioned in section 335A is made in respect of land which includes a dwelling house which is or has been the home of the bankrupt or the bankrupt's spouse or former spouse, in addition to the matters mentioned in subsection (2) of that section the court shall also have regard to the matters mentioned in paragraphs (b) to (d) of subsection (4) of this section.".

(4) This section applies whether the trust was created before or after the commencement of this Act and the functions conferred on the court by virtue of this section are exercisable on an application made before or after that time.

Right of beneficiary to occupy trust land

Right of beneficiary to occupy trust land

7.—(1) Subject to the provisions of this section, a person with a vested interest in possession under a trust (other than a mere annuitant) shall be entitled to occupy any land subject to the trust if—

(a) the purposes of the trust include making the land available for his occupation or the occupation of beneficiaries in general; or

(b) the land has been acquired by the trustees for that purpose, and the land is reasonably available for occupation by him.

(2) Where, apart from this subsection, two or more persons would be entitled to occupy land under subsection (1), then the trustees may—

(a) restrict in any reasonable manner they think fit the right of any of those persons to occupy the land or any part of it;

(b) impose such reasonable conditions on any of those persons in relation to his occupation as they think fit.

(3) In exercising their powers under subsection (2) in relation to any land the trustees shall have regard—

(a) to the intentions of the settlor;

(b) to the purpose for which the land was acquired;

(c) to the circumstances and wishes of each of the persons who are (or apart from any previous exercise by the trustees of those powers would be) entitled to occupy the land; and

(d) to any other relevant matters.

(4) Without prejudice to the generality of subsection (2)(b), the conditions which may be imposed on a person under that subsection may include conditions requiring him—

(a) to make payments to any other person by way of compensation for the restriction of that other person's rights of occupation under this section;

(b) to forego any payment or other benefit to which he would otherwise be entitled under the trust so as to benefit any other person whose rights are so restricted;

(c) to pay any outgoings or expenses in respect of the land;

(d) to assume any other obligation in relation to the land or to any activity which is or is proposed to be conducted there.

(5) The powers conferred on the trustees by subsection (2) may not be exercised—

(a) so as prevent any person in occupation of any land from occupying it, or

(b) in a manner likely to result in any person ceasing to occupy any land, unless he consents or the court has by order approved that exercise.

(6) The court shall not make an order under subsection (5) unless, having regard to the matters mentioned in subsection (3), they consider it just to do so.

(7) This section applies whether the trust was created before or after the commencement of this Act.

Ending of statutory imposition of trusts for sale

Trusts on which mortgaged property held after redemption barred

8.—(1) In section 31 of the Law of Property Act 1925 (trust for sale of mortgaged property where right of redemption barred) for the words from "trust for sale" in subsection (1) to the word "applicable", in the second place where it occurs, in subsection (2) there shall be substituted the words "on trust—

(a) to apply the income from the property as if it were interest paid on the mortgage debt; and

(b) if the property is sold, to apply the net proceeds of sale, after payment of costs and expenses, as if they were a repayment of the mortgage debt".

(2) Subsections (3) and (4) of that section shall cease to have effect.

(3) Subsection (1) applies whether the right of redemption is discharged before or after the commencement of this Act, but this section has effect without prejudice to any dealings or arrangements before that time.

Land held in personalty settlements

9. Section 32 of the Law of Property Act 1925 (implied trust for sale of land held in personalty settlements) shall cease to have effect.

Joint ownership of land without trust for sale

10.—(1) Section 34 of the Law of Property Act 1925 (effect of dispositions to tenants in common) and section 36 of that Act (joint tenancies) shall have effect subject to the following amendments (which provide that land to which those sections apply shall, instead of being held on statutory trusts for sale, be held on the trusts appropriate for giving effect to the rights and claims of interested persons).

(2) In subsection (2) of section 34 (conveyance in undivided shares to operate as conveyance to grantees on statutory trust for sale) and in subsection (3) of that section (devises and bequests in undivided shares) for the words "upon the statutory trusts hereinafter mentioned" there shall be substituted the words "upon such trusts as are appropriate for giving effect to the rights and claims of the persons interested in the land (whether beneficially or otherwise)".

(3) Subsection (4) of that section (settlement of undivided shares in land to operate only as settlement of share of proceeds of sale and rents and profits) shall be omitted.

(4) In section 36—

(a) in subsection (1) (trusts applicable to land held for persons as joint tenants) for the words "on trust for sale" there shall be substituted the words "on trust";

(b) in the proviso to subsection (2) (severance of beneficial joint tenancy) for the words "under the trust of sale affecting the land, the net proceeds of sale, and the net rents and profits until sale" there shall be substituted the words "under the trust the land"; and

(c) in the second sentence of that subsection (rights of survivor of joint tenants who is solely or beneficially interested not to be affected by trust for sale) for the words "on trust for sale" there shall be substituted the words "on trust".

(5) This section applies whether the disposition comes into force before or after the commencement of this Act.

Trusts on intestacy

11.—(1) Section 33 of the Administration of Estates Act 1925 (trust for sale on intestacy) shall have effect subject to the following amendments.

(2) For subsection (1) there shall be substituted—

"(1) On the death of a person intestate as to any real or personal estate, such estate shall be held by his personal representatives upon trust.".

(3) In subsection (2) for the words from the beginning to "shall pay" there shall be substituted the words "The personal representatives shall pay out of the ready money of the deceased and any net money arising from the disposal of any other part of his estate (after payment of costs)".

(4) In subsection (4) for the words from "including" to "retained unsold" there shall be substituted the words "and any part of the estate of the deceased which remains unsold".

(5) This section applies whether the death occurred before or after the commencement of this Act.

Trusts arising on reverter of sites

12.—(1) Section 1 of the Reverter of Sites Act 1987 (right of reverter replaced by trust for sale) shall have effect subject to the following amendments.

(2) In subsection (1)—

(a) the words "on the trust arising under this section" shall be omitted; and

(b) at the end there shall be added the words "on trust (subject to the following provisions of this Act) for the persons who but for this Act would from time to time be entitled to the ownership of the land by virtue of its reverter".

(3) Subsection (2) shall be omitted.

(4) In subsection (3) for the words "trustees for sale" there shall be substituted the word "trustees".

(5) In subsection (4) for the words "trust for sale" there shall be substituted the word "trust".

(6) Notwithstanding anything in subsection (1) of that section, this section shall not affect the operation of that section as respects any trust which has arisen by virtue of that section before the commencement of this Act.

Phasing out of Settled Land Act 1925

No new settled land

13. Land shall not be or be deemed to be settled land for the purposes of the Settled Land Act 1925 by virtue of being or being deemed to be subject to a settlement, unless it was or was deemed to be such land by virtue of being or being deemed to be subject to that settlement immediately before the commencement of this Act and has remained so since.

Dispositions formerly creating settled land to operate as dispositions on appropriate trusts

14.—(1) Where, apart from section 13, land would become settled land by virtue of being—

(a) held in trust for persons in succession; or

(b) charged (otherwise than for full consideration in money or money's worth) with the payment of any sums for the benefit of any persons,

it shall be held instead on such trusts as are appropriate for giving effect to the rights and claims of the persons interested in the land (whether beneficially or otherwise).

(2) Where an instrument coming into operation after the commencement of this Act contains an expression which immediately before its commencement would have created—

(a) a trust of any land for any person in possession—

(i) for an estate in fee simple or for a term of years absolute subject to an executory limitation, gift, or disposition over on the happening of any event;

(ii) for a base or determinable fee (other than a fee which is a fee simple absolute by virtue of section 7 of the Law of Property Act 1925) or any corresponding interest in leasehold land; or

(b) a trust of any land for any person for an estate in fee simple or for a term of years absolute contingently on the happening of any event,

that instrument shall operate instead as a declaration that the grantor or, if the instrument is a will, the personal representatives of the deceased hold the land on such trusts as are appropriate for giving effect to the rights and claims of the persons interested in the land (whether beneficially or otherwise).

(3) In subsection (2) "determinable fee" means a fee determinable either by limitation (including a trust) or condition.

Conveyances to minors

15.—(1) For section 19 of the Law of Property Act 1925 (effect of conveyances of legal estates to infants) there shall be substituted—

"Conveyances to minors

19.—(1) A conveyance of a legal estate in land to a minor alone, or to two or more minors jointly—

(a) shall not be effective to pass any legal estate, but

(b) shall operate as a declaration that the land is held on the appropriate trusts.

(2) A conveyance of a legal estate in land to a minor jointly with one or more other persons of full age shall operate to vest the legal estate in the other person or persons on the appropriate trusts, but not so as to sever any beneficial joint tenancy in the land.

(3) In this section "appropriate trusts" means such trusts as are appropriate for giving effect to the rights and claims of the persons interested in the land (whether beneficially or otherwise).

(4) Subsections (1) and (2) of this section apply—

(a) whether or not the minor or minors are beneficially entitled to the land in question, and

(b) if they are beneficially entitled, whether they are so entitled as joint tenants or as tenants in common.

(5) Nothing in this section prevents an equitable interest in land being conveyed to a minor."

(2) Where immediately before the commencement of this Act a conveyance to a minor alone or to two or more minors jointly operated by virtue of

section 27(1) of the Settled Land Act 1925 (effect of conveying legal estate to infant) as an agreement to execute a settlement in favour of, and meantime to hold the land in trust for, the minor or minors, that conveyance shall operate instead as a declaration that the land is held on such trusts as are appropriate for giving effect to the rights and claims of the persons interested in the land (whether beneficially or otherwise).

(3) Except as provided by subsection (2), this section does not affect any conveyance which came into operation before the commencement of this Act.

Effect of attempts to create entailed interests

16.—(1) Section 130(1) to (3) of the Law of Property Act 1925 (creation of entailed interests in real and personal property) shall not apply to any instrument taking effect after the commencement of this Act.

(2) Where such an instrument contains an expression showing an intention to create an entailed interest in either real or personal property then, subject to subsection (3)—

  (a) if it purports to grant any person a legal interest in tail, it shall operate instead to transfer the property to him absolutely; and

  (b) if it purports to grant any person an equitable interest in tail, it shall operate instead as a declaration that the property is held in trust for him absolutely.

(3) Where the person to whom such an instrument purports to grant an interest is a minor, section 19 of the Law of Property Act 1925 (effect of conveyances to infants) shall apply as if the instrument were a conveyance having effect as mentioned in subsection (2).

Trusts of land for charitable, public or ecclesiastical purposes

17.—(1) Without prejudice to the generality of section 13, section 29 of the Settled Land Act 1925 (by virtue of which land vested or to be vested in trustees on charitable or public trusts is deemed settled land for the purposes of that section) shall only apply to land which has continuously been held on or for the same charitable, ecclesiastical or public trusts or purposes since before the commencement of this Act.

(2) Any conveyance of land held on charitable, ecclesiastical or public trusts must state that the land is held on such trusts.

(3) Where land registered under the Land Registration Act 1925 is held on charitable, ecclesiastical or public trusts the trustees shall apply under section 58 of that Act (power to place restrictions on the register) for an entry to be placed on the register of title to prevent any transaction concerning the land being effected without any necessary consents or orders.

(4) Section 26 of the Law of Property Act 1925 (consents of two persons to exercise of trustees' powers sufficient) and subsection (1) of section 28A of that Act (which provides for the protection of purchasers from trustees with limited powers) shall not apply as respects the exercise of any powers by trustees of land held on charitable, ecclesiastical or public trusts, and where a purchaser of such land has notice that the land is held on those trusts he must see that any consents or orders necessary to authorise the purchase have been obtained.

(5) Subsections (2) to (4) do not apply to land to which section 29 of the Settled Land Act applies and none of this section applies to land to which the Universities and College Estates Act 1925 applies.

(6) Nothing in this section affects the jurisdiction of the High Court, the Charity Commissioners or any other competent authority in relation to the administration of such trusts.

Appointment of new trustees

18.—(1) Section 36 of the Trustee Act 1925 (subsections (1) and (6) of which provide for the appointment respectively of new or additional trustees by the person nominated by the trust instrument or by the trustees) shall have effect subject to the following amendments.

(2) After subsection (1) there shall be inserted—

"(1A) If—

(a) there is no person falling within paragraph (a) of subsection (1), or no such person who is able and willing to act, and

(b) all the beneficiaries under the trust are sui juris,

then all the beneficiaries acting together may in writing direct the person or persons who are entitled by virtue of subsection (1)(b) to appoint a new trustee to appoint such person or persons as may be specified in the direction, and the appointment shall be made accordingly.

(1B) Where the beneficiaries have power to give such a direction by virtue of a trustee being incapable, by reason of mental disorder within the meaning of the Mental Health Act 1983, of exercising his functions as trustee, they may, instead of giving such a direction, direct the trustee's receiver, or (if no receiver is acting for him) any person authorised for that purpose by the authority having jurisdiction under Part VII of that Act, to appoint such person or persons as may be specified in the direction to be a trustee or trustees in his place (but subject to subsection (9) of this section).

(1C) Where the beneficiaries have power to give a direction under subsection (1A) or, as the case may be, subsection (1B) of this section, the persons mentioned in paragraph (b) of subsection (1) of this section may not make an appointment without receiving a direction unless the beneficiaries are not all willing and able to give a direction.".

(3) After subsection (6) there shall be inserted—

"(6A) If—

(a) there is no person falling within paragraph (a) of subsection (6) of this section, or no such person who is able and willing to act, and

(b) all the beneficiaries under the trust are sui juris,

then all the beneficiaries acting together may in writing direct the person or persons who are entitled by virtue of subsection (6)(b) to appoint an additional trustee to appoint such person or persons as may be specified in the direction, and the appointment shall be made accordingly.

(6B) Where the beneficiaries have power to give a direction under subsection (6A) of this section, the persons mentioned in paragraph (b) of subsection (6) of this section may not make an appointment without receiving a direction unless the beneficiaries are not all willing and able to give a direction.".

(4) This section does not affect section 36 of the Trustee Act 1925 as it applies by virtue of section 64 of that Act (Settled Land Act trustees and trustees for the purposes of the management of land during a minority) and is without prejudice to proviso (ii) to paragraph 3 of Part III, proviso (iii) to paragraph 1(3) and proviso (ii) to paragraph 1(4) of Part IV of Schedule 1 to the Law of Property Act 1925 (under which the replacement of the Public Trustee requires his consent).

Power to postpone sale to apply to all trusts for sale despite contrary intention

19.—(1) For subsection (1) of section 25 of the Law of Property Act 1925 (power to postpone sale) there shall be substituted—

"(1) Notwithstanding any provision to the contrary in the instrument creating the trust, a power to postpone sale shall be implied in the case of every trust for sale of land.".

(2) In subsection (2) of that section the words from the beginning to "sale)" and from "nor" onwards shall be omitted.

(3) In subsection (4) of that section (trust either to retain or sell land to be construed as trust to sell with power to postpone sale) for the words "to sell the land with power to postpone the sale" there shall be substituted the words "with power to sell the land".

Powers etc. of trustees of land to apply to personal representatives

20.—(1) In section 33 of the Law of Property Act 1925 (provisions of Part I of that Act relating to trustees for sale to apply to personal representatives holding on trust for sale) for the words "trustees for sale" and "holding on trust for sale" there shall be substituted respectively the words "trustees of land" and "holding land on trust".

(2) In subsection (1) of section 39 of the Administration of Estates Act 1925 (powers of management of personal representatives)—

(a) in paragraph (i) (powers available before the commencement of that Act)—

(i) at the beginning there shall be inserted the words "as respects the personal estate,"; and

(ii) the words from "and such power" onwards shall be omitted;

(b) for paragraph (ii) there shall be substituted—

"(ii) as respects the real estate, all the functions conferred as respects land subject to a trust by section 28 of the Law of Property Act 1925 (taking the reference in subsection (3) to the persons interested in the land as a reference to the persons interested in the due administration of the estate and disregarding subsection (10) (contrary intention))";

(c) in paragraph (iii) for the words "conferred by statute on trustees for sale and" there shall be substituted the word "necessary".

(3) This section applies whether the testator or intestate died before or after the commencement of this Act.

Abolition of doctrine of conversion as respects trust property

21.—(1) In determining for any purpose whether property subject to a trust or held by personal representatives should be treated as personalty or realty, any duty of the trustees or the personal representatives to deal with that property so as to alter its nature in that respect shall be disregarded.

(2) Subsection (1) applies whether the trust was created or the testator or intestate died before or after the commencement of this Act.

Supplementary provisions

Interpretation

22. Except where the context otherwise requires, section 205(1) of the Law of Property Act 1925 applies for the interpretation of this Act as it applies for the interpretation of that Act.

Minor and consequential amendments and repeals

23.—(1) The enactments mentioned in Schedule 1 have effect subject to the amendments mentioned in that Schedule (which extend certain provisions applying to trusts for sale or trustees for sale to all trusts of land or, as the case may be, all trustees of land, or are otherwise consequential on or incidental to this Act).

(2) Subject to paragraph 23 of that Schedule, those amendments apply to trusts created before or after the commencement of this Act.

(3) The Lord Chancellor may by order made by statutory instrument make such modifications of any existing statutory provision as appear to him to be appropriate in consequence of the provisions of this Act.

(4) A statutory instrument made in the exercise of the power conferred by subsection (3) shall be subject to annulment in pursuance of a resolution of either House of Parliament.

(5) In subsection (3) "existing statutory provision" means any enactment contained in a public general or local Act and passed before, or in the same Session as, this Act.

(6) The enactments mentioned in Schedule 2 are repealed to the extent specified in the third column but subject to subsection (7).

(7) The repeals in sections 7(3) and 130 of the Law of Property Act 1925 do not affect the validity of any interest created before the commencement of this Act.

Short title, commencement and extent

24.—(1) This Act may be cited as the Trusts of Land Act 1989.

(2) This Act shall come into force on such day as the Lord Chancellor may by order made by statutory instrument appoint.

(3) The provisions of this Act do not extend to Scotland or Northern Ireland except so far as it affects other enactments so extending.

SCHEDULES

SCHEDULE 1

MINOR AND CONSEQUENTIAL AMENDMENTS

1. Section 32 of the Wills Act 1837 shall cease to have effect.

2. In paragraph 17(3) and (4) of Schedule 15 to the Law of Property Act 1922 for the words "on trust for sale" there shall be substituted the words "under a trust of land within the meaning of the Trusts of Land Act 1989".

3.—(1) The Settled Land Act 1925 shall have effect subject to the following amendments.

(2) In section 17—

(a) in the proviso to subsection (1) for the words "settlement, trust for sale" and the words "settlement, or trust for sale" there shall be substituted the word "trust";

(b) for the words "trust for sale" in the second place where they occur in the second sentence of subsection (1) and in subsections (2)(c) and (3) there shall be substituted the word "trust";

(c) in subsection (2)(b) for the word "settlement" there shall be substituted the word "trust";

(d) there shall be omitted—

(i) in paragraph (a) to the proviso to subsection (1), the words "a vesting instrument or";

(ii) in the second sentence of subsection (1) the words from "is settled land" to "or" and "as the case may require".

(3) In section 36—

(a) for the words "upon the statutory trusts" in subsection (2) and the words "on the statutory trusts" in subsection (3) there shall be substituted the words "on such trusts as are appropriate for giving effect to the rights and claims of the persons interested in the land (whether beneficially or otherwise)";

(b) in subsection (4), for the words "trust for sale" there shall be substituted the words "trust of land (within the meaning of that Act)";

(c) subsection (6) shall be omitted.

4.—(1) The Trustee Act 1925 shall have effect subject to the following amendments.

(2) In section 10(2), in the first sentence the words "by trustees or" and "the trustees or" and in the second sentence the words from the beginning to "mortgage; and" shall be omitted.

(3) In section 14(2) for the words "the proceeds" and "trust for sale" there shall be substituted respectively the words "proceeds" and "trust".

(4) In section 24—

(a) after the words "undivided share" there shall be inserted the words "in land or"; and

(b) for the words "trust for sale" and "trustees for sale" there shall be substituted respectively the words "trust" and "trustees".

(5) In section 27(1) for the words "or of a disposition on trust for sale" there shall be inserted the words "trustees of land (within the meaning of the Trusts of Land Act 1989)".

(6) For section 32(2) there shall be substituted—

"(2) This section applies only where the trust property consists of money, securities or land subject to a trust of land (within the meaning of the Trusts of Land Act 1989) and is not treated as land or applicable as capital money for the purposes of the Settled Land Act 1925."

(7) In section 34(2) for the words "on trust for sale of land" there shall be substituted the words "creating trusts of land within the meaning of the Trusts of Land Act 1989".

(8) In section 35 after subsection (3) there shall be inserted—

"(3A) Subsections (1) and (3) of this section shall apply in the case of a conveyance of land on trusts not including a trust for sale, where there are for the time being trustees of a settlement of the proceeds of the land if it is sold, as they apply in the case of a conveyance of land on trust for sale, taking the reference in subsection (3) to trustees for sale as a reference to the trustees of the conveyance.".

5.—(1) The Law of Property Act 1925 shall have effect subject to the following amendments.

(2) In section 2—

(a) in subsection (1)(ii) for the words "trustees for sale" and the words "the statutory requirements respecting the payment of money arising under a disposition upon trust for sale" there shall be substituted respectively the words "trustees of land" and "the requirements of section 27 of this Act respecting the payment of capital money arising on such a conveyance";

(b) in subsection (2) for the words "a trust for sale", the words "the trust for sale", in both places where they occur, and the words "trustees for sale" there shall be substituted respectively the words "a trust of land", "the trust" and "trustees".

(3) In section 3—

(a) paragraph (b) of subsection (1) shall be omitted;

(b) in paragraph (c) of that subsection for the words from the beginning to "sale" there shall be substituted the words "in any other case";

(c) subsection (2) shall be omitted;

(d) in subsection (5) for the words from the beginning to "owners" there shall be substituted the words "If the estate owners".

(4) In section 16—

(a) in subsection (2) for the words "pursuant to a trust for sale" there shall be substituted the words "by a trustee of land";

(b) in subsection (6) for the words "trustee for sale" there shall be substituted the words "trustee of land".

(5) In section 18—

(a) in subsection (1) for the words "the proceeds of sale of land, being land held on trust for sale" and "trustee for sale" there shall be substituted respectively the words "land or the proceeds of sale of land subject to a trust of land" and "trustee of land";

(b) in subsection (2) for the words "trustees for sale", in both places where they occur, there shall be substituted the words "trustees of land".

(6) In section 22(2) for the words "land held on trust for sale", "trust for sale" and "trustees for sale" there shall be substituted respectively the words "land subject to a trust of land", "trust" and "trustees".

(7) After subsection (1) of section 24 there shall be inserted—

"(1A) Subsection (1) of this section shall apply in the case of a conveyance of land on trusts not including a trust for sale, where there are for the time being trustees of a trust of the proceeds of sale of the land if it is sold as it applies in the case of a conveyance of land on trust for sale".

(8) In section 27—

(a) for subsection (1) there shall be substituted—

"(1) A purchaser of a legal estate from trustees of land shall not be concerned with the trusts affecting the land, the net income of the land or the proceeds of sale of the land whether or not those trusts are declared by the same instrument by which the trust is created.";

(b) in subsection (2) for the words "trust for sale", "the settlement of the net proceeds" and "trustees for sale" there shall be substituted respectively the words "trust", "any trust affecting the net proceeds of sale of the land if it is sold" and "trustees".

(9) In section 39(4) for the words "trusts for sale" there shall be substituted the words "trusts of land".

(10) In section 42—

(a) subsection (1)(a) shall be omitted; and

(b) in subsection (2) for the words "trust for sale" in both places where they occur there shall be substituted the words "trust".

(11) In section 66(2) for the word "trustee for sale" there shall be substituted the words "trustee of land".

(12) In section 102(1) for the words "trustees for sale" there shall be substituted the words "trustees".

(13) In section 131 after the words "but for this section" there shall be inserted the words "and section 16 of the Trusts of Land Act 1989".

(14) In section 137—

(a) in subsection (2)(ii) after the words "proceeds of sale of land" there shall be inserted the words "subject to a trust of land"; and

(b) in subsection (5) for the words "held on trust for sale" there shall be substituted the words "subject to a trust of land".

(15) In section 153(6) for the words "in trust for sale" there shall be substituted the words "as a trustee of land".

(16) In paragraph 2 of Part III of Schedule 1 for the words from "on the statutory trusts" to "until sale" there shall be substituted the words "on the appropriate trusts (within the meaning of section 19 of this Act), but not so as to sever any beneficial joint tenancy in the land".

(17) In paragraph 1 of Part IV of that Schedule for the words "upon the statutory trusts", in the first place they occur, there shall be substituted the words "on such trusts as are appropriate for giving effect to the rights and claims of the persons interested in the land whether beneficially or otherwise (in this Part of this Schedule referred to as "the appropriate trusts)" and for those words in the second and subsequent places where they occur there shall be substituted the words "on the appropriate trusts".

(16) In paragraph 1(9) of that Part for the words "The trust for sale" and "on trust for sale" there shall be substituted respectively the words "The power of sale" and "on trust".

(17) In paragraph 2 of that Part for the words "on the statutory trusts" there shall be substituted the words "on such trusts as are appropriate for giving effect to the rights and claims of the persons interested in the land (whether beneficially or otherwise)".

(18) In paragraph 2 of Part V of that Schedule for the words from "on the statutory trusts" to "court" there shall be substituted the words "on such trusts as are appropriate for giving effect to the rights and claims of the persons interested in the land whether beneficially or otherwise (the power to sell the land being exercisable only with the leave of the court)".

6.—(1) The Land Registration Act 1925 shall have effect subject to the following amendments.

(2) In section 3(xv)(a) for the words "land held on trust for sale" and "trustees for sale" there shall be substituted respectively the words "land subject to a trust of land" and "trustees of land".

(3) For section 3(xxviii) and (xxix) there shall be substituted—

"(xxviii) "trust of land" has the same meaning as in the Trusts of Land Act 1989;

(xxix) "trustee of land" has the same meaning as in the Trusts of Land Act 1989;"

(4) In sections 4 and 8(1) for the words "trustee for sale" there shall be substituted the words "trustee of land".

(5) In section 49(1)(d) for the words "in the proceeds of sale of land held on trust for sale" and "disposition on trust for sale" there shall be substituted respectively the words "in or in the proceeds of sale of land subject to a trust of land" and "trust disposition".

(6) In section 49(2) for the words "trust for sale" in the first place where they occur and the words "trustees of a disposition on trust for sale" there shall be substituted respectively the words "trust of land" and "trustees of land".

(7) In section 49(3) for the words "trust for sale" there shall be substituted the words "trust".

(8) In section 83(11)(b) for the words "land held on trust for sale" there shall be substituted the words "land held subject to a trust of land".

(9) In section 94—

(a) for subsection (1) there shall be substituted—

"(1) where registered land is subject to a trust of land, the land shall be registered in the names of the trustees."; and

(b) in subsection (3) for the words "trust for sale, the trustees for sale" there shall be substituted the words "trust of land, the trustees".

(10) In section 95 for the words "land on trust for sale" there shall be substituted the words "land subject to a trust of land".

(11) In paragraph (b) of the proviso to section 103(1) for the words "on trust for sale" and "on the execution of the trust for sale" there shall be substituted the words "subject to a trust of land" and "on a sale of the land by the trustees".

(12) In section 111(1) for the words "trustees for sale" there shall be substituted the words "trustees of land".

7. In the Administration of Estates Act 1925—

(a) in the definition of "real estate in section 3(1)—

    (i) in paragraph (i) for the words "every interest" there shall be substituted the words "subject to paragraph (ii) below, every interest"; and

    (ii) in paragraph (ii) for the words "trust for sale" there shall be substituted the word "trust";

(b) in section 41(6) for the words "trusts for sale there shall be substituted the words "trusts";

(c) in section 51(3) after the word "married" there shall be inserted the words "and without issue" and for the words "an entailed interest" there shall be substituted the words "a life interest".

8. In section 19(1)(b) of the Green Belt (London and the Home Counties) Act 1938 for the words "trustee for sale within the meaning of the Law of Property Act 1925" in the first place where they occur there shall be substituted the words "trustee of land within the meaning of the Trusts of Land Act 1989" and for those words in the second place where they occur there shall be substituted the words "trustee of land".

9. In section 1 of the Settled Land and Trustees Acts (Courts' General Powers) Act 1943—

(a) in subsection (1) for the words "trustees for sale of land" and "land held on trust for sale" there shall be substituted respectively the words "trustees of land within the meaning of the Trusts of Land Act 1989" and "land subject to such a trust of land"; and

(b) in subsections (2) and (3) for the words "trust for sale" there shall be substituted the words "trust of land".

10. In section 5(2) of the House of Commons Members' Fund Act 1948 after the word "money" there shall be inserted the word "land".

11. In sections 8(3), 8A(3) and 8B(3) of the Historic Buildings and Ancient Monuments Act 1953 for the words from "in the case" to "thereof" there shall be substituted the words "are conferred by law on trustees of land within the meaning of the Trusts of Land Act 1989".

12. In section 16(2) of the Ministry of Housing and Local Government Provisional Order Confirmation (Greater London Parks and Open Spaces) Act 1967 for the words "trustee for sale" in both places where it occurs there shall be substituted the words "trustee of land".

13. In the Leasehold Reform Act 1967—

(a) in section 6(1) for the words "statutory trusts" there shall be substituted the words "trusts";

(b) in section 24(1)(a) and in paragraph 7(1) and (3) of Schedule 2 for the words "on trust for sale" there shall be substituted the words "under a trust of land within the meaning of the Trusts of Land Act 1989".

14. In section 33(2) of the Agriculture Act 1970 after the words "trust for sale" and "trustees for sale" there shall be inserted respectively the words "or trust of land within the meaning of the Trusts of Land Act 1989" and "the trustees of land".

15. In the Land Charges Act 1972—

(a) in section 2(4)(iii)(b) for the words "trust for sale" there shall be substituted the words "trust of land";

(b) in section 17 for the words "trust for sale" there shall be substituted the words "trust of land".

16. In section 10(2) of the Land Compensation Act 1973 for the words "on trust for sale" there shall be substituted the words "under a trust of land within the meaning of the Trusts of Land Act 1989".

17. In section 11(2) of the Local Land Charges Act 1975 for the words "trust for sale" there shall be substituted the words "under a trust of land within the meaning of the Trusts of Land Act 1989".

18.—(1) In section 2(3) of the Rentcharges Act 1977—

(a) in paragraph (a) for the words from "making" onwards there shall be substituted the words "causing the land to fall within section 14(1) of the Trusts of Land Act 1989"; and

(b) in paragraph (b) for the words from "already" onwards there shall be substituted the words "already falls within that section or is settled land".

(2) In section 10(2) for the words "trust for sale" there shall be substituted the words "trust of land within the meaning of the Trusts of Land Act 1989".

(3) Nothing in sub-paragraph (1) affects the validity of any instrument made before the commencement of this Act.

19. In the Ancient Monuments and Archaeological Areas Act 1979—

(a) in section 12(3) for the words "trust for sale" there shall be substituted the words "trust of land within the meaning of the Trusts of Land Act 1989";

(b) in section 18(4)(b) for the words "trustees for sale within the meaning of the Law of Property Act 1925" there shall be substituted the words "trustees of land within the meaning of the Trusts of Land Act 1989".

20. In paragraph 9 of Schedule 1 to the Limitation Act 1980—
(a) for the words "land held on trust for sale" there shall be substituted the words "land subject to a trust of land within the meaning of the Trusts of Land Act 1989";
(b) for the words "proceeds of sale" in both places where they occur there shall be substituted the words "proceeds of its sale".

21. In section 87(4)(b), of the Highways Act 1980 the words from "and section" to "sale)" shall cease to have effect.

22. In the definition of "estate" in section 128 of the Supreme Court Act 1981—
(a) in paragraph (a) for the words "every interest" there shall be substituted the words "subject to paragraph (b) below, every interest"; and
(b) in paragraph (b) for the words "money to arise" there shall be substituted the words "the interest of a beneficiary".

23.—(1) In section 22 of the Health and Social Services and Social Security Adjudications Act 1983—
(a) in subsection (3) for the words "trust for sale" there shall be substituted the word "trust";
(b) in subsection (5) for the words "a joint tenant in the proceeds of sale of land held upon trust for sale" and "those proceeds" there shall be substituted respectively the words "an equitable joint tenant in land held on trust" and "the land";
(c) in subsection (6) for the words "a joint tenant in the proceeds of sale of land held upon trust for sale", "the proceeds is" and "interests in the proceeds" there shall be substituted respectively the words "an equitable joint tenant in land held on trust", "the land is" and "interests in the land";
(d) in subsection (8) for the words "an interest in the proceeds of sale of land" there shall be substituted the words "the interest of an equitable joint tenant in land held on trust".

(2) This paragraph does not affect the operation of that section as respects any charge created under it before the commencement of this Act.

24. In the County Courts Act 1984, in section 24(2)(c) for "30(2)" there shall be substituted "30(7)".

25. In section 19(2) of the Family Law Reform Act 1987 for the words "which is used to create" there shall be substituted the words "showing an intention to create".

SCHEDULE 2

REPEALS

Chapter	Title	Extent of repeal
7 Will. 4 and 1 Vict. c.26.	The Wills Act 1837.	Section 32.
1922 c.16.	The Law of Property Act 1922.	Section 188(30).
1925 c.18.	The Settled Land Act 1925.	In section 17, in paragraph (a) to the proviso to subsection (1), the words "a vesting instrument or" and in the second sentence of subsection (1) the words from "is settled land" to "or" and "as the case may require". Section 27. Section 36(6).
1925 c.19.	The Trustee Act 1925.	In section 10(2), in the first sentence the words "by trustees or" and "the trustees or" and in the second sentence the words from the beginning to "mortgage; and". In section 68(19) the words "and with or without power at discretion to postpone the sale".
1925 c.20.	The Law of Property Act 1925.	Section 3(1)(b) and (2). In section 7(3), the words from "This section" onwards.

Chapter	Title	Extent of repeal
		In section 25(2), the words from the beginning to "sale)" and from "nor" onwards. Section 31(3) and (4). Section 32. In section 34(2), the words from "and so" to "shares". Section 34(4). Section 35. Section 42(1)(a). Section 130(6). In section 205(1)(xxix) the words "and with or without a power at discretion to postpone the sale".
1925 c.23.	The Administration of Estates Act 1925.	In paragraph (i) of section 39(1) the words from "and such power" onwards. In section 55(1)(xxvii), the words "and with or without a power at discretion to postpone the sale".
1927 c.36.	The Landlord and Tenant Act 1927.	In section 13, in subsection (1) the words from "(either" to 1925)", in subsection (2) the words "trustee for sale or personal representative" and in the second sentence of subsection (3) the words from "and" onwards.
1932 c.27.	The Law of Property (Entailed Interests) Act 1932.	Section 1(1).
1939 c.72.	The Landlord and Tenant (War Damage) Act 1939.	Section 3(c).
1946 c.73.	The Hill Farming Act 1946.	Section 11(2).
1949 c.74.	The Coast Protection Act 1949.	In section 11(2)(a), the words from "by", in the second place it occurs, to "sale" and the words "by that section as applied as aforesaid".
1954 c.56.	The Landlord and Tenant Act 1954.	In paragraph 6 of Schedule 2, the words from "by", in the second place it occurs, to "sale" and the words "by that section as applied as aforesaid".
1957 c.59.	The Coal Mining (Subsidence) Act 1957.	In section 11(7)(a), the words from "and by" in the first place they occur to "sale" and the words "by that section as applied as aforesaid".
1967 c.10.	The Forestry Act 1967.	In Schedule 2, paragraph 1(4).
1967 c.88.	The Leasehold Reform Act 1967.	In section 6(5), the words from "or", in the first place it occurs, to "sale", in the first place it occurs, the words "or by that section as applied as aforesaid" and the words "or by trustees for sale". In Schedule 2, in paragraph 9(1), the words from "or", in the first place it occurs, to "sale" and the words "or by that section as applied as aforesaid".
1969 c.10.	The Mines and Quarries (Tips) Act 1969.	In section 32(2)(a) and (b), the words from "by that" to "sale".
1970 c.40.	The Agriculture Act 1970.	In section 30(1), the words from "(including" to "1925)".
1971 c.78.	The Town and Country Planning Act 1971.	In section 275(1)(a), the words from "and by" to "sale" and the words "by that section as so applied".
1977 c.42.	The Rent Act 1977.	In Schedule 2, in paragraph 2(b) the words

Chapter	Title	Extent of repeal
1980 c.58.	The Limitation Act 1980.	from "or if" to "sale". In section 18(1)(a) the words from "including" to "sale". In the definition of "land" in section 38(1) the words from "including" to "sale".
1980 c.66.	The Highways Act 1980.	In section 87(4)(b), the words from "and" to "sale)".
1984 c.28.	The County Courts Act 1984.	In Part II of Schedule 2, in paragraph 2, in sub-paragraph (1) the words from "section 30" to "powers)", sub-paragraph (2) and in sub-paragraph (3) the word "30(2)".
1985 c.68.	The Housing Act 1985.	In section 507(3), the words from "that section" to "sale".
1986 c.5.	The Agricultural Holdings Act 1986.	In section 89(1), the words "or the Law of Property Act 1925".
1986 c.45.	The Insolvency Act 1986.	In section 336, subsection (3) and in subsection (4), the words "or (3)" and "or section 30 of the Act of 1925".
1987 c.15.	The Reverter of Sites Act 1987.	Section 1(2).

Trusts of Land and Appointment of Trustees Act 1996

EXPLANATORY NOTES

Clause 1

1. Clause 1 contains two definitions, designed to bring all trusts except existing Settled Land Act settlements under the umbrella of the new single trust system (see report, paragraphs 1.6–1.7, 3.5, 4.3, 5.1–5.2, and 7.1).

Subsection (1)
2. In this subsection:
(a) "trust of land" is defined as any trust (express, constructive or implied) other than a settlement to which the Settled Land Act 1925 applies. (It thus includes trusts for sale, bare trusts and charitable trusts, and settlements created after commencement of the present Act (see clauses 13 and 14 below)).
(b) "trustees of land" are defined as the persons holding land on such a trust, including personal representatives holding land as trustees. (Personal representatives who have not assented in writing in their own favour as trustees continue to hold the legal estate in land as personal representatives and do not, therefore, fall within the definition: *Re King's Will Trust* [1964] Ch. 542).

Subsection (2)
3. This subsection adds the two definitions to those in section 205(1) of the Law of Property Act 1925.

Clause 2

4. This clause deals with the duration and termination of trusts of land, substituting a re-draft for the present section 23 of the Law of Property Act 1925 (duration of trusts for sale).

Subsection (1)
5. This subsection sets out the new section 23:

Subsection (1)
This effectively re-enacts the protection for the purchaser afforded by the present section 23: a trust of land is deemed to continue, so far as a purchaser is concerned, until the land has been conveyed to, or under the direction of, a beneficiary who is *sui juris* and absolutely entitled to it under that trust.

Subsections (2) and (3)
These implement paragraphs 14.1 to 14.3 of the report, which recommend that there should be a provision similar to section 17 of the Settled Land Act for all trusts of land. Trustees are empowered to convey trust land to a person who is *sui juris* and absolutely entitled to it, whether or not so required by him; however, if they do so, they must execute a deed of discharge, which will entitle a purchaser to assume that the land has ceased to be subject to that trust.

Subsection (2)
6. This applies the new provisions to all trusts of land, whenever created.

Clause 3

7. This clause deals with the duty of trustees to consult beneficiaries and contains amendments to section 26 of the Law of Property Act 1925 (consents to the execution of a trust for sale).

Subsections (1) to (4) and (6)
8. These subsections contain the amendments necessary to extend the provisions of section 26 to all trusts of land.

Subsection (5)
9. This subsection implements the recommendation in paragraph 13.5 of the report that subsection (3) of section 26 be amended so that the trustees' duty to consult applies unless expressly excluded in the trust instrument.

Subsection (7)
10. This applies the new provisions to all trusts of land, whenever created.

Clause 4

Subsection (1)
11. This subsection substitutes a re-draft for the present section 28 of the Law of Property Act 1925 (powers of management, etc, conferred on trustees for sale). The new section 28 contains eleven subsections:

12. *Subsections (1) to (4)*
These subsections implement the recommendation, discussed in paragraphs 10.1 to 10.9 of the report, that trustees of land should be given all the powers of an absolute owner in relation to trust land (subject to their general equitable duties as trustees and, in relation to the investment of proceeds of sale, to the provisions of the Trustee Investment Act 1961). Specifically mentioned is the power to purchase freeholds or leaseholds (for any term). In exercising their powers, trustees are expressly required to have regard to the interests of the beneficiaries. "Trustees of land" include trustees of the proceeds of sale of land which, prior to sale, was trust land (including land which either was, or was deemed to be, settled land) and "land" is to be construed accordingly.

13. *Subsections (5) to (9)*
These subsections effectively re-enact subsections (3) and (4) of the present section 28 (partition), with amendments so as to apply them to all trusts of land.

14. *Subsection (10)*
This subsection implements the recommendation contained in paragraph 10.10 of the report that it should be possible expressly to limit trustees' powers, by making them subject to consent or otherwise.

15. *Subsection (11)*
This makes it clear that the expression "authorised attorney" in the new subsection (7) means an attorney acting under a registered enduring power of attorney.

Subsection (2)
16. This subsection implements the recommendations in paragraph 10.10 of the report (a) that purchasers should not be affected by an express limitation of the trustees' powers unless they have notice of it; (b) that trustees should be under a duty to take reasonable steps to ensure that any limitation on their powers is brought to the attention of prospective purchasers; and (c) that if the trust land is registered, trustees whose powers are limited should be required to apply for a restriction to be entered on the register of title. The necessary provisions are contained in an additional section (28A), to be inserted after section 28 of the Law of Property Act 1925.

Subsection (3)
17. This applies the new provisions to all trusts of land, whenever created, and, where the trust is of the proceeds of sale of land, whenever the sale took place.

Clause 5

18. This clause deals with the delegation of powers by trustees of land.

Subsection (1)
19. This subsection sets out a redrafted section 29 of the Law of Property Act, implementing the recommendation discussed in paragraphs 11.1 to 11.3 of the report that the power of delegation conferred by section 25 of the Trustee Act 1925 should be extended to allow the delegation (without limit of time) of any functions in relation to trust land to any beneficiary of full age with a present, vested interest (other than a mere annuitant).

Subsection (2)
20. This subsection applies the section to all trusts of land, whenever created, but specifies that it does not affect the operation of section 29 in relation to any delegation prior to commencement.

Clause 6

21. This clause deals with the powers of the court in relation to trustees' exercise of their functions and to trust disputes.

Subsection (1)
20. This subsection implements, by means of a re-drafted section 30 of the Law of Property Act 1925, the recommendations in paragraphs 12.1 to 12.10 of the report. The new section 30 has six subsections:

21. *Subsections (1), (2) and (6)*
These are designed to ensure (a) that any person who is a trustee of, or otherwise interested in, trust land may apply to the court under the section; and (b) that the court's powers are sufficiently broad to enable it to make such order as it thinks fit, as to the exercise by trustees of any of their functions, or for the settlement of any dispute concerning the trust or trust land. "Land" includes the proceeds of sale of land which was trust land immediately prior to its sale.

22. *Subsection (3)*
This subsection sets out factors to which the court must have regard in considering whether to order sale of trust land.

23. *Subsection (4)*
This makes it clear that where the application relates to the exercise by trustees of their powers under clause 7 (below) in relation to beneficiaries' occupation of trust land, the court is to have regard also to the circumstances and wishes of the beneficiaries who have a right to occupy the land.

24. *Subsection (5)*
This specifies that subsection (3) does not apply where the application is made by the trustee of a bankrupt for the sale of land. Such applications are subject to different guidelines (see below).

Subsections (2) and (3)
25. These subsections set out the amendments necessary to implement the recommendations in paragraph 12.12 of the report that in cases of insolvency, the provisions of section 336 of the Insolvency Act 1986 should be extended to cover all applications for sale in which a beneficiary has been adjudged bankrupt, but that paragraphs (b), (c) and (d) of subsection (4) of that section should apply only where the trust land is or has been the home of the bankrupt or the bankrupt's spouse or former spouse.

Subsection (4)
26. This subsection applies the section to all trusts, whenever created and to applications made before, as well as after, commencement.

Clause 7
27. This clause deals with the right of a beneficiary to occupy trust land. It implements the recommendations contained in paragraphs 13.3 and 13.4 of the report.

Subsection (1)
28. This subsection specifies which beneficiaries are entitled to occupy trust land, and the circumstances in which the right to occupy arises.

Subsection (2)
29. This subsection deals with the situation in which two or more beneficiaries are entitled to occupy and empowers trustees (a) to restrict the occupation right of any such beneficiary; (b) to impose conditions of occupation.

Subsection (3)
30. This subsection sets out the factors to which trustees are to have regard in exercising their powers under subsection (2).

Subsection (4)
31. This subsection sets out a (non-exhaustive) list of conditions which may be imposed upon an occupying beneficiary.

Subsections (5) and (6)
32. These subsections provide that trustees may not exercise their powers under subsection (2) so as to upset any present occupation of the land unless the occupier consents or the court

approves by order; and the court may not make such an order unless, having regard to the factors set out in subsection (3), it considers it just to do so.

Subsection (7)
33. This subsection applies the section to all trusts, whenever created.

Clauses 8 to 10

34. These clauses implement, in relation to statutory trusts for sale, the recommendation in paragraph 3.5 of the report that all land which previously would have been held under an implied trust for sale should now be held under the new trust system.

35. *Clause 8* sets out the necessary amendments to section 31 of the Law of Property Act 1925 (trust for sale of mortgaged property where right of redemption barred). Subsection (3) states that the new system is to apply regardless of when the right of redemption is discharged but that dealings or arrangements made prior to commencement are not to be affected.

36. *Clause 9* states that section 32 of the Law of Property Act 1925 (implied trust for sale of land held in personalty settlements) is to cease to have effect.

37. *Clause 10* sets out the necessary amendments to sections 34 (effect of dispositions to tenants in common) and 36 (joint tenancies) of the Law of Property Act 1925. Subsection (5) applies the amendments to all dispositions, whenever made.

Clause 11

38. This clause implements the recommendation contained in paragraph 19.2 of the report that trusts for sale should no longer arise on intestacy (in relation to either real or personal property) and that the personal representatives of the deceased should instead hold the estate on trust under the new system. Subsections (1) to (4) set out the necessary amendments to section 33 of the Administration of Estates Act 1925. Subsection (5) states that the amendments apply whether the death occurred before or after commencement.

Clause 12

39. This clause implements the recommendation contained in paragraph 3.5 of the report in relation to trusts arising on reverter of sites, and sets out the necessary amendments to Section 1 of the Reverter of Sites Act 1987. Subsection (6) stipulates that the operation of trusts which have arisen under that section prior to commencement is not to be affected.

Clause 13

40. This clause implements the recommendations in the report: (a) that it should no longer be possible to create Settled Land Act settlements, although existing such settlements would not be affected (paragraph 4.3); and (b) that there should be no addition to settled land held under existing such settlements (paragraph 8.3).

Clause 14

41. This clause also implements the report's proposals in relation to the phasing out of the Settled Land Act 1925 by implementing its recommendations that: (a) all successive interests; (b) land which is charged with the payment of a rentcharge or family charge; and (c) conditional and determinable fees (other than those to which section 7 of the Law of Property Act 1925 applies), (paragraphs 4.3, 15.1 and 17.1, respectively), should now be held on trust under the new system.

Clause 15

42. This clause deals with conveyances to minors. It implements the recommendation in paragraph 5.1 of the report that minority should remain a disability and that an attempt to convey land to a minor should take effect as a declaration of trust, the land being held by the relevant trustee(s) under the new system.

Subsection (1)
43. Subsection (1) contains a redrafted section, to be substituted for the present section 19 of the Law of Property Act 1925 (effect of conveyances of legal estates to infants). *Inter alia*, the

"new" section 19 specifically refers to a conveyance to minors as tenants in common (thus covering the gap presently existing in section 27(1) of the Settled Land Act 1925). Subsections (3), (4), (5) and (6) of the "old" section 19 (making special provisions for conveyances on trust or by way of mortgage) are otiose, as the new provisions make it clear that any conveyance of any legal interest in land to a minor creates a trust in favour of the minor, and have accordingly been omitted from the "new" section 19.

Subsection (2)
44.   Under section 27(1) of the Settled Land Act 1925, the effect of a conveyance of a legal estate to a minor is to create a contract to execute a settlement in favour of the minor. Subsection (2) removes any doubt as to the position if the present Act comes into force between the conveyance and the execution of the settlement by providing that the conveyance will in those circumstances operate as a declaration of trust (thus preventing further Settled Land Act settlements coming into existence and bringing any such conveyances into line with conveyances to minors after the commencement of the Act).

Subsection (3)
45.   This stipulates that, save as provided by subsection (2), the section does not affect pre-commencement conveyances.

Clause 16

46.   This clause implements the recommendation in paragraph 16.1 of the report that the creation of new entailed interests should be prevented. It provides that an attempt to grant a legal interest in tail will operate instead as a grant of a fee simple absolute; an attempt to grant an equitable interest in tail will operate instead as a declaration of trust that the land is held on trust for the grantee absolutely.

Clause 17

47.   This clause deals with trusts of land for charitable, public or ecclesiastical purposes. It expressly confirms that the recommendation in the report as to the phasing out of the Settled Land Act 1925 extends to land held under charitable trusts (see paragraph 18.1) and implements the recommendations in paragraph 18.2 of the report in relation to special provisions applicable only to charitable, ecclesiastical and public trusts.

Subsection (1)
48.   This subsection states that section 29 of the Settled Land Act (land vested or to be vested in trustees on charitable or public trusts to be deemed settled land for the purposes of that section) is not to apply to land unless it applied to it immediately before the commencement of the present Act and has continued to do so since.

Subsection (2)
49.   This subsection stipulates that any conveyance of land held on charitable, ecclesiastical or public trusts must state that the land is held on such trusts. (Section 29(1) of the Settled Land Act 1925 contains a similar provision).

Subsection (3)
50.   This subsection provides that where registered land is held on charitable, ecclesiastical or public trusts, the trustees are to apply for an entry to be placed on the register of title to prevent any transaction concerning the land being effected without any necessary consents or orders.

Subsection (4)
51.   Subsection (4) states that section 26 of the Law of Property Act 1925 (consents of two persons to exercise of trustees' powers sufficient) and section 28A of that Act (protection of purchasers from trustees with limited powers) shall not apply in relation to the exercise of powers by trustees of land held on charitable, ecclesiastical or public trusts, and where a purchaser of such land has notice that it is held on such trusts, he must see that any necessary consents or orders have been obtained.

Subsection (5)
52.   Subsection (5) states that subsections (2) to (4) do not apply to land to which the Settled Land Act applies and that none of the section applies to land to which the Universities and College Estates Act 1925 applies.

Subsection (6)

53. Subsection (6) confirms that nothing in the section affects the jurisdiction of the High Court, the Charity Commissioners or any other competent authority in relation to the administration of such trusts.

Clause 18

54. This clause deals with the appointment of new trustees and implements the recommendation in paragraph 9.1 of the report that section 36 of the Trustee Act 1925 be amended so as to enable beneficiaries who are ascertained, *sui juris* and unanimous to exercise, by direction, a right of appointment that takes priority over that currently accorded to existing trustees. Subsections (1) to (3) set out the necessary amendments and additions to section 36 of the Trustee Act 1925. Subsection (4) stipulates that the changes do not affect section 36 as it applies by virtue of section 64 of the same Act and is without prejudice to certain transitional provisions contained in Schedule 1 to the Law of Property Act dealing with the replacement of the Public Trustee.

Clause 19

55. This clause implements the recommendation in paragraph 3.7 of the report that in an express trust for sale of land, a power to retain should be implied, contrary intention notwithstanding. Subsections (1) to (3) set out the necessary amendments to section 25 of the Law of Property Act 1925 (power to postpone sale).

Clause 20

56. This clause implements the recommendation in paragraph 19.3 of the report that personal representatives should be provided with the powers conferred on trustees of land under section 28 of the Law of Property Act 1925 (as amended). Subsections (1) and (2) set out the necessary amendments to section 33 of the Law of Property Act 1925 (application of Part I of that Act to personal representatives) and subsection (1) of section 39 of the Administration of Estates Act 1925 (powers of management of personal representatives), respectively. Subsection (3) makes it clear that the changes apply whenever the testator's or intestate's death occurred.

Clause 21

57. This clause implements the recommendation in paragraph 3.6 of the report that the doctrine of conversion should be abolished in relation to all property subject to a trust or held by personal representatives.

Clause 22

58. This clause deals with interpretation (except where context otherwise requires, section 205(1) of the Law of Property Act 1925 to apply for the interpretation of this Act).

Clause 23

59. This clause deals with minor and consequential amendments, and repeals (set out in Schedules 1 and 2, respectively).

Clause 24

60. This clause deals with the short title, commencement and extent.

INDEX

References preceded by "s" or "Sch" relate to the text of the 1996 Act; other references
relate to page numbers (and should be read as though preceded by 47–).